Roles Women Play:
Readings Toward
Women's Liberation

Contemporary Psychology Series
Edward L. Walker, Editor

The frontiers of psychology are advancing—advancing in response to persistent and fundamental social problems, advancing as a result of improved technology in both research and application, advancing through individual creative effort.

Brooks/Cole Publishing Company will make contemporary ideas, research, and applications widely available to students and scholars through the Contemporary Psychology Series.

Psychological Aspects of International Conflict
Ross Stagner, Wayne State University

An Anatomy for Conformity
Edward L. Walker, The University of Michigan
Roger W. Heyns, University of California, Berkeley

Delinquent Behavior in an American City
Martin Gold, The University of Michigan

Feminine Personality and Conflict
Judith M. Bardwick, The University of Michigan
Elizabeth Douvan, The University of Michigan
Matina Horner, Harvard University
David Gutmann, The University of Michigan

Roles Women Play: Readings Toward Women's Liberation
Michele Hoffnung Garskof, Quinnipiac College

Roles Women Play: Readings Toward Women's Liberation

Edited by

MICHELE HOFFNUNG GARSKOF

Quinnipiac College

Brooks/Cole Publishing Company
Belmont, California

A division of Wadsworth Publishing Company, Inc.

L.C. Cat. Card No: 75–146974
ISBN 0–8185–0009–3
Printed in the United States of America

5 6 7 8 9 10—75 74

ACKNOWLEDGMENTS

The photograph by W. Cobb (1970) and the woodcut by Sharon Jones (1967) in Sections One and Two are reproduced by permission of *Off Our Backs: A Women's Liberation Bi-Weekly*, Box 4859, Cleveland Park Station, Washington, D.C. 20008. The art in Section Three, cover montage, and book design are by Linda Marcetti.

To the memory of Diana Oughton

Preface

In this book I have tried to bring together some of the important material about women that I found relatively inaccessible when I first set out to teach a course on the psychology of women. In my course I wished to stress the interrelationship of economic and social factors in the evolution of the psychology of women as it is now and as it could be. This, too, is the orientation of the book.

I wish to thank all the women in the course, especially Anne Gordon Greever, for their help and patience in that experiment. In addition, the manuscript was helpfully reviewed by Jane Prather of San Fernando Valley State College and Bernice Podel of Chico State College. I was pleased to be working with a woman production editor at Brooks/Cole; Adrienne Harris and I worked well together because of our mutual involvement in the issues treated in the book. I also wish to thank my husband, Bert, who, although he could not type, helped me in many ways.

Michele Hoffnung Garskof

Contents

Roles Women Play:
Readings Toward
Women's Liberation

Introduction

In the past few years the United States has experienced a dramatic increase in public awareness of its social problems. Antiwar demonstrators have brought the validity of the Viet Nam war into question, and now a great number of people oppose it. Black Americans have pushed their struggle for freedom to the front pages of every newspaper, to Congress, and to the streets. Inequalities between the rich and the poor, the black and the white, the industrial nations and the third world have become glaringly obvious. At the same time, awareness of the inequality between the sexes has heightened, and the women's liberation movement has become an identifiable force in the battle against social injustice. Now, with increasing frequency, newspaper and magazine headlines bear such terms as "women's liberation," "new feminists," "NOW" (National Organization of Women), or "WITCH" (Women's International Terrorist Conspiracy from Hell).

What is the women's movement? What do women want? Do you really think men and women aren't different? Why are men and women different? Could the sexes be equal? These are questions I am asked repeatedly as a psychologist and as a woman. This book is an attempt to help answer these questions.

The women's movement is an informal association of groups of women who have come together for a variety of reasons, and with varying emphases, to express and act upon their concern over the discrimination they are subjected to because they are female. Although there is variation in the specific demands presented by the different groups around the country, there is also a large degree of consistency. Equality is the key word—equal educational opportunity, equal job opportunity, equal work for equal pay, equal freedom from household tedium, equal control over sexual and reproductive functions.

No one, no matter how radical, denies the existence of physical differences between males and females. Their genitals are obviously different. In addition, women tend to have larger breasts, to be smaller and less muscular, to have less body hair, and to have smaller lungs than do men. There are also differences in the sex hormones secreted by each. Women today do not question the existence of these biological differ-

ences, but rather they question the psychological and sociological implications of these differences.

Women do the majority of the menial work in society. Dishwash-
ing, clothes washing, vacuuming, shopping, typing, keypunching, and
similar activities take up most of women's waking hours. In the rare
situations in which women are trained to be professionals, they have
great difficulty finding responsible positions, and even when they break
through these first two barriers, they are accorded less prestige and
money than their male counterparts.

The first rationale for such discriminatory practices is that a
"woman's place is in the home" anyway. Women are "natural"
mothers, wives, cooks, and housekeepers. But how natural are these
roles for women? Should 53 percent of the adult population be house-
bound? The present rates of alcoholism, drug addiction, attempted
suicide, psychiatric care, divorce, and disturbed children in the suburbs
suggest that women do not happily adjust to being kept in even the
nicest homes. The women's liberation movement rejects such traditional
assumptions about how a woman should fill her life. The movement is
one of many signs that women cannot be kept "in their place"—that
woman's place is in the world.

A second rationale is that the feminine personality is not suited for
positions of authority. Women in our society are considered to be
dependent, emotional, childlike, passive, and nurturant, while men are
considered to be relatively independent, rational, adult, active, and
productive. Therefore, it is reasoned, men must make the decisions,
although women may help to carry them out. When women do fill
positions of authority or exhibit signs of active independence, they must
live under the stigma of being "unfeminine." And in the areas where
women regularly assume authority, men consider the jobs unimportant
and therefore sex-type them as "woman's work."

Do psychological differences between the sexes really exist? And, if
they do exist, what causes them? Traditionally, psychologists have found
a positive answer to the first of these questions, and, instead of going on
to the second question, they have proceeded to create theories that
"justify" these psychological differences through tying them to the
apparent biological differences. Freud's theory of psychosexual development has been the most influential example of this type of formulation.
Young children of both sexes go through a period of strong sexual
attraction to the parent of the opposite sex. However, a little boy is able
to eventually resolve his Oedipal complex and to identify with his
father, but a little girl can never resolve her Electra complex. She feels
castrated; her lack of a penis dooms her to inadequate development. In
Freudian terms, a woman is only an incomplete man destined to suffer
through life continually motivated by penis envy.

The women's liberation movement rejects the hypothesis of biological determinism and replaces it with sociological determinism. From birth boys and girls are treated differently and are taught different skills, expectations, ideas about themselves, hopes and dreams. Little girls are prepared to be mothers, housekeepers, low-level workers, sex objects, and consumers, while little boys are encouraged to be doctors, lawyers, engineers, and executives. In this way, girls and boys are each taught the psychological characteristics necessary for them to be successful in their predetermined roles. Different learning experiences result in different behaviors. It follows, therefore, that changing the social conditions into which girls and boys are born and raised can transform their "natures." Most women's liberation proposals and demands address themselves to how societal conditions should be changed so that individuals, regardless of their sex, can develop their full human potential.

This book is a collection of readings that together explore my second question: what causes the psychological differences between the sexes? The material is divided into three sections, none of which approaches being exhaustive. Because of the large importance of social factors, the first section emphasizes the various roles that women do play in our society today. The second section discusses the socialization of women, some of the psychological data that have been gathered on women, some of the traditional psychological theories that have been constructed, some evidence against those theories, and some directions for further scientific investigation. Section Three is devoted to some proposals for changing the differential treatment of girls and boys, women and men. It looks toward the liberation of women.

Section One

Woman's Place in Society

It is impossible to begin to study the psychology of women without first looking objectively at the roles that women fill in our society. In her book *The Feminine Mystique* (1963), Betty Friedan called attention to the discrepancies between the image of American womanhood and the reality of the lives women lead. Both inside and outside of the home, women fill a variety of roles that do not fit on the imagined pedestal. Floor scrubber, bed-pan emptier, factory-line worker, and bargain hunter are just a few of these. Although most psychologists ignore these discrepancies between fairy tale and life—insisting they are nonpsychological factors—this section will be devoted to understanding the roles that women *actually* play.

In our society, women are exploited as buyers and sellers of products. Any glance through a magazine or any evening of television viewing will provide an array of female bodies in a variety of seductive poses advertising everything from deodorant to dog food, from cars to computers. The implication is clear—if you buy the object that is for sale, your chances of obtaining the other object, the woman, will increase.

A woman is valued for her body. She can make babies, she can make beds, and she can "be made." In order to maintain herself as a desirable sex object, it is necessary for her to buy lotions, perfumes, padding, diet pills, girdles, garters, curlers, straighteners, eye makeup, and much more. No one is born to fit the image of the "American beauty"; it is necessary to strive to become closer to it. And in our society, striving means buying. In the first article, "Woman as Secretary, Sexpot, Spender, Sow, Civic Actor, Sickie," Marilyn Salzman-Webb presents a women's liberation group's analysis of the roles women play and how they are interrelated.

Motherhood, usually defined as bearing and rearing the young, has traditionally been considered to be the "primary" function of women. Women become pregnant, give birth, produce milk; therefore, they should care for the young until maturity is reached. This last assumption is held to be true despite the fact that there is no evidence that the biological process of becoming a mother prepares a woman psychologically and sociologically to be a mother. Many "natural" mothers are convicted every year of mistreating their children. "Unnatural" mothers, those who adopt children or serve as foster parents, are not as a group less adequate mothers than are natural mothers. There are many psychological factors that have been identified as characteristics of good mothers, such as maturity and self-respect, but these qualities do not coincide with the ability to conceive. The mythology of motherhood is the subject of the second article, "The Unmothered Woman," by Ethel Albert.

Closely associated with the role of mother is the role of wife. Just as child rearing is thought to be an integral part of motherhood, so is housekeeper-cook-laundress thought to be a part of wifehood. All "successful" women, regardless of their talents, training, and inclinations, are expected to direct households.

Wife and mother are the two roles of which we are all most conscious, though not necessarily in the terms presented. However, they are not the only ones that women play. Most women work outside of the house in roles supplementary to their "womanly" responsibilities; more than 40 percent of the work force is female. Yet the kinds of jobs open to women are limited. Positions of responsibility, prestige, and high pay are considered male jobs and only a very few "token" women have been allowed to obtain them. The jobs that are sex-typed as female include menial, subordinate and low-prestige positions—secretary, nurse, teacher; not executive, doctor, principal, or professor. Most women are employed on temporary or part-time bases so that the workers receive no fringe benefits or salary increases. Even when men and women do the same work, the paychecks and prestige are considerably lower for women than for their male co-workers. The third article, "The Sex Map of the Work World," by Caroline Bird, deals specifically with the woman as worker. It lays bare some of the grim details of sexist economic oppression and destroys with facts many of the myths that we have all been taught to accept.

Reference

Friedan, B. *The feminine mystique*. New York: W. W. Norton, 1963.

Woman as Secretary, Sexpot, Spender, Sow, Civic Actor, Sickie

Marilyn Salzman-Webb

Marilyn Salzman-Webb has done graduate study in psychology. She is an active member of Washington, D.C. Women's Liberation, a member of the staff collective of *Off Our Backs: A Women's Liberation Bi-Weekly* since its inception in early 1970, and a free-lance writer whose most usual topic has been women.

. . . Our Women's Liberation group in Washington, D.C. has been concerned with the emptiness of women's lives. We've looked at ads, heard the personal testimonies, and tried to understand why we all, in one way or another, have lived alone and isolated, keeping those stories of our days locked up inside. How did we come to this situation; why do we live depersonalized, dehumanized existences? How does society reinforce this emptiness?

Through months of talk, study and reflection, we have come to the understanding that we, as women, are brought up to behave in specific ways. We are trained for particular roles in this society, and we are given very few alternatives. We label these roles Secretary, Sexpot, Sow,

> *I have a Bachelor's degree in French literature. The smartest thing I ever did, however, was to take a typing course my junior year in high school; without it I would never be able to find a job. (secretary, age 24)*

Spender, Civic Actor and Sickie. Each role reinforces the others, but they are all interrelated. Spender is a function of all the others, while Sickie is their failure. All of them are limiting and dehumanizing to us as thinking, feeling human beings.

Why, if these roles are limited and dehumanizing, have they been perpetuated? It would be easy simply to see men as the immediate enemy and the cause of women's oppression; yet this would imply that the cause is rooted in something inherently evil in men. It is necessary, therefore, to look into the present social system and to examine how, over a long period of time, society programs people, men and women, into specific roles that fit its needs for maintaining itself.

Ever since I had Kevin I lie in bed at night and plan what I'm going to do the next day. When I need to go to the drugstore to buy some more Pampers, that's a big thing. I plan my whole day around it. I can't believe that's become an excursion out for me now. (new mother, age 21, college graduate)

Social order grows out of basic human needs. In early human history, these needs were quite simple: food, shelter, and physical protection. To survive, ancient humans devised ways to care for themselves, creating simple forms of social organization to meet these basic needs. As methods for meeting basic needs became more sophisticated, social organization changed to adapt most efficiently to changes in methods of production.

In *Origins of the Family, Private Property and the State,* Engels describes the change from a primitive, communal society, with group

Ye Gods—what do I do [all day]. Well, I get up and out of bed at 6 A.M. I get my son dressed and then get breakfast. After breakfast I wash dishes, then bathe and feed my baby. She's 3 months old. Then I start the procedure of house cleaning. I make beds, dust, mop, sweep, vacuum. Then I do my baby's wash. Then I get lunch for the three of us. Then I put my baby to bed, and the little boy to bed for his nap. Then I usually sew or mend or wash windows or iron and do the things I can't possibly get done before noon. Then I cook supper for my family. After supper my husband usually watches TV while I wash dishes. I get the kids to bed. Then—if I'm lucky—I'm able to sit down, watch TV or read a magazine. Then I set my hair and go to bed. (a 22-year-old housewife, quoted in Workingman's Wife, *p. 34)*

marriage and collective work for collective ends, to a property-oriented, pairing social structure that developed class differentiations of work and life-style.

Tribes, Engels said, divided labor so that men cared for cattle and women maintained communal farms and cared for children and domestic chores. In this early period, there were no status differentiations between men's and women's work; both were necessary for survival, and both contributed to the good of the whole community.

Then early forms of trading began. Cattle became the early unit of exchange around which all other forms of trade were measured. Trade broke down the concept of work for the necessity of the community, and developed the notions of bartering and property. If one could trade something for something else, one owned what one traded. Since cattle, which was the assigned responsibility of men, became the unit of trade, it followed that men became the first owners of property. This subtle shift spelled the end of communal production and the beginning of private wealth vested in the hands of men.

Property owned by men could not be passed to their sons if paternity was uncertain. Thus the economic development of trade slowly changed the family structure from a kind of group commune to pairing and marriage. Whereas before, sexual relations were free and open within the group, now strict fidelity was demanded to insure known paternity and thus heredity lineage. Women became, like cattle, the property of men.

Several groups or classes emerged: those men who owned cattle, and those who did not. Secondary to this were women who were the property of either the owners or the laborers. The wealthy began to live differently from the workers; they developed sports and "refined" tastes, engaged in wars and consumed the products of others' work. The workers engaged in arduous drudgery with no leisure time and no energy for anything more than survival. Religions and customs developed which reinforced this emerging class society.

Marx emphasizes that the superstructure of society develops around the economic base, or the means of production. There is cultural lag; customs may carry over even after the previous productive form has been outdated; but those who adapt most quickly to new forms of production develop a new social organization that reflects that new economy. The owners of this new productive form thus gain the power to define, by providing the means by which others can survive, how social organization will develop.

Our own history and our own society today reflect the power of the productive process to define us in our guts. American women are used for profits, and we are programmed to make our capitalist system run most effectively for the good of those who reap the benefits of our work.

Quite early, London merchants who put money into the "new world" realized that men alone would not build a stable colony, but would remain shifting adventurists unless women could be provided to settle them down. In 1619 they sent "Agreeable persons, young and incorrupt . . . sold with their own consent to settlers as wives, the price to be the cost of their own transportations." (Flexner, p. 3)

These women, and the many more who came, either by being kidnapped in England, or in search of a husband, or by selling themselves as indentured servants, became, like slaves, the property of the men they lived with. In marriage, they had few civil rights; they, like slaves, did not exist as human beings under law. They were expected to behave with deference and obedience; they had little education and were expected to breed and to do their share of the work.

The patriarchal extended family was the basic social and economic unit. All goods the family used were produced by its members; and work was divided so that women cared for the house and farmyard, while men brought home lumber, meat, grain and wool. The house was a small factory that employed old men, women and children and produced all the family needed.

With the invention of the spinning jenny, the power loom and other industrial machines, and with a rising demand for mass-produced items, a new era in American production began. Women who saw their lives waning under the thumb of men at home flocked to the new mills to gain some economic independence and freedom.

> Mass production made it easier and often cheaper to purchase the family's needs than to rely on home production. This meant that the family's greatest need was *cash* income to buy processed foods and manufactured goods. Because the new factory system needed workers, women and even children were encouraged to seek employment. (Wells, p. 4)

But "freedom" to work and to leave the demanding private family unit was deceptive. Factories merely moved hard labor from the home to the central workplace, and made money for the mill owners, while the workers were still impoverished.

Since the typical workday for the factory girl lasted from sunup (4:30 A.M.) to sundown, it completely altered family relationships. Workers had only a few short hours together, and they had to live within textile villages that were entirely run and owned by the factory. Single women, whose wages were always lower than men's, earned from $1 to 3 per week, out of which they had to pay $1.50 to 1.75 for board in the company-owned houses. Economic freedom did not appear, and the living conditions of workers grew steadily worse.

Expanded industry created a new middle-class and freed growing numbers of women from domestic drudgery, giving them time to work in new "service" occupations. The Civil War (wars always being times when women are enlisted to take on the work of fighting men) opened up new economic roles for women. They began teaching and hospital work and, with the invention of the typewriter in 1867, they entered new clerical fields.

Although two world wars have changed the situation for short periods, women have remained in the same occupations they held before World War I. They did clerical and factory work and they continuously expanded the new "soothing" professions like social work, nursing, and teaching. Propaganda and mass mobilizations for the "war effort" got women to fill in while men fought, but they were quickly sent home again when the men returned.

Without a whimper, women believed what they were told and followed the needs of a changing economy. When women were wanted during World War II, companies provided child care facilities; when the male workers returned, there were no more child care programs. Social scientists were popularized who maintained that motherhood was a full-time, all-important job. Freud was useful in the process, as were Margaret Mead and the functional sociologists who eulogized that what existed was good.

As capitalism became more sophisticated and further rationalized, it demanded that other values replace these. Early competitive capitalism was consolidated by growing monopolies and large corporate conglomerates.

The corporation has replaced the old family structure and early competitive small business around which community was organized and socialization occurred. A new corporation man or woman must learn to work collectively in each corporation for the profit of that firm. He must repress bald competitive urges and fit smoothly into his niche in a well-oiled machine geared for maximum efficiency. He must find outlets for his tension in situations other than the workplace. Here we see the ultimate form of personal adaptation, defined by the productive process for the higher profits of some and the survival of the rest.

But the development of the productive corporation and the corporate personality isn't by any means the whole story. At the turn of the century, in his search for new markets, Henry Ford discovered that if he paid his workers more than the bare minimum for survival, they could afford his automobiles. They could be markets as well as workers to maximize his profits. The consumption economy had deep roots in the past; the rich had always consumed in quantity. But the notion of the mass market appeared only at the turn of the century. The gearing up for the sales effort began, and it has since become one of modern capitalism's nerve centers.

Thus the advertising industry arose, first to announce new products, then to convince the prospective buyer of the absolute necessity of the product, and finally to encourage waste consumption.

Since society demands that woman's place be in the home, her economic function easily became that of consumer; each household was seen as both a production and a consumption unit.

> Nothing makes markets like a marriage. There's new business in setting up house, and future business in raising a family. All together it's big business, appliances and house furnishings to stepped-up insurance and bigger cars. (*New York Times* ad for *TV Guide*, Nov. 6, 1968)

Today the advertising promotion and sales business eats up most of the spending of large corporations. Baran and Sweezy estimate that expenditures for sales efforts, if market research, public relations and commercial design are included, had reached the phenomenal figure of over $20 billion by 1966. Corporate workers were complaining that the sales departments were taking over business by reaching back into design and product development to maximize product turnover.

This sales effort fit in nicely with the developing corporate and worker personalities. As workers had to suppress their human tensions, both physically and mentally, and as feelings of powerlessness grew in the face of ever-expanding economic conglomerates and political manipulations, people came to see purchasing power as their only outlet for freedom of choice. Trends of mass consumption culture were set by an elite leisure class that had fostered the myth of the American Dream where "anyman" could be a success and live surrounded by cars and appliances. Conspicuous consumption clouded the class nature of American society and allowed a worker to feel he had it made when he could buy a TV and lounge in his prefabricated backyard.

In middle-class America, "the duties of vicarious leisure and consumption devolve upon the wife alone . . . for the good name of the household." (Veblen, p. 68) She is the ceremonial consumer of goods which the husband produces. Her dress, her household goods, her "refinement," her ladylikeness and "culture" are symbolic of the household's ability to pay. Her job is to expand the consumption economy and to reinforce the American Dream.

If the economy needed people to consume, and if the mark of success were to be set by the "style" of the rich in which women played the role of an expensive mannequin of leisure culture, and if the economy needed women to stay at home and reduce the pressures of unemployment, it followed that popular culture would proclaim women's fashions and products for the home to be key concerns of the American woman. The statistics show that we have listened well: during the '60's there was a massive boom in consumer goods, particularly clothing and household commodities. Women make 75% of all consumer purchases.

Roles Women Play: Secretary

Twenty-eight million women now work in America. They work in almost every job listed by the Bureau of the Census, but contrary to a now popular ad, "you have *not* come a long way, baby." Most women are employed in the same occupations we've had for centuries. We do the crap work of society!

Clerical work is the largest single occupation of women workers. In 1960, 31% of all women who worked were secretaries, bookkeepers, stenographers, and clerk-typists.

The next largest occupation of women is service work—over 15% of working women are waitresses, cooks, bartenders, and hospital attendants, not including nurses. In 1960, two out of three women in the service category were waitresses, and most of the jobs in this category were only part-time.

Fourteen percent of women workers do factory work—they are operators, assemblers, and other kindred workers, always with wages lower than those of men. We are the first fired and the last hired. Blacks get more attention than we do.

Slightly over 13% of us are professionals. Forty-two percent of all professionals were teachers (except college) in 1965, and seven out of ten of these teachers taught in elementary schools. Since then, secondary schools and junior high schools have become even more the domain of men.

One-fourth of the professionals were in the health professions, the largest single occupation being nursing, followed by dental and medical technicians. ". . . Women hold only a small proportion of the positions as engineers, technicians (other than medical and dental) and scientists, despite the numerous job openings created by the tremendous interest in research and development." (*Handbook on Women Workers*, p. 95)

In 1963, over sixty percent of those women who had earned BA's in 1958 were classified as full-time housewives: they held no job at all. The statistics further indicate that even if we weren't working as housewives and wanted to work, our preparation was not the best for professions other than those listed above.

Forty-three percent of us majored in education in the school year 1963–64. Twenty-two percent were in the humanities and the arts; fourteen percent were in social sciences. We aren't given much on-the-job training in comparison to men with BA's. They give us a typing test and men a management training test when we look for jobs straight out of college.

The prospects for us as workers aren't good. The earning gap between men and women has widened continually. In 1964, the median income of male workers was $6,283; for female workers it was $3,710.

Women's jobs are usually part-time, so real earnings are further decreased since we aren't given fringe benefits like health and life insurance plans given full-time male workers.

Furthermore, not only have we stagnated in "women's vocations," we have regressed. In 1940, 40% of all working women worked in service jobs; today that figure has reached 54%. Plus there has been a decline in the percent of women professionals with PhD's, since 1930. We have greater unemployment than men even when we are the sole support of our families, and that is very often. Forty-two percent of working women support themselves and others, and an additional 24% have husbands who earn less than $5,000 a year.

How did we get in this position? How did we get the scut-work of society? We have been placed in the lowest paying, lowest skilled, and most boring jobs in America, a country overburdened with boring jobs anyway, by workforce *channeling!*

> The fact is that the 'woman's place is in the home' myth is a phony rationalization for paying lower wages and providing worse working conditions for women than men . . . (Employers) use the feminine mystique to mold women into 'their place' in industry, the place of the reserve labor pool. They can be thrown in or out of the labor market at will, used as part-time or temporary workers, kept in the lowest-paying jobs with a minimum of resistance, and their rate of exploitation is the highest (women have lower median income than black people). (Wells, p. 9)

Our media, education, families, in fact our entire socialization is for this channeling in adult life. "You are nobody unless you marry"—love comics tell you that all the time. "You are a poor housewife and mother unless you buy things"—magazines just assume that. "You are to be pretty, not as smart as men, sexy, and not compete with men in any way." "Your job will fit into what is feminine and ladylike—it is innate, you know, that women love kids."

Role Number Two: Sexpot

> "Ain't she sweet
> Makin' profit off her meat.
> She's just America's prime commodity,
> Ain't she sweet."
>
> (*sung by Women's Liberation at the Miss America Pageant, 1968*)

We are to entertain men; we are the playgirls of America. One lucky girl each month makes it into *Playboy's* centerfold, but each of us wants to be there and to be the Myth America of every man's dreams.

From the prostitute to the advertising model to the socialite hostess, women have been able to make it in life by selling their sexiness. We have been made to see our bodies as commodities. We are to entertain men and to sell products—use your bod, kid, not your mind.

Besides the more blatant sex-roles of the call girls, we serve as sex entertainers in many other jobs, such as airline stewardesses (United's flights "for men only") or special receptionists ("Hertz has one leg up on Detroit.") Katherine Gibb's high class secretarial schools teach girls to dress to be expensive-looking in a luxury office.

Sex sells everything from cigarettes to farm machinery, and it sells "beauty products" to maintain the image. "The call of the Wild Streak: It's irresistible. Now! The first complete kit to fashion-streak your hair. Like all good lures, the Wild Streak by Clairol is beautifully simple. No retouching for up to six seductive months. Why hide the secret siren inside of you? Answer the call of the Wild Streak. You're not the type to be timid. And this is no time to be tame." (*Cosmopolitan*, the sex seller of them all.)

Get it? Women are to be screwed and not heard. That's part of it. The other part is that they're to buy all the products they can afford to make sure they are desirable enough to get a man.

> A good housewife knows how to be an expensive mistress. Are you so busy being devoted to your husband you never make reckless demands? That's a mistake! Try acting spoiled now and then. Simply have to have some wildly beautiful extravagance. This extraordinary Natural Russian Crown Sable should fill the bill admirably. How will your husband feel about suddenly having an expensive mistress? He'll complain about the cost of maintenance. And he'll be a lot more attentive. (*New York Times* ad, Nov. 24, 1968)

This ad, to sell an air conditioning system, in *Fortune* magazine, the Bible of Big Business, speaks for itself.

> "What a way to heat your building," said above two men taking off their glasses to look at a new miniskirted secretary. "Miss Johnson is a warm-blooded animal. Her thermostat is set at 98.6°. She burns food and generates a lot of heat. So much, in fact, that she and her co-workers overheat modern, tightly insulated buildings and cause the air conditioning to turn on. Even when it's cold outside . . ." (So these guys sell spot air conditioning to cool areas where all the hot chicks are, so to speak.)

You can find others in every magazine, but the point is that the selling we do is billion dollar business. The buying we do to keep up the sexual sell is even higher. It's American business, patriotic and a sure way to whip up marriage consumer units. "Here, kids, try this. The first one's free." We are the woman behind the great man. We are the whore of American Capitalism!

And whore we become to society if we give in. Many men view sex as freeing women—that is, if we are free with sex we are truly liberated, and our identity problems are gone. *Playboy* proclaimed "The New Girl" in one of its recent issues. She is "unabashedly sexy, charmingly individualistic, and a joy to the men in her life." They make us feel that we will be loved if we screw; that's what all our sexual gearing up is supposed to be for—or is it?

Society on the surface keeps sex under the cover—literally. We don't talk about it; it's dirty. Because we've made it a commodity, we've also made love a commodity, along with beauty, trust, and human interrelatedness. If we're discreet, that's ok, but God help the woman who gets herself pregnant. Then she's treated like the whore people thought she was all along. Over 10,000 women each year, at lowest estimates, have abortions. Most of these are illegal, done in some doctor's office, if the girl is lucky, and in some hotel room or rundown tenement, if she's not. Whole institutions are built up around unwanted pregnancies— isolated homes for a woman "to go on vacation" for nine months, abandoned children's homes, etc. We are left to make it alone or die; society could care less.

Birth control information is kept a dark secret for most women. Only if she's black or poor is it pushed; then for rather hazy reasons that often resemble genocide. Teenage girls cannot get birth control devices in most cities. Unless you are married or engaged, most college clinics will not help you out, either.

Role Number Three: Spender

And so we buy to make ourselves appealing, to get a husband 'cause that man in our life will presumably give the emptiness meaning.

> Properly manipulated (if you're not afraid of that word), American housewives can be given the sense of purpose, creativity, identity, the self-realization, even the sexual joy they lack—by buying things. (so proclaims an ad executive Betty Friedan interviewed)

Department stores are the Broadway shows and the circuses of the American housewife. A shopping trip is an excursion into fantasy, a relief from vacuuming and diaper-changing, a chance to get dressed up and spend a day without the kids. They are a pacifier for powerlessness, a chance to choose one of many identical brands of toothpaste and pretty bathroom tissues. We hope our new pantsuit will get us the attention, the love, the security that life has robbed from us. It's a very pretty system that saps our human potential and adds to the gross national product.

Fortune magazine predicts consumers will spend over $36 billion for fashion goods this coming year. They further say that consumer outlays for fashion goods have risen by $15 billion or 40% in the past four years, a rise equal to the last fifteen years put together. Home goods sales have risen $11 billion in the same period. Consumer purchases have been eating up greater percentages of disposable income (income after necessities are satisfied) yearly.

Capitalism hasn't yet been able to devise a well planned system for workers to buy back the products they produce. It has thus created the system of credit and installment buying, so that products can move from factory to home, leaving the burden of forking up the money with the little guy. Besides, it makes bank profits—those big guys stick together.

Today over 21% of the average family's income is used to pay back installments, mortgages, personal loans and other consumer debts. Consumer debt has risen at a fantastic rate in this same period. In 1950, $14 billion in installment and consumer credit was "spent." By 1966, this figure was up to $74 billion.

Since women spend the major amount of this money, it is clear they have us going in the right direction for their purposes, but we've been selling our souls to the company stores.

> Before a girl marries, she buys. Major and small appliances. Living, dining and bedroom furniture. A TV set. Rugs and carpeting. China. Silver. Linens. Draperies. Household furnishings of every description. She must buy them. She's moving into her first home—an empty house or apartment. (The ad tells American Business to advertise in *Modern Bride Magazine*—the magazine that sells it to unsuspecting newlyweds.)

The Fourth Role: Sow

Our programmed role of housewife and mother helps them hold us up for the sales. We creatively redecorate our homes to provide sanctuary for our men who hate their jobs, or to lure them back if they are among the few who find total escape in their work. We learn to see our lives in terms of others—our kids will have it better than we, our husbands are winning us social status no single girl could have.

Marriage is a property relationship. Kids are the products we produce; if we fail with them, we are no good. So we'd better make motherhood a full-time profession, smother them with love and toys or we will fail for sure.

The economy plays on this insecurity about motherhood. The youth market, according to *Business Week*, is now worth $15 billion a year, just for teenagers alone. As allowances went up, with the family's disposable income, advertisers began to appeal directly to youth to exercise their newly found freedom by buying. Parents are pressured to raise allowances, as well as to buy toys and new foods for smaller children, who are counted on by TV advertisers to push their parents to buy. No part of the family is sacred to the advertisers, and Mommy is made to buy, not only for herself but for every member of the family.

Family relationships are put under severe strain. The husband has to earn enough to keep up with and to surpass the Joneses. His wife has to soothe him to help him regain the confidence and identity that are destroyed by his dehumanizing office or factory job. She must produce "beautiful children" who do well in school and who don't become delinquents, hippies, or—horror of horrors—commie protesters. She has to look pretty, on top of all her domestic drudgery, to keep a good image for the family and to keep her man by being the expensive mistress he might otherwise seek.

It's no wonder relationships collapse; but even the collapse is now a commodity. An ad for Sony TV reads, "It's nice to be alone with the one you love." It shows a man and a woman in bed, facing opposite directions watching different programs on their little, private TV's. They're wearing earphones so as not to disturb the continuity of the corporate message with extraneous noise—like talk, perhaps?

Taking the Fifth: Civic Actor

So what can homebound mothers do besides buy? If we're disturbed about America, or if we want some stimulation and interest outside the home, we can join the PTA, the church, the League of Women Voters, or volunteer to help retarded children. If we want a change, we can join an organization that will pressure Congress or elect a candidate. That's important for women to do—after all, we are 53% of the population. Civic affairs is now the great American pacifier, second only to consumption. It rests on the myth that power and decision-making are accessible in this country.

Political scientists want us to believe that we live in a pluralistic society. If one wants change, one organizes a pressure group strong enough to effect that change. That's democracy!

But real power doesn't lie with the state, Congress, the courts or pressure groups. The power that counts—the power to define how the rest will work and live—lies with private corporations. Their assumptions about economic growth determine how production will occur, and they define how we all work and live. This is *the* central decision.

C. Wright Mills describes the system this way:

> There is no effective countervailing power against the coalition of the
> big businessmen—who as political outsiders, now occupy the com-
> mand posts—and the ascendant military men—who with such grave
> voices now speak so frequently in the higher councils. (*The Power
> Elite*, Mills, p. 267)

Even John Kenneth Galbraith, that stalwart of American "liberalism,"
knows where it's at.

> The industrial system . . . is inextricably associated with the state. In
> notable respects the mature corporation is an arm of the state. And
> the state, in important matters, is an instrument of the industrial sys-
> tem. (*The New Industrial State*, p. 296)

Galbraith demonstrates the common practice for corporate executives and millionaires to move in and out of government at top administrative and decision-making levels. The permanent establishment of the
military and the growth of the aerospace and defense industry were not
coincidental.

> The mature corporation . . . depends on the state for trained man-
> power, the regulation of aggregate demands for stability in wages and
> price. . . . The state, through military and other technical procure-
> ments, underwrites the corporation's largest capital commitments in
> its area of most advanced technology. (p. 308)

The state trains corporate manpower, gives fat contracts for corporate development, and makes damn sure national and international
policy help corporate growth. Talk about socialism, the rich have it for
sure. The state and the corporation are usually one and the same group
of people changing caps every so often.

That the vote is meaningless was made most clear by this past
presidential election. McCarthy supporters saw that even a candidate
with popular support, shown in state primaries, had no way of breaking
through the party structure to get the nomination. Most states did not
even have primaries; and in many of those that did, it was not manda-
tory that delegations to the conventions support the primary election
candidate. Local party structures are controlled not by us, but by those
same men who speak for big business or who support it.

Wallace supporters saw that it was nearly impossible for any third
party to win against the weight of entrenched look-alikes like the
Democrats and Republicans.

The vote has been the biggest myth grabbed by the American
people. Sure, we get to choose between two or even three candidates
every few years, but elections don't let us decide on central political

issues. Those decisions will be made privately, untouched even by public debate. Remember that Johnson, during the 1964 Presidential election, was the peace candidate, and that he won because voters were appalled as Goldwater promised escalation in Vietnam.

And what about Congress, that great representative voice of the people?

> . . . as social types, these (Congressmen) are not representative of the rank and file citizen. They represent those who have been successful in entrepreneurial and professional endeavors. Older men, they are of the privileged white, native-born, of native parents, Protestant Americans . . . They are, in short, in and of the new and old upper classes of local society. (Mills, p. 248)

Senator Gale McGee, on the Senate floor on Feb. 4, 1969, said:

> In the US Senate today there are said to be 27 millionaires. This is up from what it was two years ago, and that was up from the preceding election, and so on. My point is we are gradually forfeiting service in our National Congress to the millionaires. (*Congressional Record*)

And these are the campaigns women, as the majority of campaign workers, staff.

> More and more the fundamental issues never come to any point of decision before the Congress, or before its most powerful committees, much less before the electorate in campaigns. (Mills, p. 255)

No Congress ever declared war in Vietnam, and you can bet your next picket sign many Congressmen don't even know about the wars we are presently waging in Laos, Cambodia, Bolivia, Guatemala and Peru.

PTA's aren't any better. Business is glad for us to work for free to make for better schools. Better schools make better students who will become better workers—especially new white collar workers who are now much in demand.

Forward Together, we will create a more rationalized capitalism. Women—help staff nicer social institutions and keep up the image of citizen participation in democracy, but don't come near where real decisions are made. Remember, your place is in the home.

The Collapse of Roles: Sickie

When these roles fail to satisfy, as they do, women resort to the salves of all oppressed groups. They take to drugs and drink, and if they can afford it, to psychiatry.

Indices of rising drinking and drug use, let alone psychiatric care, show that during the last two decades American consumption has zoomed way ahead of any previous predictions.

Psychiatry, the art of fitting people back into their socially designated places, is expanding by leaps and bounds. New institutes, like Esalen, and new forms of therapy—dance, group, drug, Rogerian, etc.—are growing wildly and women flock to them to find some happiness and security.

A study now under way at George Washington University indicates that much larger proportions of women are on drugs and in psychiatric care than men.

Any society finds ways of dealing with its maladjusted, but never has a society seemed so maladjusted as ours. "Over one-half of all the hospital beds in this country are occupied by mental patients. There are 500,000 psychiatric patients housed in public and private mental hospitals at any given time." (Shofield, p. 4) This doesn't include the hordes of us going to local shrinks.

As of 1951, the World Health Organization estimated that the United States had the greatest number of alcoholics as a percent of total adult population in the world. Alcoholism and other drug use has risen sharply since that year.

Consider "crime." Taxpayers shell out over $12 million each day just on maintaining prison systems, and $4 billion annually for "law enforcement." That's higher, percentage-wise, than any other country in the world. This doesn't include the "welfare prison system," where women who are poor are subject to prying scrutiny in their homes all hours of the day. Many "criminals" are women—prostitutes unable to make a decent living elsewhere or forced into it by the system of sexual objectification.

Something is terribly wrong with this whole system—a system that forces us to conform or be labeled sick or locked up for "deviance."

Could it be that we have been programmed to self-destruct when our tolerance for living in this America gets very low? That is much better than the route of revolution, in the eyes of the corporate rulers and their professional "crisis managers."

It should be clear that the roles we see as our only alternatives in this society are quite essential to the continuation of the status quo. We fit in all too well. We continue to play these roles because we have learned them from childhood. We are afraid to be concerned about our condition for fear of being called frustrated, unsexy, feminist, communist, or other synonyms for bad. Because we have been brought up to think of ourselves as inferior, we block our minds and come to believe we are.

Remember the times in elementary school when girls were the smartest in the class? Somewhere between then and high school we learned that smartness doesn't pay off for our prime goal in life—that of getting and keeping a man—at least not the kind of smartness we learned in schools. We learned that girls with brains didn't have dates; that cheerleaders were the envy of all girls in the school. We learned to see each other as competitors for that all-important man, and to be wary of each other. That's how the programming began, but it got much more complex as we got older.

The roles we have described are functional to capitalism, whether or not women play them. Someone has to consume; someone has to be surplus labor with depressed wages. The system is capable of giving us as women a token of integration, just as it has begun to give blacks. We must not be misled by our new supposed freedoms. We must create a new society where no one has to play these roles, and where we, as women, can all develop to the highest of our human potential.

What shall we do?

Because we have been kept from each other, and because we are in the unique position of having to live a daily "desegregated" life with a representative of the system of male supremacy (a house slave, while we are field slaves), we must meet and organize for mutual support, solidarity and major social change.

We should have three main goals in mind:

One: To increase our understanding, from our own personal experiences, of the way in which we, as women, have been programmed and oppressed, and to analyze the social institutions that create the context of our oppression.

Two: To devise methods of changing our situation by changing the corporate economic structure so these roles are not necessary. We must create an economic revolution that will end a system that exploits most people for the good of a few.

Three: We must create a cultural revolution in the process, that will destroy the centuries of social programming we have undergone. It has been this programming that has made us see ourselves as inferior to men, that created the institution of marriage as a property relationship, that caused us to get little satisfaction from our work and leisure, that caused us to feel completely powerless and to accept that state of being.

The cultural aspect of the revolution has happened in very few other revolutions—usually the superstructure that developed under a previous economic system was maintained even after economic upheaval and reorganization. To prevent this from occurring in America, we must be organized before, during and after the initial struggles. We must all band together in Women's Liberation Groups, not as caucuses or auxiliaries of other organizations, but in our own organization that allows us to define our own goals and to determine our own programs. We must be active individually in other revolutionary organizations and take leadership roles in determining their programs, but each of us must be a part of a revolutionary woman's movement if real change in our condition is to occur.

What Should We Do?

Women in each class, in each culture (Black, Third World, Indian), will have to determine the most appropriate means of struggle for themselves. Revolutionary battles cannot begin until real wages are at least equal to those of men. Fight on those issues, and raise the questions we have outlined above about the kind of work we do and the conditions we live under. Don't wage union fights on *only* bread and butter issues.

Students and middle-class women have been meeting in small groups, no larger, usually, than twenty, to analyze the roots of their oppressions as women. Such groups usually begin by focusing on people's immediate concerns, problems, and experiences, and then dig deeper by asking how those emerged . . . what institutions in society caused these conditions. What each participant once thought was her personal, individual problem, is in fact a social problem, shared by most in the group. It is a problem with institutional roots.

Secondly, the programming we each have undergone becomes clear. We can then build actions around the institutions that reinforce this programming—abortion laws, low wages, hiring discriminations, Bridal Fairs, Wall Street, Virginia Slims ads, etc.

We can build support services so that additional women can join with us. We should develop abortion funds and referral services, birth control information centers, child care facilities—all while pressuring appropriate institutions like the government and the work place to provide these services. This pressuring is not an end in itself; nor are the services we provide or the services the government and business may be forced to provide. Our goal is to raise consciousness by our own actions, and no action should be taken unless it is clear how that consciousness-raising process will be accomplished.

We must reach out and talk with other women. We can give courses on women's history at a local Free University, on campus, or in citywide forums. We can hold dorm meetings, workplace meetings, talk to women at trade and professional schools and prisons and try to develop new ways of communicating with each other (e.g., making films or "comic books").

We must act, as someone said at one of our conferences, as if the revolution had already begun. We must break through the Myth America image and create new ways of living and struggling with each other and with our brothers, as we destroy a system that will allow no growth of this kind. We must relearn how to be human beings, and we must create the conditions so that others, too, can learn. *Viva la revolución!*

Bibliography

Baran, Paul and Paul Sweezy, *Monopoly Capitol*, Monthly Review Press, New York, 1966.

Beard, Mary, *Woman as a Force in History*, New York: The Macmillan Co., 1946.

Bird, Caroline, *Born Female*, New York: David McKay Co., Inc., 1968.

Engels, Friedrich, *Origins of the Family, Private Property and the State.*

Flexner, Eleanor, *A Century of Struggle*, Cambridge: Harvard University Press, 1959.

Friedan, Betty, *The Feminine Mystique*, New York: Dell, 1963.

Galbraith, John Kenneth, *The New Industrial State*, Boston: Houghton Mifflin Co., 1967.

Handbook on Women Workers, United States Dept. of Labor, Washington, D.C., 1965.

Jones, Beverly, *Towards a Female Liberation Movement*, part I, Nashville: SSOC, 1968.

Komarovsky, Mirra, *Blue Collar Marriage*, New York: Random House: 1962.

Mills, C. Wright, *White Collar*, New York: Oxford University Press, 1951.

————, *The Power Elite*, New York: Oxford University Press, 1965.

Packard, Vance, *The Hidden Persuaders*, New York: Pocket Books, Inc., 1957.

————, *The Waste Makers*, New York: Pocket Books, Inc., 1960.

Rainwater, Lee, et al., *Workingman's Wife*, New York: MacFadden Books, 1959.

Shofield, William, *Psychotherapy: The Purchase of Friendship*, New Jersey: Prentice-Hall.

Sinclair, Andrew, *The Emancipation of American Women*, New York: Harper and Row, 1965.

Veblen, Thorstein, *The Theory of the Leisure Class*, New York: Mentor, 1899.

Weber, Max, *The Protestant Ethic and the Spirit of Capitalism*, New York: Charles Scribner's Sons, 1958.

Wells, Lyn, *American Women: Their Use and Abuse*, Nashville: SSOC, 1969.

The Unmothered Woman

Ethel M. Albert

Ethel M. Albert is Professor of Anthropology and Speech at Northwestern University. She holds a Ph.D. from Columbia University where philosophy was her major area and sociology/anthropology her minor area. Dr. Albert is the author of dozens of professional articles, several of which are on women.

It is by now a commonplace that times tend to change faster than attitudes. The twentieth century has seen far-reaching modifications in ideas about human nature and values, both in the social-behavioral sciences and in the opinions of the general public. Yet, these revised attitudes have lagged far behind changes in science and technology, as well as those in society, economy, and polity. In the midst of rapid, widespread, and unpredictable change, it is not enough merely to catch up. We must try to anticipate future developments and to reshape our thinking to fit tomorrow's realities.

No crystal ball is needed to foresee a heavy demand on our rationality and intellectual courage in the immediate future. Repeated warnings of the likely effects of the steadily rising worldwide population curve have evoked pleas for population control measures. But this is not enough. The spread of technology and progress in automation have transformed the way of life of a substantial part of mankind and are rapidly altering life in every corner of the globe. Between them, population increase and technological progress are leading to a world in which there will be more and more people with less and less work to do. A grim wit has observed that if the shadow of the mushroom-shaped cloud that constantly hovers above us should become substance, we will not have to worry about the biologic avalanche or much of anything else. This threat to survival represents still another grave problem for our times.

In the past, the practical problems of society have stimulated progress in the theoretical sciences. We are confronted now by threats to our well-being and to our very existence that dwarf the predicaments of earlier eras. They represent an obligation and an opportunity to advance our knowledge of ourselves and to use it to bring our runaway world under control.

Chapter 4 of *The Challenge to Women*, edited by Seymour M. Farber and Roger H. L. Wilson, © 1966 by Basic Books, Inc., Publishers, New York. Reprinted by permission.

The ordeal by reason has been undergone by successive generations as science developed. Our forebears survived the shock of learning that there are mountains on the moon, that the earth spins on its axis and revolves about the sun, that the face of the earth and the creatures who inhabit it have not always been as they now appear but have evolved through long ages. Now it is our turn, and the nature of human nature is the storm center. To achieve a truly reliable, rational account of ourselves, we must be willing to sacrifice the comfort of familiar notions. Our "eternal truths" and "abiding values" may have no more foundation than the belief that the earth is flat. Subjected to the tests of factual observation and rational analysis, they may turn out to be mere stereotypes and stale platitudes.

In the history of ideas, nothing is sacred—not even motherhood. This is an ideal subject for the study of warring stereotypes and pious slogans. In itself, the concept of motherhood has undergone many ups and downs. Moreover, it is bound into a culture pattern of belief that involves a whole set of interlocking ideas about human nature. Attitudes toward motherhood determine attitudes toward childlessness. Beliefs about women are tied to beliefs about men. What we think is good about maternity determines what we think is bad about childlessness and is related to the fact that we hardly give a thought to paternity. Defects in our beliefs and attitudes about any one of the interlocking concepts of the pattern will be reflected in errors about the others.

As a category, the unmothered or childless woman is about as meaningful and useful as the category of "dresses that are not green," or "sounds that are not music," or "people who are not six feet tall." The "unmothered woman" is in truth a noncategory. It is merely the negative of stereotypes of motherhood, also a noncategory. A quick, informal inventory will only confirm the contention that we are dealing with a term that has no corresponding referent in reality. Consider: among childless women, some are so because they cannot have children, some as a matter of choice; some are devoted to careers, some not; some are young and perhaps only temporarily childless, while others are not so young but have lost their children to time or to accident or disease; some women have no children because they do not like men and cannot or will not marry. A prostitute early afflicted with gonorrhea of the sort that leads to sterility will be childless; but so is the nun childless, from unutterably different causes; and so, too, is the carefree but careful bachelor girl.

The category of mothers, considered in its physiological, psychological, and social aspects, is in reality hardly more uniform. Nevertheless, motherhood is presented to us as though it were the same for all women and as though all women were equally fitted for it. For what it is worth, there is some choice among current stereotypes of motherhood.

Largely as an overreaction against the antifeminine feminism of the suffragettes, young women today are being offered what their conservative grandmothers believed was the only truly feminine role, marriage and the family. A mechanized version of the madonna ideal is part of the package. Sufficient publicity has been given to the idealization of motherhood to make description here superfluous. Rejection or criticism of the madonna ideal has in some instances taken the form of wholesale and bitter condemnation of "momism." Freudianism and other psychoanalytic and psychological theories must bear their share of responsibility for perpetuating some very negative and unscientific notions in the name of science. If we were to credit some of what is said in the name of psychology, we would have to believe that mothers are monsters, the very opposite of madonnas. The notion that women are fit for nothing but motherhood, that they envy males and use motherhood and wifehood to avenge themselves on the superior sex—all this and the rest that goes with it sounds oddly familiar. A moment's thought will tell us that the radical Freudian model of the female, far from being the latest thing in science, is a faithful replica of an ancient, patriarchal tradition. Extending from Asia to Europe and part of Africa and exported to the New World, it is a time-honored attitude that dishonors women, no matter what they do or do not do.

The unmothered woman fares badly, whichever stereotype is favored. On the madonna theory, a childless woman is missing the greatest if not the only joy available or proper to a woman. On the monster theory, an unmothered woman is unfeminine, unfulfilled, and no doubt a castrating female to boot. Not even a glance is wasted on the unfathered male, on the distinctly counterfactual assumption that paternity is a matter of supreme indifference to men. Stereotypic thinking obscures our vision of human beings as real people, as individuals with distinctive personalities and life histories, with highly variable physiological characteristics and abilities.

Flatly stated, no conception of human nature can be trusted if it ignores the fact that humankind is characterized by an immense range and variety of individual differences. Simplistic categories do not reveal but conceal the nature of human nature. If a theory advanced in the name of science confirms ancient or stereotypic beliefs, it should on principle be suspect. As Henri Poincaré pointed out, the closer an idea is to what appeals to common sense, the further it is likely to be from science. At all events, in our present situation, we do not need laborious experimental or statistical studies to get a clear conception of the contents and effects of stereotypes of the unmothered woman in our society. We all possess a great many facts of direct observation and common knowledge that will, if we only let them, admirably serve the purpose of dissolving this noncategory.

It is reasonable to assume that a "natural," "normal" life for human beings of both sexes includes marriage and the family. Emphatically, this does not imply that anyone who is not married or who is childless is "unnatural" or "abnormal." Let us examine the sense in which the notions of natural and normal are used before attempting to draw conclusions about those whose life patterns are not typical.

Used in so many ways over several thousands of years, the notion of the "natural" has become a verbal muddle. In one sense, it means that human beings belong to the natural order like other creatures and are not endowed with separate and supernatural qualities. In a sense more relevant to our problem, natural means what is biologically possible, easy or agreeable, as it should be. On the other hand, "doing what comes naturally" may land you in jail. In what sense is it natural for women to have children? Nobody would contend that it is unnatural for women to have children or natural for men to have them. The relevant sense and significance of assertions of the naturalness of childbearing and the potential for nonsense and error can best be seen in the contrast between what is natural and what the ancient Greeks called conventional —that is, between what is given by nature in contrast to what is devised by human intelligence and technique.

The natural fitness of women for bearing and raising children takes on an uneasy meaning when it is viewed in relation to the roles of obstetricians, pediatricians, and gynecologists. What is the function of these specialists and of others concerned with maternal and infant health, if motherhood is so natural? Even with expert assistance, women may die in childbirth; children may be miscarried or stillborn; or childbearing may gravely impair maternal health. We can measure the lack of naturalness of childbearing by comparing the rates of maternal and infant mortality and morbidity in societies that have modern medical science with those closer to a "state of nature." In the absence of medical science, the rates of maternal and infant mortality and the wretchedly low health level of women who bear children from menarche to menopause are quite enough to dampen enthusiasm for nature as a science teacher. We will find her no better as a moral guide.

Biologically determined inability to bear children is not uncommon. Nature herself has made some women sterile and has crippled the health of others so that they risk life if they attempt to bear children. These unmothered women cannot very well be called unnatural in the literal sense of the term, since they are biologically, hence naturally, unmothered. In some other quite slippery sense, sterile women are sometimes viewed as unnatural and as such may be subjected to unwanted pity or humiliation. In much the same way, when a romantic and rosy notion of nature is held, women who have serious difficulties having children may be reproached as failing or even as refusing to be natural. As an example of natural behavior, they may have held up to them some peasant woman half way around the world who simply interrupts her daily tasks for a brief hour to have her baby. To be sure, there is not usually a follow-up inquiry into the health of the peasant mother or her baby. Domesticated animals—cows and mares—need help to deliver their young. But all this talk of the naturalness of maternity is really not very meaningful. Mothers or unmothered women are individuals. Biologically—that is, naturally—they are differentiated from each other on a long continuum of variability. At the comfortable and happy end are women who in fact bear children with relative ease and safety; at intervals along the continuum are those who encounter various degrees of physical hardship; and at the other end are those who cannot have children. This is continuity, not a simple dichotomy in biological nature of mothers and childless women.

Mother Nature, unfortunately, is more the monster than the madonna type in regard to the relation of psychological to biological variations. She has made no natural law to fit personality and life history to physiological endowment. A biologically sterile woman may have all the character attributes of an ideal mother, as some have demonstrated in their excellent care of adopted children. But these children are often so-called unwanted children. This must remind us that biological maternity is not correlated very neatly with psychological or social aptitude or liking for motherhood. Having babies is one thing, raising them another. There are women who murder their own infants, and some who beat and starve their offspring, and not a few who regularly mistreat and neglect their children. Such women have been called "unnatural mothers." But what does this signify? They are surely nobody's ideal of motherhood, but we evade a wider truth if we merely dismiss them as unnatural.

In some sense, whatever human beings are or do is natural. But many types of conduct are and must be socially defined as criminal, or immoral, or otherwise subject to sanctions. It is criminally wrong for a woman to destroy an unwanted infant; it is socially wrong for a woman to neglect her children out of boredom with the domestic routine or dislike of the hardships imposed by maternity. Even in its extreme forms, psychological unfitness for motherhood in women who have actually become mothers biologically is too frequent to allow us to exclude it from a description of motherhood. Real flesh-and-blood mothers cannot simply be divided between good and bad or natural and unnatural. Again, we need a continuum, finely graded, to represent with fidelity the variations we know exist in nurtural feelings, adequacy to the tasks of child-care, interest in the home and family life, and other psychological and social aspects of child-rearing. Places at the upper end of this continuum must be reserved for some childless women and for some men, fathers and nonfathers.

If some mothers are not maternal and if some nonmothers are nurtural, something must be wrong with the statement that nature intended women to be mothers. It is far too shaky a notion to serve as the basis of a description of human nature. If we mean by "nature" biology or physiology, we would be well-advised to say so. But if we mean by natural or unnatural a positive or negative value judgment disguised as a statement of fact, we have a more difficult task of clarification before us.

Reinforcing and to some extent overlapping with the confused notions of natural and unnatural is a nearly incredible misuse of the concepts of normal and abnormal. To be sure, most women are mothers, hence only relatively few are childless; most mothers are probably at least reasonably good, hence only relatively few are either very good or very bad. These are merely statistical generalizations. To convert any descriptive statement into a normative one, to convert a statement of "what is" into a rule of "what ought to be," is a violation of one of the most elementary rules of logic. Normal and natural seem to refer to what is; but they function in both positive and negative form as unexamined judgments of what ought to be.

Clearly, we need norms and standards for the sane conduct of life. It is not possible to make effective individual or social decisions on the view that anything goes, that "that that is, is right." But to convert the central or "normal" part of the curve of normal distribution into a rigid rule to govern conduct and judgment of it is to create problems, not to solve them. The idea of the normal becomes a Procrustes' bed that makes misfits of us all. If we see from a table of normal heights that a child is somewhat undersize for his age, we do not set about stretching him to fit the norm. Or if a child is oversize for his age, we do not cut off his head or feet or try to shrink his body to make it conform to the norm. Yet, let anyone depart a millimeter from the notion of normal personality, and we call in the head-shrinker. This is a very bad pun. There is little else to laugh at in our overpsychologized modern life. A rigid conception of what is normal and the accompanying label of "abnormal" for any departures from it impose wholly unnecessary burdens of guilt, shame, anxiety, or inconvenience on otherwise perfectly nice, normal, human beings.

Any scientific concept can be distorted and misused. To reject the abuses does not entail rejecting the concept. We are here concerned particularly with those abuses of the concept of normal personality, by laymen or professionals, that merge with stereotypic thinking in their narrow tyranny over individual adjustment patterns, hence in their lack of factual reliability and their potential for inflicting harm. A review of the factual grounds of some of the more common epithets applied to the childless woman, often in the guise of learned diagnoses of abnormality, should reveal the weaknesses we suspect. In the interest of economy of effort, we may deal at the same time with two questions: Are the various characteristics attributed to the unmothered woman usually or always correctly attributed? Are they also found among mothers? This simple test of "agreement and difference" for the validity of generalizations has long been useful in ridding us of spurious hypotheses.

The unmarried, unmothered woman should in all propriety be an isolate. In common parlance, loneliness is her inescapable fate. Doubtless, there are childless women who are lonely, some of the time or most of the time. But we must not confuse being alone or living alone with being lonely. In our overpopulated, densely packed world, the charms of solitude have by necessity been foregone and have been nearly forgotten. There can, of course, be too much of a good thing, even of the peace and quiet of solitude. But this is a relative matter. Individuals differ in their requirements for solitude and company. Living alone, particularly if there is a job or career that fills the day with the usual crush of human contacts, is a necessity for some and a luxury for others—one that they would not give up without a struggle. These are our stubborn spinsters and bachelors, and no amount of well-intentioned matchmaking will tear them away from the privilege and pleasure of solitary dwelling. On the other side of the ledger, those who have a real need for solitude, male or female, suffer intensely in the typical family life of our day, in which there is no adequate provision for privacy, peace or quiet. Further, as we perfectly well know, modern family life seems almost calculated to impose real loneliness on mothers and sometimes on fathers and children as well. It is that especially painful kind of loneliness that is suffered in the midst of company. A young woman who devotes herself to her family, to the virtual exclusion of other concerns and company, may be utterly isolated in the very bosom of her family, even if she never has a minute to herself. Sharing few interests with husband or children, she may know better than many an unmothered woman what loneliness is. Where the "joys of motherhood" notion of normal feminine life prevails, a lonely mother cannot admit, either within her own thoughts or aloud, that she is not happy. Far from receiving solace for her suffering, if she should dare to speak of it to a party-line adherent to the psychological norm, she can expect reproach and criticism for failing to derive supposedly normal satisfaction from the supposedly normal way of life for women. She is, in fact, more cruelly treated than the unmothered woman, who, if she is lonely, is conforming to the expected pattern.

In contemporary society, we need a new category, that of the "demothered woman," the woman whose children are grown and have left the parental home to found families of their own. Such "technological unemployment" for mothers occurs at an age when modern women are still relatively young and vigorous. Sad but relevant is the probability of widowhood at some point, since the life expectancy of women is greater than that of their husbands in our society. A woman who has given her earlier years entirely to her family may find herself alone, with twenty to forty years of life yet before her. Changing a way of life does not come easily in middle age. Yet, no individual can be expected to sit around for two or more decades, idly waiting for the end in the chill comfort of the knowledge that she has done her duty by society and posterity.

The predicament of the demothered woman is very striking evidence of the anachronism in the view that the normal life for women is motherhood and nothing else. In our grandmother's time, the size of family and the hardships of household management, as well as the great hazards to maternal health, combined to keep the average woman busy with her family during the entire course of her natural life. Her older daughters' older children might easily have been older than her own younger offspring. Despite the biologic avalanche on a worldwide scale, and despite the recent upward trend in American family size compared to what it was a generation ago, modern women, with few exceptions, have very small families. This, added to the technological lightening of the burdens of keeping house, the spread of education to both sexes and to the college level as the aspiration of our young people, the remarkable improvement in maternal health and great extension of life expectancy, results in demothering a substantial number of mothers, as I observed above, when they still have twenty to forty years of useful time ahead of them.

In respect to her way of life and personality, the voluntarily childless woman may be very similar to the biologically sterile woman and the demothered woman, even to some mothers. In stereotype, however, she is in a class apart. If one must be voluntarily childless, the easiest way is to admit, if not to insist upon, being a miserable and maladjusted wretch. It helps no end to have no figure, to wear neither cosmetics nor jewelry, and to dress badly, preferably with a few safety pins conspicuously substituting for buttons. With or without these badges, the woman who is voluntarily childless, and that by her own admission, must of course be "unfeminine," whatever that means. She no doubt has suffered childhood trauma, the all-purpose causal factor of abnormality, and probably has some sort of father fixation. Those who marry and give it up as a bad job are, of course, disillusioned, bitter, probably frigid, man-haters, maybe secret drinkers. Careers are, needless to say, some sort of overcompensation.

Alas for this sort of pseudo-learned stereotyping, there is no very convincing correlation between femininity, sexiness, marriage, and motherhood, nor between singleness or childlessness and bitterness, man-hating, neurosis, and secret drinking. The traditional image of the frowsy, eccentric, tight-lipped old maid—whatever language is used to describe this caricature—is not very apt for the modern career woman. Actually, even in the good old days when spinsters were really spinsters, some terribly plain girls caught husbands, and some pretty ones did not, could not, or would not. Some of the most unpromisingly flat figures respond to maternity with greater ease and less pain than the curvaceous Titian ideal. Bitterness, frustration, and man-hating no doubt exist in the psychological make-up of some unmothered women, but they have no monopoly on these unhappy states. Some of the most bitter and most frustrated women, some of the most efficient and dedicated man-haters, are found among wives and mothers. Many childless women appear to be quite content with their lives and even to like men, both as persons and as males. Secret or public drinking, repression, neurosis, frigidity, nymphomania, homosexuality, and the other abnormalities, singly or in various combinations, that supposedly "explain" the unmothered woman are generously shared with wives and mothers. With a slight vocabulary adjustment, men, too, may join the distinguished company. Motherhood is no protection, childlessness no special hazard to our embattled psyches. There is real meaning in the notion of the abnormal, but it is not so easily defined or described or identified as some would lead us to believe. The relativity of normal behavior to the specific characteristics of the person is well established in more thoughtful quarters.

For a voluntarily childless woman to say anything in favor of her way of life may lead to suspicions of "sour grapes," or of defensiveness or some such thing. But it is necessary and it should be possible to communicate in some way how a woman, even approximately in her right mind and bearing few if any stigmata of acute maladjustment, may actually prefer to remain childless. This is, in fact, a very poor way of stating the case. To prefer some other design for life to motherhood is not so astonishing. It may even appear rational if we consider it in the light of the great opportunities for choice open to all or most of us in the modern world. It is also reasonable in the light of the fact that nature has endowed human beings of both sexes not only with reproductive organs but also with eyes, ears, hands, a marvelously complex higher nervous system, and more. A woman who finds in herself no interest in children and housekeeping but who has a magnificent singing voice, or a high I.Q., or nimble fingers, or an eye for color is doing the rational thing when she chooses what she can do well in preference to what she cannot do well. The same principle applies whether a woman is biologically or psychologically unfitted for motherhood. And it applies also to women who have an interest in children and other interests as well. What we do with our lives depends on our specific set of abilities and disabilities.

The inappropriateness of the notion, in whatever form, that all young women must marry and have children to be "natural" and "normal" is further evidenced by data on the actual life patterns of women in our society. Married or unmarried, mothers or not mothers, a significant proportion of our feminine population spend a very considerable part of their time and energy on matters other than motherhood. Not a few derive more satisfaction from their jobs or careers than from their families. A great many can enjoy their families as much as they do precisely because they are also engaged in other satisfying activities. Either most women, then, are not "normal," or the notion of normal needs to be broadly and realistically defined.

Defective representations of the normal harm precisely those who are least able to defend themselves. Not the strong, the clear-eyed, the realistic, or the mature woman—these will sooner or later see through the fictions and steer clear of them. Even so, there is probably an unavoidable waste of time and energy and a disagreeable choice between speaking out against prevailing modes of thought instead of tending to business or accepting the nasty hypocrisy of doing what she wishes and giving lip service to fashionable fictions. But the gentle, the timid, the uncertain, those who want very much to do what is right, and, worst of all, the young and confused, cannot easily swim against the current. If their aspirations and preferences do not conform to what they have been misled to believe is normal, they suffer secret self-doubt and are fair game for the make-believe scientific diagnoses of self-styled experts in psychology.

Parlor psychoanalysis has become a game that any number can play. In addition to points won by displaying jargon, players can improve their score by using the unverifiability of statements about the unconscious. Just about anything, from a toothache to pregnancy, can be "explained" as psychosomatic. In the excitement of this heady game, "psychosomatic" and "imaginary" illnesses are confusedly and cruelly treated as the same thing. The principal contribution of popular psychological extensions of ancient stereotypes, imperfectly concealed by new names, is the addition of two new types of emotional disturbance to the already lengthy list: psychological hypochondriasis and iatrogenic psychoneurosis.

If our theories are to make sense and our guides to behavior are to be free from the needless tyranny of fixed and narrow ideas, we need reliable information to guide us. It is wrong to overdraw the joys of motherhood and the pains of childlessness. It is equally wrong to overdraw the joys of the career woman, with or without a family, and the pains of maternity. The decision to devote one's life to a career should not be lightly made. Few human beings of either sex have that intensity of devotion to a life-work that makes them self-sufficient or nearly so. A combination of family and career is feasible only for a woman who has a cooperative husband, a reasonably good income, considerable physical strength, a strongly organized personality, and other characteristics none too generously granted to mere mortals. In the present heavily competitive and demanding world of business and the professions, the women are surely no less subject than the men to the penalties of tension and overwork. They are no less a prey to the situational uncertainties and self-doubts that make business and professional life at the same time exciting but a very rough game. Certainly, a career cannot rationally be viewed in the pure idealistic light of the socially and economically underprivileged suffragettes of an earlier day. A career means hard work. It is not a privilege to work hard, but part of a realistic description of the actualities. It would be most injudicious to ignore the fact that it is still generally true that a woman has to be "twice as good to get half as far." Neither for mothers nor for career women is this world a utopia.

Once we dismiss a one-track notion of what is normal, we can see that the only thing that unequivocally differentiates mothers from unmothered women is that the former do, whereas the latter do not, have children. This is not saying much, but there is really nothing more to say about it. Stereotypes, in whatever form they appear, are objectionable because they are incorrect. They are thus unsuited for purposes of theory construction. The truth hurts, we are told, but myths and fictions may hurt much more, certainly in the long run. By their very nature, stereotypes are a demand for conformity, a blind force that cannot guide intelligently either individual development or the control of socially undesirable behavior. On the contrary, the discrepancies between facts and fictions about human nature and behavior create tensions and represent a serious waste of human resources.

In a subsistence society, there are few choices for anyone. The demands of survival make family life the only feasible way for women or for men. For neither sex is there any need of elaborate provision for individual variation, and for neither sex is there the possibility of conflict between parenthood and career, between one way of life or another. In a simple world, simple patterns are not stereotypes, nor are they unrealistic. Once the conditions of life permit choice, its intelligent exercise demands more complex models. Choice also involves courage, for even the wisest and best-informed can make the wrong decision. An insistent demand for conformity saps courage and destroys individuality and responsibility.

In no case are the beliefs and habits of thought appropriate for a simple farming or hunting society serviceable in a complex technological society. The standard of the natural and the normal being offered to today's young women was already out of date in the nineteenth century. It has no positive function in the world of today. Worse than that: we can only gape in open-mouthed incredulity at the sheer folly of urging young women, irrespective of their talents and tastes, to have families, and larger families at that, when we are confronted by the problems of rising population. If this is rational, what is irrational?

Here, precisely, is the crux of the matter. Verbal arguments and criticisms in themselves are not necessarily significant. But they are called for, and called for loudly, when logic and evidence are against a theory. Theory is "mere" theory if it does not work well, either in controlled experiment or in practical application. The principle of verification—in effect, test by experience—is the same in physics, medicine, psychology, and anything else that claims the name of science. At least since Freud, psychoanalytic theory and some psychological theories have claimed immunity from this critical scientific test. Parenthetically, psychiatry and neurophysiology are not in question here. We would not under any circumstances accept a claim to immunity from empirical verification or verifiability from others. Imagine a physician insisting that his diagnosis of a bodily illness is correct, even though there is no confirmable evidence for it, and that his cure is right even when it fails, on the ground that the failures are due only to the recalcitrance of his patients. If we refuse such a position to the physicians of the body, we cannot in reason permit it to the physicians of the mind, or to educators of our young people, or to parents or others charged with the tasks of facilitating human adjustment in this complex world.

It is part of the American way to face up bravely and actively to any problematic state of affairs and when something is wrong to set to work to correct it. But we have to be very sure indeed that we know what is wrong, lest the cure prove worse than the disease. We are all children of our times; many of us, having shared the general enthusiasm for the promise of psychoanalytic and psychological theory, understand very well the seductiveness of their teachings. When a theory ceases to be science and becomes an "ism," a doctrine, a shibboleth, it must lose our support. Single-minded devotion to an idea or ideal is admirable, but it must not make us deaf and blind. The belief that the mentally and emotionally ill as well as the physically ill can and should be cured needs no defense. However, when it is so interpreted that a school psychologist undertakes to "cure" a girl of an excess of creativity or independence of judgment, or of intellectual excellence, it has missed its mark. When a physician is so persuaded of the power of mind over matter that he forgets that people have bodies and that human bodies can get out of order with no assistance from the psyche, when virtually all his patients suffer from the same disease—psychosomatic illness—the ideal has missed its mark. When any of us think that we can diagnose or cure the unprecedented disorganization of individuals and society in all their complexity and variety by using a simple verbal formula for what is normal or natural, we are betraying the whole meaning of science and grinding into the dust the ideal of resolute attack on the troubles that besiege us.

But no truth is so complete and so powerful that it can stand alone as the whole truth and nothing but the truth. The truth of any idea is part of a complex network of truths. When a belief, no matter how long or how deeply we have cherished it, has failed the test of experience, it must be reexamined and perhaps surrendered altogether. It is morally and intellectually inexcusable to persist in a way of thinking without examining it or to clutch it to our bosom when there are serious doubts of its logical or factual reliability.

The right to make a mistake has perforce to be granted to everyone, even scientists and educators, parents and physicians, since we are after all only human and since the truth is hard to come by. As the philosopher Spinoza observed, "all things excellent are as difficult as they are rare." The criticism of some trends in current thinking about human nature that has been offered above is doubtless in many respects defective and inadequate. That does not matter: it is a confession of ignorance, an insistence on ignorance, about the nature of human nature. And the active awareness of ignorance is the indispensable condition of a rational quest for reliable knowledge. We know a little, but not enough.

To the extent that we share a common set of social perceptions that are out-of-date, incompatible with the dominant trends of our time, and inconsistent with our higher values, we owe each other as much candor and as much accurate information as we can possibly muster. This is a minimal condition to enable us to work together to correct defects and solve problems. It is nobody's task to "debunk" motherhood. It is everyone's task to be accurate and realistic about it. It is nobody's task to prove that the unmarried, unmothered state is so far superior to that of the married mother that all women should forthwith abandon having husbands or babies. The critical issues are not really here at all. They arise from the overwhelmingly difficult predicament of our rapidly changing modern society, which is already out of breath trying to keep up with itself.

Usually, neither having children nor not having them is a direct response to population statistics. No merit badges need be distributed to unmothered women, nor need we form an association of "Women against Motherhood." It is highly doubtful whether a sensible and realistic view of maternity and of its alternatives or combinations with

other activities could bring about a sufficient downward trend in repro-
duction to solve our population problems. The biologic avalanche is a
challenge to all of us, but it entails far more than mere population
control. We are in trouble, for we have a strange new world to live
in—women and men, mothers and the unmothered—in brief, humanity. The surrender of our comfortable misconceptions is at best a beginning, and it is after all a small price to pay, if it simultaneously improves
our understanding of human-kind, facilitates individual development,
enables us to realize some of the highest values of our society—and gives
us at least a fighting chance to come to terms with tomorrow.

The Sex Map of the Work World

Caroline Bird

Caroline Bird studied at Vassar, the University of Toledo, and the University of Wisconsin. She has been on the staff of the *Journal of Commerce, Newsweek,* and *Fortune* and now writes frequently for many popular magazines. In addition to *Born Female,* she has written *The Invisible Scar,* a book about the long-range effects of the Depression on American society.

It isn't polite to admit it, but money is one of the reasons why sex is important. The fact is that women simply do not get hold of as much money that they can legally call their own as do the men in their lives. Very rich widows sometimes do, and so do very poor Negro women, who can get work when their husbands can't, but they are treated as exceptional cases.

Everyone seems to think that this country is full of idle rich women living on money inherited from a husband or father. Such women are highly visible on Caribbean cruises or at resorts, and stockbrokers and other salesmen often cite the vast assets that idle rich women are supposed to control.

The sad fact of the matter is that idle rich women are very rare. Census breakdowns prove this. If you modestly define as idle rich any person with an independent income of $10,000 a year or more for which he did not work, there were only 87,269 idle rich women in the United States in 1966, or one-tenth of one percent of all the women 14 years old and older. That same year there were 96,252 idle rich men in the same situation lolling around the United States, and since there were seven million fewer men than women 14 years old and older in the population, your chances of being idly rich were a shade better if you were male. In 1966, most people in the upper income brackets worked for at least part of their money.

However women come by money—whether by inheritance, by earnings, or as dependents—they simply don't get as much money or as unequivocal control of it as men. This isn't supposed to matter, but in an increasingly money-driven society, it *does* matter. If it really didn't matter, no one would giggle when saying that women "really own" the country (they don't, of course, not even if you count property nominally owned by women but controlled by men), or that "women are the reason why men want money," or that "Mrs. Consumer makes or breaks business" because she is the family purchasing agent.

Money is divided along sex lines so sharply that the statistics are worth a close look. In 1966, the most recent year for which census breakdowns are available, nearly 40 percent of adult women had no independent income at all. Most of them, of course, were supported by husbands who handed them money to spend or bought them what they needed without legally transferring funds to them. The other 60 percent had incomes of their own, from investments, earnings, welfare payments, alimony, or some other source, but half of these received less than $1,638 during the year. Adult men did much better: 92 percent had income from some source, and their median income—half above, half below—was $5,306.

Many conditions contribute to this gap. First of all, most income is earned, and men are the earners. Many more men than women earn money, and men spend more of their time earning than women. Most of the women who earn work only part time, or part of the year. In 1966, 60 percent of all the men reporting income from any source were full-time, year-round workers, compared with only 30 percent of all the women with income of their own. What's more, the men earned almost twice as much money for the same effort. In 1966, half the women working full time earned only $4,000 or less, compared with $7,000 for men. This difference reflects the fact that women are often limited to work that pays less than the work done by men, and also that women are not paid as much as men even if they are doing the same work.

Many employers see nothing wrong in a dual pay scale. In 1961, for instance, one third of 1,900 employers queried by the National Office Managers Association frankly admitted that they systematically paid men more than women. That year, the Women's Bureau reported sizable differentials between the wages paid men and women for jobs carrying identical titles. Male bank tellers, for instance, earned from $5 a week more in Atlanta to $31 a week more in Milwaukee.

The gap widens at the upper brackets. Women scientists and engineers are paid $2,500 to $3,000 less a year than men in the same positions, according to an article in the Winter 1965 issue of the *Harvard Medical Alumni Bulletin*, by Ruth Kundsin, a bacteriologist. An executive recruiter reports that the managers of a manufacturer in northern New Jersey saved money by hiring a woman to serve as their chief financial officer at $9,000 a year. When she left, they had to pay $20,000 to get a man to do her job. When *he* left, they went back to a woman at $9,000 and they then replaced *her* with a man at $18,000. According to the recruiter, all four employees were good at the job.

Employers have long assumed that there is a ceiling on the financial "worth" of a woman. When President Grover Cleveland was pioneering the nonpolitical Civil Service in the 1880s, the first administrators were quoted as saying that no woman appointee could be paid more than $1,200 a year. In 1919, Senator Reed Smoot established a salary ceiling for the staff of the Women's Bureau. "No woman on earth is worth more than $2,000 a year," he told Mary Anderson, the first director.

The dollar figures have inflated, of course, but the notion of a ceiling persists to this day. In 1967, for instance, the leading public relations placement agency told a woman looking for a job that $12,000 was the most any employer in this field would pay to hire a woman from the outside, while salaries for men were negotiated on an individual basis. Many women who have founded businesses of their own say they did so to get out from under an arbitrary salary ceiling, and the census figures bear them out. Women earning top incomes are slightly more apt to be self-employed than men making the same money.

Wherever distinctions of pay can be drawn, women draw the lower-rated job. A study reported by the Women's Bureau shows that in 1964 women sales workers earned 60 percent less than men sales workers; women managers, officials, and proprietors earned 45 percent less than men in those classifications, and women clerks earned 44 percent less than men clerks. Unions are quite candid. Women earn less, they report, because they are assigned to jobs that pay less.

Men and women often do exactly the same thing in all but name and pay. In some organizations, for instance, both men and women process applications for employment. Both have the same authority, but the men are called "interviewers" and are paid more than the women, who are merely "clerks." A woman lawyer who worked for the Government during the war recalls with amusement that men who adjusted minor differences with war contractors called themselves "expediters" "negotiating" contracts, while women who did the same thing, at lower pay, said they were "writing a change order." Management consultants frequently turn up men and women doing the same job under differing titles when they analyze what each employee really does.

"Women's jobs" pay less than "men's jobs" of comparable education. A college education has been a reliable economic elevator for all minority groups, but according to a calculation for a recent year, California women with four or more years of education beyond high school averaged $4,151, only $300 more than California men who had left school at the end of the eighth grade. At the same time, California men with four or more years of college averaged $8,108. In California, as in the nation, teaching is the most popular vocation for educated women. Teaching is defined as a "woman's job," and like nursing, another woman's profession, it pays less than other occupations requiring comparable education.

"Women's work" pays less than "men's work" of comparable skill and steadiness. A taxi driver has to be about as skillful as a cleaning woman who can run the machinery of a mechanized home. Moving up the skill ladder, a trained nurse has invested more time and money in her education, and her responsibility is at the very least as great as that of an electrician—but the electrician earns more money per hour. Part of the reason for the gap is that transport workers and electricians are more apt to be unionized.

The gap between the pay of men and women is wider than it seems on the basis of take-home pay. Half of all the people who work in offices, factories, or establishments of any kind except farms are now covered by a pension or retirement plan other than Social Security, but few of these plans protect the families of women employees as well as they protect the families of men. The plan may force a woman to retire earlier, even though a woman can expect to live longer and in better health than a man.

During her 1967 investigation of pension plans, Congresswoman Martha Griffiths dramatized the inequity by asking Government men who testified before her pension committee, "Why should I be paying to support your widow, when you aren't paying to support my husband?"

The Social Security system favors widows over widowers of workers in a similar way. If a working woman elects to take benefits as a widow rather than as a worker—and she often comes out better that way—she doesn't get any benefits for Social Security payments that have been deducted from her earnings. But when she dies, her husband does not benefit from her payments in the same way she benefits from his. Unless he can prove that he is indigent, he gets nothing at all from her Social Security account. But why shouldn't her heirs benefit from all that she has paid in—just as a man's heirs do, whether indigent or not?

Pension plans entirely paid by the company discriminate against women workers in a more subtle but nonetheless effective way, Mrs. Griffiths charged. A typical "noncontributory plan" will vest, or set aside, funds for an employee only after he or she has worked for ten years and reached age 40. This sounds fair enough. If a woman stays ten years and is 40 years old, she gets the pension the same as a man. The fact is, of course, that a woman usually doesn't stay long enough to get the pension. When she leaves, the company hires another woman, and uses the money that would have gone to fund a pension for her job to finance bigger pensions for the men.

Employers see nothing wrong with this arrangement. Their position is that pensions reward long service and protect a man's dependent wife and children. If this is so, Mrs. Griffiths contends, then the pay gap between long-service and short-service employees (in practice, men workers and women workers) is wider than their paychecks indicate. If, on the contrary, the pension is really deferred salary, then the girls who leave are literally cheated out of part of their pay.

Women workers lose out in much the same way on group life insurance, available now to 90 percent of all clerical and production workers. Many of these policies provide larger benefits for men than for women workers and pay less to widowers than widows. And insurance plans that give higher-salaried employees more coverage often allot them additional insurance on the basis of long service, a proviso that discriminates against women workers who have lost their seniority during child-rearing years or even for taking a few weeks off to have a baby.

At the 1967 Congressional hearings on pension plans, a spokesman for American Telephone and Telegraph testified that differentials were adopted "in recognition of different needs and roles of men and women in society." But whatever the intent, the effect is to cut women's pay.

When unions bargain with employers, they add to the dollars in a worker's paycheck all the various fringe benefits—vacations, holidays, sick leave, bonus rights, rights to overtime and premium pay, stock options, savings plans, health and life insurance, rights to buy meals, products, or services at a discount, allowances for uniforms or expenses.

In 1963 a government estimate put employer expenditures on supplementary compensation for nonfactory workers at 24 percent of the payroll. This invisible pay has been rising faster than the dollars workers take home, so those who don't get the "fringes" lag farther and farther behind those who do.

This lag increasingly divides the working world into two groups: first-class workers who have rights to their jobs and the benefits that go with them, and intermittent, second-class workers who, like the poor, are out of the system and entitled only to be paid for the work actually performed. What seems to be growing is a sharp class distinction between work that is less skilled, less responsible, less permanent, and so carries lower pay and fewer fringe benefits, and the more skilled, more responsible, permanent work that carries high pay and a stake in the future of the enterprise.

This cleavage between the ins and the outs worries idealists. It is often used to condone riots in city ghettos. But the fact is that most of these "workers anonymous" without job protection are not Negro men primed for revolution. Most of them are docile wives and mothers. White and Negro women outnumber men in restaurants, hotels, stores, and many other fields where the work is not steady.

Whatever the field, whatever the function, whatever the training, however contribution is measured—by piece rate or time rate or commission—women wind up with less money than men doing the same work. According to the Department of Labor, only 14 percent of the women receiving unemployment compensation earned enough to qual-

ify for the maximum benefit allowed by the various states in 1965, while
59 percent of the men did. Although one out of ten families is headed
by a woman, and the Women's Bureau says that nearly half the women
working really need the money, a woman worker is nearly twice as likely
to be unemployed as a man, and she gets second-class treatment even
then. In 37 states, for instance, she cannot draw unemployment insurance if she is fired for pregnancy.

Women are supposed to be worth less pay because they aren't as
steady workers as men, but continuing U.S. Public Health Service
studies of time lost from work because of illness or injury show that age,
occupation, and salary make more difference than sex. Women seem to
be out sick more than men because they hold the dull, ill-paid jobs that
invite "sickness." Some studies show that men in clerical jobs are
actually out sick more than women and that women over 45 years old
were out sick substantially less frequently than men their age.

It's the same way with turnover. Women quit because they are
confined to jobs that anyone would readily quit. Employers can't expect
to reduce the turnover of any particular job by hiring men instead of
women. Men will resign to get another job almost as often as women
will leave for family reasons. The Bureau of Labor Statistics concludes
that absenteeism and turnover rates depend much more on the nature
of the job than on the sex of the job-holder.

The uncertainty women feel about their job futures handicaps
them in another way. Rather than take a lower-paid job that permits
them to earn while learning, as career-oriented men often do, they
choose dead-end jobs that pay well right from the start, such as
stenographic work. Professor Jacob Mincer, of Columbia University,
who has calculated the money investment in "human capital," found
that women invested only one-tenth as much as men in on-the-job
training defined this way. When women do train on the job, they are
more likely than men to bear the costs themselves, rather than have
them financed by employers. Thus a typist pays a business school to
learn how to operate a typewriter, but the man who repairs it is usually
trained at the expense of a manufacturer. Hairdressers, nurses, teachers,
and many other skilled women are in fields which are entered from
vocational schools that charge tuition. Men, on the other hand, may
qualify as skilled craftsmen by serving as apprentices on the job.

William H. Miller, marketing vice president of American Oil
Company, believes that this "statistical discrimination" is unfair:

> So some women do take time out from the jobs to have children.
> Some men leave one company to go to another or to start a business of
> their own; some men crack up on a job and must be replaced; some
> men become seriously ill or die before they reach the normal age of

retirement. Some become alcoholic. But management doesn't refuse to hire or promote men just because these things happen.

Reasons for dividing jobs on a sexual basis can be pretty far-fetched. Years ago, when girls unexpectedly turned out to be good at typing, people said, "Of course! Girls can type because they are good at playing the piano!" Women themselves claim they are better at paperwork because of a feminine "instinct" for order in the home.

Women's "knack for detail" has been cited as the reason why they should do everything from the filing to computer programming. Fannie Klein, a woman member of the New York City bar, once declared that if a woman were appointed to the Supreme Court, she would be able to handle the "painful and minute details under judicial consideration that men ordinarily leave to their assistants and secretaries." But there is neither agreement on exactly what this knack is, nor evidence that men do not possess it, too.

Very little scientific work has been done on differences between the productivity of men and women in specific jobs. Personnel directors are more apt to go by characteristics such as finger dexterity, strength, speed, coordination, language, and other skills for which sex differences have been established by academic psychologists. But sex-based differences are seldom the critical factor in on-the-job performance.

People have fixed ideas about whether a job should be done by a man or a woman, but their reasons are as arbitrary as a Frenchman's attempt to explain what's so feminine about *la table*. In 1962, a Presidential order requesting all Federal appointing officers to give reasons for requesting a man or a woman for a job opening cut down requests for candidates of a certain sex to one percent of their former volume. Apparently many of the reasons looked lame in writing. Reasons for preferring a man given by the one percent included travel, arduous duty, geographical location, exposure to weather, and lack of facilities for mixed groups.

Explanations for sex-typing are often given in the tone of voice a teller of fairy tales uses to warn his audience that what he says is not to be taken literally: women cannot be railroad yardmasters because they might have to "work at night." Everyone knows, of course, that women telephone operators and trained nurses have always taken night shifts.

A British firm explained to a United Press reporter that it did not hire women executives because all its executives had to make "frequent visits to extreme tropical climates, for which women would not be suitable." No one offered evidence that women suffer more than men in the tropics, nor did anyone mention that wives frequently follow their husbands to jobs in the tropics.

A foreign visitor noticed that workers on electronic circuits in a factory were all women. "It's close work, and women have the finger dexterity for it," the visitor was told. Later on in her tour she visited a medical school class in brain surgery and remarked that the students were all men. "But they've got to be men," the answer came. "Brain surgery takes a steady hand!"

Women are seldom accountants, it is often said, because they have "no head for figures"—a failing which does not prevent them from doing the less prestigious bookkeeping work which really does require a head for figures.

Women practically never manage supermarkets or grocery stores, because "they couldn't move those heavy boxes around in the back room," but except in the smallest stores or in emergencies, the manager doesn't tote boxes himself.

In 1956, a *Fortune* reporter found that corn-husking was a woman's job in Eureka, Illinois, but a man's job in Jackson, Wisconsin, while textile spinning was done by women in Chattanooga mills and by men in North Carolina. Women pharmacists and dentists are common in many European countries, but they are rare in the United States.

The most general explanation of the division of labor between men and women in all societies has been advanced by Talcott Parsons, of Harvard, a leader in sociological theory. Parsons believes that every culture, including the primitive tribes observed by Margaret Mead, assigns men what he calls "instrumental-adaptive" roles and women what he calls "expressive-integrative" roles. Men are "instrumental" or active in doing things to the physical environment and "adaptive" in making policy for the family, the firm, the nation, or the group. By contrast, women are "expressive"—or concerned with registering emotions and "integrating the group." According to Parsons, women generally manage "the internal motivational tensions of the members of a group and their solidarity with each other."

These terms translate quite easily into the popular masculinist stereotypes which have been advanced to keep women "privatized" or unrecognized in law or public affairs. According to Jessie Bernard in *Academic Women*, women are in charge of "domestic relations." They help the insiders get along with each other and keep the place organized. Men are in charge of "foreign relations." They negotiate with the outsiders, the customers, the suppliers, the government, the adversaries, or the allies. The inside-outside principle holds up when it is tested on existing occupational sex labels.

The occupations most completely monopolized by women are the personal services where women do for pay exactly what they would do for their own families. Not unexpectedly, more than 90 percent of all nurses, baby-sitters, household workers, hotel maids, dressmakers, milliners, and dietitians are women.

Women also tend to monopolize those jobs of limited responsibility which involve greeting and serving outsiders in much the same way that a wife welcomes visiting acquaintances of her husband. More than 90 percent of receptionists, attendants in doctors' and dentists' offices, airline flight attendants, and demonstrators, more than 80 percent of persons employed to wait on tables, more than 75 percent of cashiers are women.

Like the 100-percent female "bunnies" who wait on table in Playboy clubs, these women hold their jobs in part because they help to bring in and please customers. The mild titillation of a feminine presence is an admitted factor in offices where the men to be pleased are not paying customers. In 1961, more than a quarter of the 1,900 employers queried told the National Office Management Association that sex appeal figured in some jobs in their offices.

The public image of the millions of women who work in offices is the private secretary or office wife to a policy-making male boss. No clearer definition of the "integrative" function Parsons ascribes to women could be stated than W. M. Kiplinger's "Salute to Secretaries" at the National Secretaries Association meeting of February 1967:

> Secretaries are marvelous people. They are ornamental and they are useful. They take down what you say and improve upon it. They know where to put in the double l's, the commas and the paragraphs. They hold the mad letters until tomorrow. They answer the telephone, sidetrack the bores and put through those on the important list. They remember the birthdays and anniversaries. They remind you that it's time to get going for the lunch date. They see when you need a haircut.

Secretaries may be specially prized, and the top secretaries exceptionally well paid, because they give men who can afford to pay well the subservient, watchful, and admiring attention that Victorian wives used to give their husbands. But increasingly, office wives are rebelling, too. According to an anecdote printed in *Reader's Digest*, one secretary had long resented her boss's boast that he hired girls for their looks and then taught them to type. One day when he was interviewing a particularly handsome male job-seeker, she slipped a note on his desk which read, "Hire him, we'll teach him engineering."

A few brilliant managements have systematically exploited the man-woman relationship. Henry Luce tapped the talents of women with journalistic ability by creating a new wifely role for them. Under Time, Inc.'s system of "group journalism," work was divided along sex lines: men developed ideas and did the writing, and to keep their minds free and untrammeled by details each was supplied with a girl researcher to take notes on interviews, set up appointments, look up facts, and ultimately check the writer's statements against available evidence. Experience as a researcher has developed some competent women writers, but most of them became writers only after leaving Time, Inc.

The writer-researcher team is powerful because it mirrors the contemporary ideal of American marriage. Researchers are not mere handmaidens. They have their own area of authority, and writers are not allowed to forget it. If a writer insists on using a fact his researcher cannot substantiate, she may keep the story out of the magazine by refusing to put a red dot over the disputed word on her "checking copy" of the manuscript.

This complementary relationship of "separate but equal" is not universal. In his comparative study of the occupational roles of women in three cultures, Chester L. Hunt, of West Michigan University, found that American women supplemented men, while Japanese women served them as subordinates, and Filipino women were their occupational equals. Americans may be especially self-conscious about the role of women in part because it is so much harder to supplement another person than to serve, direct, or even treat him as an autonomous equal.

Journalism is one of the few occupations which has a woman for every two men, roughly the ratio of women to men in the labor force generally, yet particular jobs can be rigidly sex-typed within the field. Personnel and labor relations workers, managers in apparel and accessory stores, personal service workers, and foremen in textile and apparel manufacturing have this average sex ratio, too. Yet women in these occupations are sometimes more aware of the limitations of their sex than women in fields where women either predominate or are so rare that like women engineers, they can be taken as exceptions to every rule.

Are there any principles that explain the meanderings of the sex boundaries? One is the idea that women should work inside and men outside. Another earmarks service work for women and profit-making for men. Other rules reserve work with machinery, work carrying prestige, and the top job to men. Most sex boundaries can be explained on the basis of one or another of these three rules.

Take the inside-outside concept. It divides the work of women and men along many axes: cooperation-competition; helping-fighting; welfare-profit; and hence, in our time, public sector-private sector. Let's see how it works.

Competitive private enterprises are apt to be dominated by men, especially if the risk is high and there is a big profit to be made. The automobile and appliance industries fall into this category, and they are frankly hostile to women above the rank of secretary. Investment banking, canning, and large-scale real estate speculation are other highly competitive, profit-oriented businesses where the pace is regarded as "too fast" and the going "too rough" for women in policy-making spots. Retailing and garment-making are high-risk, fast-paced, profit-oriented industries which do promote women, but it must be added that the women buyers or designers who share in the rewards are deprecated as "hard" and "masculine."

Cooperative, helping, welfare work is dominated by women, especially when it is done for little or no money. This idea even carries over into the field of medicine.

In the United States, medicine is still largely private enterprise, and nowhere else do physicians make so much money. At the 1960 Census, for instance, physicians and surgeons led all other occupations in earnings: their median income was nearly $15,000 a year, compared with less than $10,000 for dentists, the next highest-paid occupation. Unlike physicians in some countries, our doctors have to invest their own money in their education and make it "pay out" in private practice. Those who don't have the capital themselves are usually financed through their training and internship by the "sweat capital" of working wives. Nowhere else in the world is medical training so long, so expensive, and so little supported by public funds. And few countries make it quite so hard as we do for women to become doctors.

One reason, of course, is that women are reluctant to invest as much in their own professional training as men. Russia has a high proportion of women doctors partly because since Czarist days the Russian medical system has had a second grade of physician for routine illnesses whose training is shorter, partly because under Communism the Government bears the total cost of medical education for women doctors as well as men. But an additional and significant reason is the strong welfare orientation of Russian medicine. Medical care is a free service that cannot be considered a business. Britain, Yugoslavia, and other countries with socialized medicine also have a higher percentage of women doctors than we.

The welfare-profit boundary is convincing because it exists even in American medicine and law. The few women we do attract to medicine tend to enter Government service or teaching rather than private practice. It's the same way with our women lawyers. They are more apt to work for the Government, nonprofit organizations, or on salary than in what lawyers call the law "business" of serving clients on a fee basis.

The welfare-profit boundary exists within business organizations as well as in broad industry categories. In selling, men are more apt to be compensated by commission than women. The line is dramatic in department stores. Men manage high-priced, high-margin merchandise such as appliances and furniture, while women buyers usually manage departments where the margin is lower.

We had a bit of fun asking our friends why it was that men usually sell women's shoes, while women may sell men's underwear. One acquaintance surmised that there was probably "something masculine about leather." Another thought that women especially valued the attention of men to their legs and the opinion of men on the sexiness of their shoes. The fact is that women's shoes carry a high enough margin to be worth selling on a commission basis, while men's underwear is sold by a salaried clerk.

Organizations which distinguish between "sales" and "service" often assign sales to men and service to women. Office machine manufacturers, among many others, send men out on the road as "salesmen," but follow up with women "service representatives," who teach customer employees how to use the products. Another nonprofit service that women dominate is the adjustment of complaints. They have an easier time holding customers to the rules because a woman isn't expected to have the authority to break regulations.

The service-profit boundary divides personnel work. In business concerns, women hire the routine workers, but men recruit the executives. Women run employment agencies serving job-seekers, but most executive recruiters paid by employers are men. In labor unions or in management departments set up to deal with labor relations, women watch out for employee health, education, and welfare of various kinds, but seldom appear on either side of the bargaining table when contracts are being negotiated and substantial money is at stake.

The service-profit boundary works in banks. Able women sometimes get good jobs in escrow and trust work where the funds of women and children must be protected against risks. They have less chance in the loan department, where profit for the bank can be made and the bank's resources must be risked. The Invisible Bar even separates receiving money from paying money. Banks employed women as receiving tellers before they were allowed to be paying tellers. As late as 1942, the U.S. Department of Labor classified the job of "paying teller" as only "apparently" suitable for women. Everywhere, it seems, "mamma can take the money in, but only papa can pay it out." The town clerk who receives taxes is often a woman, but the clerk who pays the town bills is usually a man. And it's the same way with cashiers and paymasters.

The inside-outside boundary between "domestic" and "foreign" relations runs along the same lines as the service-profit boundary. Men compensated on commission are the "outside" purchasing agents and salesmen who visit vendors and customers to make the deals that result in profit or loss; women on straight salary buy and sell routine, fixed-price items over the phone. It works the same way in newspaper advertising departments: want ads for the classified section are solicited and filled by women telephone workers; display ads are solicited by men on commission who travel and entertain prospects.

Everywhere the women stay inside, "at home" in the office, the organization, the profession, the country, while men work "outside." Advertising agencies employ both men and women to check television commercials, but the men in the bull pens check out-of-town shows that require travel to cover and, say the girls, have to spend fewer hours glued to the screen. Factories don't like to hire women as expediters because this liaison job requires a lot of "running around" from department to department. And it took a major labor shortage as well as equal opportunity laws to convert the Fuller Brush man into a Fullerette and to create jobs for girl letter carriers and gas station attendants.

Women stay "inside" their occupational groups in a figurative way as well as inside the office physically. In organizations, they hold the office of secretary, which deals with the membership. They sometimes become presidents of professional societies which exist to assert the solidarity of an occupational group; in the past few years, women have headed the Society of Magazine Writers and the New York Society of Security Analysts. By contrast, trade associations representing whole industries with Government or the public "outside" the industry seldom, if ever, have a woman chief. When Jessie Bernard compared the publications of male and female college professors, she discovered that more men published in journals "outside" their fields than women. She found that the men were more apt to interpret their specialties to the lay public as "men of knowledge," while women were more apt to teach it to students.

Men are "instrumental" in a literal sense. They will do anything that can be done by *machinery*, including, as we have seen, attending the birth of babies by "instrument." Engineering is the American profession with the fewest women, and the heavy, highly mechanized industries are the ones most opposed to women policy-makers. In railroads, steel, shipping, aviation, space, automobiles, and metal-working the opposition to women above the secretarial or pretty-girl level is categorical. One president of a metal-working company shrugged women off as "totally unsuited to most manufacturing operations." The bad language of men in machine shops is so frequently and seriously cited as a bar to women that it sometimes looks as if men cuss deliberately to prove that no women are present.

The male affinity for machinery is a mystique accepted by both sexes. Women sometimes don't realize that they can change a tire until they have to do it because there is no man around to do it for them. "Women drivers" are a staple joke even for those who know that the most sophisticated studies seldom disclose a significant difference between the accident rate of men and that of women. American women have to drive cars because American life would come to a halt if they didn't, but the notion that a man ought to do it is so strong that a wife usually slides over and gives the wheel to her husband when she picks him up in the car.

As machines have been invented to do women's work, men have taken it over. In 1968, the most sophisticated machine of all, the computer, was bringing men back into clerical work. "You always see *men* sitting at the consoles in the ads for computers," an office manager explained. Ida Hoos, a social scientist who has analyzed the impact of automation on employment, foresees fewer office *girls* but more work for the repair*man*.

It's interesting to see what happens when, as has frequently been the case in America, a job changes sex. "I wonder what's going on in banks," a woman telephone company supervisor said to us. "A bank teller used to be important, but now women do it. They must have changed the teller's job."

"Not really," George Ward of the American Bankers Association replied when we put the question to him. "The teller has always really had a contact job. What's changed is public acceptance of women."

A woman bank teller, accosted on the floor of the bank, disagreed with this view. "It's just money," she said. "Bank salaries haven't risen as fast as salaries in other fields. They can get women cheaper."

A woman personnel officer of a Newark bank told us she didn't discriminate. In her bank all tellers, men and women both, started at $68 a week and advanced regardless of sex to a ceiling of $140. Most of the tellers were women, she said, only because there weren't enough men to go around.

It was not always so. In 1940, women tellers were few and far between. When World War II came, some banks tried to get draft deferment for their tellers on the ground that they were essential. But by the end of the war, women bank tellers were common and everybody liked them. A lot of women stayed on.

What happened next resembled nothing so much as the stampedes that used to occur when a neighborhood shifted from white to Negro. In 1950, bank tellers were almost evenly divided between the sexes. In the next ten years—a decade not marked by gains for women in employment—the job of bank teller passed from men to women. By 1960, 70 percent of the bank tellers in the country were women. In 1966, the First National City Bank of New York was buying display advertising in the help-wanted column:

HOUSEWIVES
TIME ON YOUR HANDS?
CHILDREN GROWN?
TRAIN TO BE A TELLER

Pleasant and interesting work meeting the public
No experience necessary—We will train you

The solidly masculine "important job" had become not only "just a high-grade clerk's job," but a job suitable for bored or rusty housewives.

What has changed? The clue is in Mr. Ward's definition of the job of the teller as the bank's contact with the customer. The old teller was a gatekeeper to money, protected by a literal cage. The bank he guarded financed production. Now it finances consumption and sells bookkeeping services to householders.

By the end of the 1960s, banks have become as friendly, noisy, and informal as supermarkets. Money is just another item on a shopping list. Today everyone has a checking account. Everyone borrows money. Paying the bills has become a housekeeping chore for wives instead of a ritual symbolizing the husband's leadership of the house. The bank is a service station, not a temple. You have a friend at the Chase Manhattan who knows how to fix it so you can fly now and pay later. The banker is no longer a glassy-eyed father judging your character and intentions. He is a kicky playmate.

Or a permissive mother. Banks don't exploit the sex appeal of their tellers as blatantly as airlines exploit the sex appeal of stewardesses, but tellers are supposed to sell, and it helps if they are attractive. In 1966, *The New York Times* business section reported that The Meadow Brook National Bank, "in accord with a theme of peppy conservatism," had retained a fashion consultant to restyle the hair and makeup of the bank's tellers at its Manhasset and Great Neck, Long Island, branches.

Although the lady bank tellers seem to indicate that there are a rising number of women in men's jobs, this is not the case. Women have flocked into the labor market to fill the demand for women's jobs like teaching and nursing or to fill jobs which were too new to be assigned to either sex, as was once the case with typewriting. In his statistical study of the sex ratios of Census occupations from 1900 to 1960, Dr. Edward Gross, Professor of Sociology at the University of Washington, found that men have invaded women's working territory more often than the other way around, while maintaining their monopoly on traditionally male occupations, with the exception of a few odd and unlamented jobs like running elevators.

And so it is today. Men are now invading nursing, secretarial work, teaching, and library work. Teaching is an important example, but library work is closely allied and a more compact field to study. What's been happening in these decorous institutions is more dramatic than meets the casual eye.

In 1940, more than 90 percent of the American librarians were women. At the end of the war, library schools eager to get their share of the tuition money provided under the GI Bill of Rights went out to recruit veterans. The graduate course was only a year, there were plenty of jobs and, since former soldiers couldn't be called sissies, veterans charged unembarrassed into library work. Sometimes they chafed under the direction of elderly female librarians, but more often they by-passed them by getting newly created library jobs at higher pay.

Why the change? Libraries had become important. The war had raised the prestige of knowledge. Government and business were investing in research. Instead of offering genteel entertainment to individuals, librarians had become, in the public mind, the gatekeepers of that knowledge that is power. The change in role unlocked a great deal of money. Federal funds were lavished on library building. Universities with Government research contracts and private companies investing in scientific research were expanding library services. Big "Librarian Wanted" ads appeared in *The New York Times*.

The machine mystique changed libraries, too. When knowledge became a competitive weapon, it was slated for mechanization. Now specialists called Information Technologists talk of putting knowledge into giant computers from which any fact can be extracted without the trouble of shuffling index cards. They are, of course, men who regard cataloguing as dull, "detail" work suitable only for women. The cataloguers who have been coping with the avalanche of printed material say that the Information Technologists are going through all the stages of trial and error which went into present indexing systems. The dialogue has a homely ring. It is repeated every time a husband refuses to take his wife's warning against a short cut that she has already tried and found wanting.

"Young man, be a librarian," Arnold Gingrich advised *Esquire* readers in a 1964 publisher's editorial. "Most of the top jobs in the profession want male librarians to fill them." Young men took the advice. By 1967 men headed 39 of the 46 biggest public libraries and all 74 of the members of the elite Association of Research Libraries. Administrators said they were hiring men because there were not enough trained women librarians to go around. At the same time, bankers were saying they had to hire women bank tellers because there weren't enough *men* to go around. And while Mr. Ward's cheery explanation that "women are better accepted in jobs" could conceivably account for the increase in women tellers, it couldn't account for the increase in male librarians.

In banks the changeover was good-humored, but a sex war rages in the library field.

"I say, kick the women out!" a state librarian wrote candidly to a colleague. "How are you going to get any worthwhile man to go into a field dominated by old women? We need more men in the library game." Whether he's right or not, the sex ratio in the library "game" has become a topic for survey, comment, and acrimonious debate. The same hostility shows up in public school systems and women's colleges. The young men seethe under petticoat rule, while the older women complain, with some justification, that the young men aren't as loyal, dedicated, competent, or manageable as the old maids they replaced.

Money makes a difference, of course. The men women replaced in banks went on to better jobs. The women that men replace in libraries and schools have nowhere better to go, and remain as obstacles to higher pay schedules for the men. But prestige is involved as well as money. Anthropologists find that women's work in one part of the world may be men's work in another, but whatever men do is regarded as more important than what their womenfolk do. In many Oriental cultures, including the Japanese, for instance, women make decisions about family spending because handling money is undignified in these societies. In some primitive tribes economic activity of any kind is held in such low esteem that women do all the productive work. In his study of women's work in three cultures, Chester Hunt found that Filipino women are more apt than ours to be doctors, lawyers, storekeepers, merchants, bankers, and pharmacists, and he thought the reason was that Filipinos do not value professional achievement as much as we do. They are agricultural, not industrial. In England, learning was long believed to be an aristocratic privilege, rather than a common right; consequently its high status has drawn a larger percentage of men into teaching than we have here.

The Invisible Bar has sometimes liberated women from the shackles of prestige. A thousand years ago, Lady Murasaki, a Japanese noblewoman, wrote *The Tale of Genji*, one of the world's greatest novels. She was freed to write as creatively as she pleased because it didn't matter what she set down in the "woman's language," vernacular Japanese. If she had been a man, she would have had to write in the much more limiting court Chinese.

In general, institutions don't like to get the reputation for "having a lot of women." Critics of the Federal Civil Service warn that the best men may not consider careers in Government if "too many women" advance in it. For more than a century, opponents of coeducation argued that the admission of women would drive the best men out of a college or a field of study. In 1968, admissions officers of coeducational schools continue to watch their sex ratio out of an uneasy feeling that "too many women" may lower standards. The standards involved are not academic ones, because women generally average better grades than men.

A bird's-eye view of the sex map of occupations shows how outmoded home roles limit women at work. Women are least accepted in work involving machinery, negotiation, travel, risk, profit, and substantial sums of money. But the most striking boundary of all is occupational *status*. In a field as masculine as railroading, women are employed to clean the railway cars. In fields as feminine as cosmetics, a man is usually found in the president's chair.

Men dominate the top of the professions of cooking, dressmaking, and child study. During the 1960s schools of home economics and social work sought men deans in order to "improve the status of the professions." Women work as commercial artists, but seldom rise to become art directors. They write advertising copy, but they seldom become partners in advertising agencies. The managing editors even of women's magazines are often men. Successful actors graduate from the screen to directing, but the only actress-directors who come easily to mind are Ida Lupino, who was born in Britain, and Mai Zetterling, who is Swedish.

If you rank the number of individuals in any occupation on the basis of income, they fall into a pyramid, with lots of people at the lowest bracket on the bottom and fewer at every rise until you reach, theoretically at least, the one individual who exceeds all others at the top. The higher you go, of course, the thinner the ranks. That is the iron law of success. But as you go up the ladder you find a lower percentage of women on every rung.

A handy example is the Federal service, which employs 650,000 women, promotes them according to explicit rules, and grades the many different occupations in the Government by income brackets. In 1966, women dominated the lower grades, but they thinned out at every rise in grade until they were only 1½ percent of those earning $20,000 or more. Students of the Federal service say that conditions are similar to those in private employment.

The bigger the job, the less likely it is to be filled by a woman. This means that women at the top are exceptional among women. It also means that the elite of any group can assume that it is stag; the few women at the top can be ignored or treated as exceptions. Yet there are always *some* women up there. The fascinating thing about it is that whether the measure is money, power, prestige, or achievement, and whatever the field, the proportion of women at the top is remarkably constant and low. In the mid-1960s, women were:

—Less than 10 percent of all the professional or *"knowledge" elites* except classroom teachers, nurses, librarians, social workers, and journalists; 9 percent of all full professors; 8 percent of all scientists; 6 percent of all physicians; 3 percent of all lawyers; 1 percent of all engineers.

—Five percent of the *income elite* of the individuals with incomes of $10,000 or more, including all the rich widows and the five former wives of Jean Paul Getty, the oil man who has not disclaimed the title of richest man in the world.

—Five percent of the *prestige elite* listed in *Who's Who in America* for 1967, down from 6 percent in 1930.

—Two percent of the *power elite* of business executives listed in

Standard & Poor's Directory of leading American corporations; less than 4 percent of all Federal civil servants in the six highest grades; 1 percent of Federal judges; 1 percent of the United States Senate.

These women at the top look as if they are exceptions to all the rules of the map. A closer look at who and where they are and how they got there discloses that they are all of them exceptions that prove the rule.

Section Two

Psychology, Sociology, and Women

The articles in the first section documented some of the discrimination that women encounter strictly because they are female. The expertise of psychologists has been called upon again and again to explain the psychological reasons for such discrimination. This section will address itself to what psychologists have told us about women and the roles they are "able" to fulfill; it will also point out why what psychologists tell us is of little value.

The behavior of an individual is determined by the complex interaction of inherited predispositions (as has been demonstrated by behavior geneticists), learning experiences, and the social context in which the individual must act. Traditionally, theories about personality have tended to overemphasize either the importance of inherited predispositions, as do Freudian theories, or, like social learning theory, to overemphasize the importance of learning experiences. In the first case, instincts are considered to determine a normal sequence of psychosexual development, this development being different for boys and girls because of girls' physiological inferiority. Thus, Freudian theorists hold that sex differences are biologically determined. In the second case, psychologists describe the differences in the socialization of males and females but do not question or investigate the loss of human potential and the frustration that accompanies the training of women to fit the female mold.

Both types of personality theories have been devised by psychologists and psychiatrists who themselves are products of a society that is strongly biased against women. It is apparently too much to expect that the theories not reflect these biases, for objective evaluation of the theories (when it has been done) has shown them to be inadequate. Masters and Johnson (1966), in their research on human sexual response, provide a clear example of how a highly valued and almost universally accepted theory like Freud's can be refuted by scientific evidence. They show that Freud's definition of the female sexual response as a dual phenomenon (a definition based solely on his experience with neurotic women and the influences of the Victorian era) is in fact inaccurate. The way in which Freud's incorrect conceptions of female sexuality have had a major influence on us all is the subject of the first article in this section, "The Politics of Orgasm," by Susan Lydon.

In Freudian psychotherapy, the doctor-patient interaction designed to cure psychological problems is linked to societal expectations. The doctor identifies a person as disturbed because she (or he) is not "adjusted." Thus, in this model, a woman who feels dissatisfied with her suburban home and family, a young wife who does not want children, or a woman who is sexually aggressive is likely to be labeled "disturbed." The definitions of who is "sick" and what constitutes a "cure" have similar built-in biases.

Other kinds of therapy may have more potential for helping people than does Freudian psychotherapy. For example, the existential-phenomenological theories are designed to encourage self-awareness and self-discovery in the individual as an individual, rather than to rely on a stereotyped model of human fulfillment. However, because therapy is an intricate interaction between therapist and client, it must be noted that the values of the therapist always affect the relationship. And the fact that therapists are almost exclusively white, middle-class, middle-aged men means that in practice nonwhites, poor people, young people, and women are likely to be discriminated against in therapy.[1] In the second article, "Psychology Constructs the Female, or the Fantasy Life of the Male Psychologist," Naomi Weisstein explains why therapy has been ineffective for helping women and for aiding the construction of theories that accurately describe women.

In the same article, Dr. Weisstein also criticizes personality psychologists for relying upon the inner dynamic of the individual to explain behavior and points out the importance of the social environment —the context in which a person is placed—as a determinant of how the person will behave. Some social situations elicit a certain kind of behavior that others do not; the same individual acts differently depending on the social context in which she or he is found. When placed in a position of responsibility, many people assume the decision-making role, even though these same individuals might act submissive and dependent in other situations. To the extent that girls and women are repeatedly placed in submissive roles, they indeed act submissively. Since an important aspect of the social setting is how others expect the individual to behave, females, because of society's definition of them, are rarely given opportunities to demonstrate self-reliance or leadership. As girls learn to internalize the values of their society, they bring into every social context their own expectations of themselves as females. This internaliza-

---

[1] This fact was recently pointed out by the Association of Women Psychologists at the 1970 meeting of the American Psychological Association.

tion decreases even more the probability of their demonstrating potential behaviors that do not fit the image of the society. The third article in this section, "Training the Woman to Know Her Place: The Power of a Nonconscious Ideology," by Sandra L. Bem and Daryl J. Bem, is designed to show how women are molded from birth to fit the image that society has of them. The fact that women reject this image in so many ways (drugs, alcohol, sexual adventurism) is a forceful demonstration that more than learning factors are at work—that women are not by nature what society forces them to be.

Another approach that psychologists have taken to the study of personality is to try to identify traits that would enable them to predict how an individual will behave in other situations. This attempt has been largely unsuccessful, for a person can score one way on one task and in an opposite way on another task testing the same trait. The fourth article, "Femininity and Successful Achievement: A Basic Inconsistency," by Matina S. Horner, discusses achievement-motivation research using female subjects in which social conditions of testing have been found to be an important variable.

It is necessary for us to look for new ways to find answers to the old questions about the psychology of women. In the last article of this section, "The Social Construction of the Second Sex," Jo Freeman proposes directions for future social science research based upon some existing studies. The other articles in this section also suggest directions for psychological study, but the most basic principle that can be drawn from our present understanding of psychology is that there is no definitive way to know if or how men and women differ psychologically until we eliminate the differences in their training. The next section will be devoted to the implementation of such changes.

Reference

Masters, W. H. & Johnson, V. E., *Human sexual response*. Boston: Little, Brown and Co., 1966.

The Politics of Orgasm

Susan Lydon

Susan Lydon was graduated from Vassar in 1965. Her articles have appeared in many places, including *London Life,* the *London Times, Ramparts,* the *New York Times,* and *Rolling Stone.* At present she is residing in Berkeley with her daughter Shuna.

Tiresias, who had been both man and woman, was asked, as Ovid's legend goes, to mediate in a dispute between Jove and Juno as to which sex got more pleasure from lovemaking. Tiresias unhesitatingly answered that women did. Yet in the intervening 2,000 years between Ovid's time and our own, a mythology has been built up which not only holds the opposite to be true, but has made this belief an unswerving ideology dictating the quality of relations between the sexes. Woman's sexuality, defined by men to benefit men, has been downgraded and perverted, repressed and channeled, denied and abused until women themselves, thoroughly convinced of their sexual inferiority to men, would probably be dumfounded to learn that there is scientific proof that Tiresias was indeed right.

The myth was codified by Freud, as much as by anyone else. In *Three Essays on the Theory of Sexuality,* Freud formulated his basic ideas concerning feminine sexuality: for little girls, the leading erogenous zone in their bodies is the clitoris; in order for the transition to womanhood to be successful, the clitoris must abandon its sexual primacy to the vagina; women in whom this transition has not been complete remain clitorally-oriented, or "sexually anaesthetic" and "psychosexually immature."

> The fact that women change their leading erotogenic zone in this way, [Freud wrote] together with the wave of repression at puberty, which, as it were, puts aside their childish masculinity, are the chief determinants of the greater proneness of women to neurosis and especially to hysteria. These determinants, therefore, are intimately related to the essence of femininity.

In the context of Freud's total psychoanalytic view of women—that they are not whole human beings but mutilated males who long all their lives for a penis and must struggle to reconcile themselves to its lack—

the requirement of a transfer of erotic sensation from clitoris to vagina became a *prima facie* case for their inevitable sexual (and moral) inferiority. In Freud's logic, those who struggle to become what they are not must be inferior to that to which they aspire.

Freud wrote that he could not "escape the notion (though I hesitate to give it expression) that for women the level of what is ethically normal is different from what it is in men . . . We must not allow ourselves to be deflected from such conclusions by the denials of the feminists, who are anxious to force us to regard the two sexes as completely equal in position and worth."

Freud himself admitted near the end of his life that his knowledge of women was inadequate. "If you want to know more about femininity, you must interrogate your own experience, or turn to the poets, or wait until science can give you more information," he said; he also expressed the hope that the female psychoanalysts who followed him would be able to find out more. But the post-Freudians adhered rigidly to the doctrine of the master, and, as in most of his work, what Freud hoped would be taken as a thesis for future study became instead a kind of canon law.

While the neo-Freudians haggled over the correct reading of the Freudian bible, watered-down Freudianism was wending its way into the cultural mythology via Broadway plays, novelists, popular magazines, social scientists, marriage counselors, and experts of various kinds who found it useful in projecting desired images of women. The superiority of the vaginal over the clitoral orgasm was particularly useful as a theory, since it provided a convenient basis for categorization: clitoral women were deemed immature, neurotic, bitchy, and masculine; women who had vaginal orgasms were maternal, feminine, mature, and normal. Though frigidity should technically be defined as total inability to achieve orgasm, the orthodox Freudians (and pseudo-Freudians) preferred to define it as inability to achieve vaginal orgasm, by which definition, in 1944, Edmond Bergler adjudged between 70 and 80 percent of all women frigid. The :litoral *vs.* vaginal debate raged hot and heavy among the sexologists—although Kinsey's writings stressed the importance of the clitoris to female orgasm and contradicted Bergler's statistics—but it became clear that there was something indispensable to the society in the Freudian view which allowed it to remain unchallenged in the public consciousness.

In 1966, Dr. William H. Masters and Mrs. Virginia E. Johnson published *Human Sexual Response*, a massive clinical study of the physiology of sex. Briefly and simply, the Masters and Johnson conclusions about the female orgasm, based on observation of and interviews with 487 women, were these:

1) That the dichotomy of vaginal and clitoral orgasms is entirely false. Anatomically, all orgasms are centered in the clitoris, whether they result from direct manual pressure applied to the clitoris, indirect pressure resulting from the thrusting of penis during intercourse, or generalized sexual stimulation of other erogenous zones like the breasts.

2) That women are naturally multi-orgasmic; that is, if a woman is immediately stimulated following orgasm, she is likely to experience several orgasms in rapid succession. This is not an exceptional occurrence, but one of which most women are capable.

3) That while women's orgasms do not vary in kind, they vary in intensity. The most intense orgasm experienced by the research subjects were by masturbatory manual stimulation, followed in intensity by manual stimulation by the partner; the least intense orgasms were experienced by women during intercourse.

4) That the female orgasm is as real and identifiable a physiological entity as the male's; it follows the same pattern of erection and detumescence of the clitoris, which may be seen as the female equivalent of the penis.

5) That there is an "infinite variety of female sexual response" as regards intensity and duration of orgasms.

To anyone acquainted with the body of existing knowledge of feminine sexuality, the Masters and Johnson findings were truly revolutionary and liberating in the extent to which they demolished the established myths. Yet four years after the study was published, it seems hardly to have made much of an impact at all. Certainly it is not for lack of information that the myths persist; *Human Sexual Response*, despite its weighty scientific language, was an immediate best-seller, and popular paperbacks explicated it to millions of people in simpler language and at a cheaper price. The mythology remains intact because a male-dominated American culture has a vested interest in its continuance.

Dr. William Masters had searched for a woman co-worker for his research because, as he said, "No male really understands female sexuality." Before Masters and Johnson, female sexuality had been objectively defined and described by men; the subjective experience of women had had no part in defining their own sexuality. And men defined feminine sexuality in a way as favorable to themselves as possible. If woman's pleasure was obtained through the vagina, then she was totally dependent on the man's erect penis to achieve orgasm; she would receive her satisfaction only as a concomitant of man's seeking his. With the clitoral orgasm, woman's sexual pleasure was independent of the male's, and she could seek her satisfaction as aggressively as the man sought his, a prospect which didn't appeal to too many men. The definition of normal feminine sexuality as vaginal, in other words, was a part of keeping women down, of making them sexually, as well as economically, socially, and politically subservient.

In retrospect, particularly with the additional perspective of our own time, Freud's theory of feminine sexuality appears an historical rationalization for the realities of Victorian society. Culture-bound in the Victorian ethos, Freud had to play the role of *pater familias*. Serving the ethos, he developed a psychology that robbed Victorian women of possible politics. In Freud's theory of penis envy, the penis functioned as the unalterable determinant of maleness which women could symbolically envy instead of the power and prestige given men by the society. It was a refusal to grant women acknowledgment that they had been wronged by their culture and their times; according to Freud, woman's lower status had not been conferred upon her by men, but by God, who had created her without a penis.

Freud's insistence on the superiority of the vaginal orgasm seems almost a demonic determination on his part to finalize the Victorians' repression of feminine eroticism, to stigmatize the remaining vestiges of pleasure felt by women, and thus make them unacceptable to the women themselves. For there were still women whose sexuality hadn't been completely destroyed, as evidenced by one Dr. Isaac Brown Baker, a surgeon who performed numerous clitoridectomies on women to prevent the sexual excitement which, he was convinced, caused "insanities," "catalepsy," "hysteria," "epilepsy," and other diseases. The Victorians had needed to repress sexuality for the success of Western industrialized society; in particular, the total repression of woman's sexuality was crucial to ensure her subjugation. So the Victorians honored only the male ejaculation, that aspect of sexuality which was necessary to the survival of the species; the male ejaculation made women submissive to sex by creating a mystique of the sanctity of motherhood; and, supported by Freud, passed on to us the heritage of the double standard.

When Kinsey laid to rest the part of the double standard that maintained women got no pleasure at all from sex, everyone cried out that there was a sexual revolution afoot. But such talk, as usual, was deceptive. Morality, outside the marriage bed, remained the same, and children were socialized as though Kinsey had never described what they would be like when they grew up. Boys were taught that they should get their sex where they could find it, "go as far" as they could. On the old assumption that women were asexual creatures, girls were taught that since they needed sex less than boys did, it was up to them to impose sexual restraints. In whatever sex education adolescents did manage to receive, they were told that men had penises and women vaginas; the existence of the clitoris was not mentioned, and *pleasure* in sex was never discussed at all.

Adolescent boys growing up begging for sexual crumbs from girls frightened for their "reputations"—a situation that remains unchanged to this day—hardly constitutes the vanguard of a sexual revolution. However, the marriage-manual craze that followed Kinsey assumed that a lifetime of psychological destruction could, with the aid of a little booklet, be abandoned after marriage, and that husband and wife should be able to make sure that the wife was not robbed of her sexual birthright to orgasm, just so long as it was *vaginal* (though the marriage manuals did rather reluctantly admit that since the clitoris was the most sexually sensitive organ in the female body, a little clitoral stimulation in foreplay was in order), and so long as their orgasms were *simultaneous*.

The effect of the marriage manuals of course ran counter to their ostensible purpose. Under the guise of frankness and sexual liberation, they dictated prudery and restraint. Sex was made so mechanized, detached, and intellectual that it was robbed of its sensuality. Man became a spectator of his own sexual experience. And the marriage manuals put new pressure on women. The swing was from repression to preoccupation with the orgasm. Men took the marriage manuals to mean that their sexuality would be enhanced by bringing women to orgasm and, again co-opting feminine sexuality for their own ends, they put pressure on women to perform. The endorsement by the marriage manuals of the desirability of vaginal orgasm insured that women would be asked not only, "Did you come?," but also, "Did you conform to Freud's conception of a psychosexually mature woman, and thereby validate my masculinity?"

Rather than being revolutionary, the present sexual situation is tragic. Appearances notwithstanding, the age-old taboos against conversation about personal sexual experience still haven't broken down. This reticence has allowed the mind-manipulators of the media to create myths of sexual supermen and superwomen. So the bed becomes a competitive arena, where men and women measure themselves against these mythical rivals, while simultaneously trying to live up to the ecstasies promised them by the marriage manuals and the fantasies of the media. ("If the earth doesn't move for me, I must be missing something," the reasoning goes.) Our society treats sex as a sport, with its record-breakers, its judges, its rules, and its spectators.

As anthropologists have shown, women's sexual response is culturally conditioned; historically, women defer to whatever model of their sexuality is offered them by men. So the sad thing for women is that they have participated in the destruction of their own eroticism. Women have helped make the vaginal orgasm into a status symbol in a male-dictated system of values. A woman would now perceive her preference for clitoral orgasm as a "secret shame," ignominious in the eyes of other women as well as those of men. This internalization can be seen in the literature: Mary McCarthy's and Doris Lessing's writings on orgasm do not differ substantially from D. H. Lawrence's and Ernest

Hemingway's, and even Simone de Beauvoir, in *The Second Sex*, refers to vaginal orgasm as the only "normal satisfaction."

Rather than working to alleviate the pressure on them, women have increased it. Feeling themselves insecure in a competitive situation, they are afraid to admit their own imagined inadequacies, and lie to other women about their sexual experiences. With their men, they often fake orgasm to appear "good in bed" and thus place an intolerable physical burden on themselves and a psychological burden on the men unlucky enough to see through the ruse.

One factor that has made this unfortunate situation possible is ignorance: the more subtle and delicate aspects of human sexuality are still not fully understood. For example, a woman's ability to attain orgasm seems to be conditioned as much by her emotions as by physiology and sociology. Masters and Johnson proved that the orgasm experienced during intercourse, the misnamed vaginal orgasm, did not differ *anatomically* from the clitoral orgasm. But this should not be seen as their most significant contribution to the sexual emancipation of women. A difference remains in the *subjective* experience of orgasm during intercourse and orgasm apart from intercourse. In the complex of emotional factors affecting feminine sexuality, there is a whole panoply of pleasures: the pleasure of being penetrated and filled by a man, the pleasure of sexual communication, the pleasure of affording a man his orgasm, the erotic pleasure that exists even when sex is not terminated by orgasmic release. Masters and Johnson's real contribution was to stress an "infinite variety of female sexual response." One should be able to appreciate the differences, rather than impose value judgments on them.

There is no doubt that Masters and Johnson were fully aware of the implications of their study to the sexual liberation of women. As they wrote, "With orgasmic physiology established, the human female now has an undeniable opportunity to develop realistically her own sexual response levels." Two years later this statement seems naive and entirely too optimistic. Certainly the sexual problems of our society will never be solved until there is real and unfeigned equality between men and women. This idea is usually misconstrued: sexual liberation for women is wrongly understood to mean that women will adopt all the forms of masculine sexuality. As in the whole issue of women's liberation, that's really not the point. Women don't aspire to imitate the mistakes of men in sexual matters, to view sexual experiences as conquest and ego-enhancement, to use other people to serve their own ends. But if the Masters and Johnson material is allowed to filter into the public consciousness, hopefully to replace the enshrined Freudian myths, then women at long last will be allowed to take the first step toward her emancipation, to define and enjoy the forms of her own sexuality.

Psychology Constructs the Female, or the Fantasy Life of the Male Psychologist[1]

Naomi Weisstein

Naomi Weisstein graduated Phi Beta Kappa from Wellesley College, received her Ph.D. (with departmental distinctions) in psychology 2½ years later from Harvard University, and took a year's postdoctoral fellowship at the Committee on Mathematical Biology, the University of Chicago, courtesy of the National Science Foundation. However, these honors did not counteract the fact that she is a woman, for the twelve institutions to which she had been recommended for a job would not hire her. What to do? Join women's liberation, and fight for a just society. Currently, she teaches psychology at Loyola University, Chicago, and does research in visual perception. Her articles have appeared in prestigious professional journals. She has been active in women's liberation since 1966, and she plays piano in the Chicago Women's Liberation Rock Band.

It is an implicit assumption that the area of psychology which concerns itself with personality has the onerous but necessary task of describing the limits of human possibility. Thus when we are about to consider the liberation of women, we naturally look to psychology to tell us what "true" liberation would mean: what would give women the freedom to fulfill their own intrinsic natures. Psychologists have set about describing the true natures of women with a certainty and a sense of their own infallibility rarely found in the secular world. Bruno Bettelheim, of the University of Chicago, tells us (1965) that "We must start with the realization that, as much as women want to be good scientists or engineers, they want first and foremost to be womanly companions of men and to be mothers." Erik Erikson of Harvard University (1964), upon noting that young women often ask whether they can "have an identity before they know whom they will marry, and for whom they will make a home," explains somewhat elegiacally that "Much of a young woman's identity is already defined in her kind of attractiveness and in the selectivity of her search for the man (or men) by whom she wishes to be sought . . ." Mature womanly fulfillment,

[1] This is a revised and expanded version of "Kinder, Kuche, Kirche as scientific law: psychology constructs the female," published by the New England Free Press, 791 Tremont Street, Boston, Massachusetts (1968).

for Erikson, rests on the fact that a woman's ". . . somatic design harbors an 'inner space' destined to bear the offspring of chosen men, and with it, a biological, psychological, and ethical commitment to take care of human infancy!" Some psychiatrists even see the acceptance of woman's role by women as a solution to societal problems. "Woman is nurturance . . .," writes Joseph Rheingold (1964), a psychiatrist at Harvard Medical School, ". . . anatomy decrees the life of a woman . . . when women grow up without dread of their biological functions and without subversion by feminist doctrine, and therefore enter upon motherhood with a sense of fulfillment and altruistic sentiment, we shall attain the goal of a good life and a secure world in which to live it." (p. 714)

These views from men who are assumed to be experts reflect, in a surprisingly transparent way, the cultural consensus. They not only assert that a woman is defined by her ability to attract men, they see no alternative definitions. They think that the definition of a woman in terms of a man is the way it should be; and they back it up with psychosexual incantation and biological ritual curses. A woman has an identity if she is attractive enough to obtain a man, and thus, a home; for this will allow her to set about her life's task of "joyful altruism and nurturance."

Business certainly does not disagree. If views such as Bettelheim's and Erikson's do indeed have something to do with real liberation for women, then seldom in human history has so much money and effort been spent on helping a group of people realize their true potential. Clothing, cosmetics, home furnishings, are multi-million dollar businesses: if you don't like investing in firms that make weaponry and flaming gasoline, then there's a lot of cash in "inner space." Sheet and pillowcase manufacturers are concerned to fill this inner space:

> Mother, for a while this morning, I thought I wasn't cut out for married life. Hank was late for work and forgot his apricot juice and walked out without kissing me, and when I was all alone I started crying. But then the postman came with the sheets and towels you sent, that look like big bandana handkerchiefs, and you know what I thought? That those big red and blue handkerchiefs are for girls like me to dry their tears on so they can get busy and do what a housewife has to do. Throw open the windows and start getting the house ready, and the dinner, maybe clean the silver and put new geraniums in the box. *Everything to be ready for him when he walks through that door.* (Fieldcrest 1966; emphasis added.)

Of course, it is not only the sheet and pillowcase manufacturers, the cosmetics industry, the home furnishings salesmen who profit from and make use of the cultural definitions of man and woman. The example above is blatantly and overtly pitched to a particular kind of sexist stereotype: the child nymph. But almost all aspects of the media are normative, that is, they have to do with the ways in which beautiful people, or just folks, or ordinary Americans, or extraordinary Americans should live their lives. They define the possible; and the possibilities are usually in terms of what is male and what is female. Men and women alike are waiting for Hank, the Silva Thins man, to walk back through that door.

It is interesting but limited exercise to show that psychologists and psychiatrists embrace these sexist norms of our culture, that they do not see beyond the most superficial and stultifying media conceptions of female nature, and that their ideas of female nature serve industry and commerce so well. Just because it's good for business doesn't mean it's wrong. What I will show is that it *is wrong;* that there isn't the tiniest shred of evidence that these fantasies of servitude and childish dependence have anything to do with women's true potential; that the idea of the nature of human possibility which rests on the accidents of individual development of genitalia, on what is possible today because of what happened yesterday, on the fundamentalist myth of sex organ causality, has strangled and deflected psychology so that it is relatively useless in describing, explaining or predicting humans and their behavior. It then goes without saying that present psychology is less than worthless in contributing to a vision which could truly liberate—men as well as women.

The central argument of my paper, then, is this. Psychology has nothing to say about what women are really like, what they need and what they want, essentially because psychology does not know. I want to stress that this failure is not limited to women; rather, the kind of psychology which has addressed itself to how people act and who they are has failed to understand, in the first place, why people act the way they do, and certainly failed to understand what might make them act differently.

The kind of psychology which has addressed itself to these questions divides into two professional areas: academic personality research, and clinical psychology and psychiatry. The basic reason for failure is the same in both these areas: the central assumption for most psychologists of human personality has been that human behavior rests on an individual and inner dynamic, perhaps fixed in infancy, perhaps fixed by genitalia, perhaps simply arranged in a rather immovable cognitive network. But this assumption is rapidly losing ground as personality psychologists fail again and again to get consistency in the assumed personalities of their subjects (Block, 1968). Meanwhile, the evidence is collecting that what a person does and who he believes himself to be will in general be a function of what people around him expect him to be and what the overall situation in which he is acting implies that he is. Compared to the influence of the social context within which a person lives, his or her history and "traits," as well as biological makeup, may simply be random variations, "noise" superimposed on the true signal which can predict behavior.

Some academic personality psychologists are at least looking at the counter evidence and questioning their theories; no such corrective is occurring in clinical psychology and psychiatry. Freudians and neo-Freudians, Adlerians and neo-Adlerians, classicists and swingers, clinicians and psychiatrists, simply refuse to look at the evidence against their theory and practice. And they support their theory and their practice with stuff so transparently biased as to have absolutely no standing as empirical evidence.

To summarize: the first reason for psychology's failure to understand what people are and how they act is that psychology has looked for inner traits when it should have been looking for social context; the second reason for psychology's failure is that the theoreticians of personality have generally been clinicians and psychiatrists, and they have never considered it necessary to have evidence in support of their theories.

Theory without Evidence

Let us turn to this latter cause of failure first: the acceptance by psychiatrists and clinical psychologists of theory without evidence. If we inspect the literature of personality, it is immediately obvious that the bulk of it is written by clinicians and psychiatrists, and that the major support for their theories is "years of intensive clinical experience." This is a tradition started by Freud. His "insights" occurred during the course of his work with his patients. Now there is nothing wrong with such an approach to theory *formulation*; a person is free to make up theories with any inspiration which works: divine revelation, intensive clinical practice, a random numbers table. But he is not free to claim any validity for his theory until it has been tested and confirmed. But theories are treated in no such tentative way in ordinary clinical practice. Consider Freud. What he thought constituted evidence violated the most minimal conditions of scientific rigor. In *The Sexual Enlightenment of Children* (1963), the classic document which is supposed to demonstrate empirically the existence of a castration complex and its connection to a phobia, Freud based his analysis on the reports of the father of the little boy, himself in therapy, and a devotee of Freudian theory. I really don't have to comment further on the contamination in this kind of evidence. It is remarkable that only recently has Freud's classic theory on the sexuality of women—the notion of the double orgasm—been actually tested physiologically and found just plain wrong. Now those who claim that fifty years of psychoanalytic experience constitute evidence enough of the essential truths of Freud's theory should ponder the robust health of the double orgasm. Did women, until Masters and Johnson (1966), believe they were having two different kinds of orgasm? Did their psychiatrists cow them into reporting something that was not true? If so, were there other things they reported that were also not true? Did psychiatrists ever learn anything different than their theories had led them to believe? If clinical experience means anything at all, surely we should have been done with the double orgasm myth long before the Masters and Johnson studies.

But certainly, you may object, "years of intensive clinical experience" is the only reliable measure in a discipline which rests for its findings on insight, sensitivity, and intuition. The problem with insight, sensitivity, and intuition is that they can confirm for all time the biases that one started out with. People used to be absolutely convinced of their ability to tell which of their number were engaging in witchcraft. All it required was some sensitivity to the workings of the devil.

Years of intensive clinical experience is not the same thing as empirical evidence. The first thing an experimenter learns in any kind of experiment which involves humans is the concept of the "double blind." The term is taken from medical experiments, where one group is given a drug which is presumably supposed to change behavior in a certain way, and a control group is given a placebo. If the observers or the subjects know which group took which drug, the result invariably comes out on the positive side for the new drug. Only when it is not known which subject took which pill is validity remotely approximated. In addition, with judgments of human behavior, it is so difficult to precisely tie down just what behavior is going on, let alone what behavior should be expected, that one must test again and again the reliability of judgments. How many judges, blind, will agree in their observations? Can they replicate their own judgments at some later time? When, in actual practice, these judgment criteria are tested for clinical judgments, then we find that the judges cannot judge reliably, nor can they judge consistently: they do no better than chance in identifying which of a certain set of stories were written by men and which by women; which of a whole battery of clinical test results are the products of homosexuals and which are the products of heterosexuals (Hooker, 1957), and which, of a battery of clinical test results *and* interviews (where questions are asked such as "Do you have delusions?"—Little & Schneidman, 1959) are products of psychotics, neurotics, psychosomatics, or normals. Lest this summary escape your notice, let me stress the implications of these findings. The ability of judges, chosen for their clinical expertise, to distinguish male heterosexuals from male homosexuals on the basis of three widely used clinical projective tests—the Rorschach, the TAT, and the MAP—was *no better than chance*. The reason this is such devastating news, of course, is that sexuality is supposed to be of fundamental importance in the deep dynamic of personality; if what is considered gross sexual deviance cannot be caught, then what are psychologists talking about when they, for example, claim that at the basis of paranoid psychosis is "latent homosexual panic"? They can't even identify what homosexual anything is, let alone "latent homosexual panic."[2] More frightening, expert clinicians cannot be consistent on what diagnostic category to assign to a person, again on the basis of both tests and interviews; a number of normals in the Little & Schneidman study were described as psychotic, in such categories as "schizophrenic with homosexual tendencies" or "schizoid character with depressive trends." But most disheartening, when the judges were asked to rejudge the test protocols some weeks later, their diagnoses of the same subjects on the basis of the same protocol differed markedly from their initial judgments. It is obvious that even simple descriptive conventions in clinical psychology cannot be consistently applied; that these descriptive conventions have any explanatory significance is therefore, of course, out of the question.

As a graduate student at Harvard some years ago, I was a member of a seminar which was asked to identify which of two piles of a clinical test, the TAT, had been written by males and which by females. Only four students out of twenty identified the piles correctly, and this was after one and a half months of intensively studying the differences between men and women. Since this result is below chance—that is, this result would occur by chance about four out of a thousand times—we may conclude that there is finally a consistency here; students are judging knowledgeably within the context of psychological teaching about the differences between men and women; the teachings themselves are simply erroneous.

You may argue that the theory may be scientifically "unsound" but at least it cures people. There is no evidence that it does. In 1952, Eysenck reported the results of what is called an "outcome of therapy" study of neurotics which showed that, of the patients who received psychoanalysis the improvement rate was 44%; of the patients who

---

[2] It should be noted that psychologists have been as quick to assert absolute truths about the nature of homosexuality as they have about the nature of women. The arguments presented in this paper apply equally to the nature of homosexuality; psychologists know nothing about it, there is no more evidence for the "naturalness" of heterosexuality than for the "naturalness" of homosexuality. Psychology has functioned as a pseudo-scientific buttress for our cultural sex-role notions, that is, as a buttress for patriarchal ideology and patriarchal social organization: women's liberation and gay liberation fight against a common victimization.

received psychotherapy the improvement rate was 64%; and of the patients who received no treatment at all the improvement rate was 72%. These findings have never been refuted; subsequently, later studies have confirmed the negative results of the Eysenck study. (Barron & Leary, 1955; Bergin, 1963; Cartwright & Vogel, 1960; Truax, 1963; Powers & Witmer, 1951.) How can good clinicians and psychiatrists, then, in all good conscience, continue to practice? Largely by ignoring these results and being careful not to do outcome-of-therapy studies. The attitude is nicely summarized by Rotter (1960) (quoted in Astin, 1961): "Research studies in psychotherapy tend to be concerned with psychotherapeutic procedure and less with outcome . . . to some extent, it reflects an interest in the psychotherapy situation as a kind of personality laboratory." Some laboratory.

The Social Context

Thus, since clinical experience and tools can be shown to be worse than useless when tested for consistency, efficacy, agreement, and reliability, we can safely conclude that theories of a clinical nature advanced about women are also worse than useless. I want to turn now to the second major point in my paper, which is that, even when psychological theory is constructed so that it may be tested, and rigorous standards of evidence are used, it has become increasingly clear that in order to understand why people do what they do, and certainly in order to change what people do, psychologists must turn away from the theory of the causal nature of the inner dynamic and look to the social context within which individuals live.

Before examining the relevance of this approach for the question of women, let me first sketch the groundwork for this assertion.

In the first place, it is clear (Block, 1968) that personality tests never yield consistent predictions; a rigid authoritarian on one measure will be an unauthoritarian on the next. But the reason for this inconsistency is only now becoming clear, and it seems overwhelmingly to have much more to do with the social situation in which the subject finds himself than with the subject himself.

In a series of brilliant experiments, Rosenthal and his co-workers (Rosenthal & Jacobson, 1968; Rosenthal, 1966) have shown that if one group of experimenters has one hypothesis about what they expect to find, and another group of experimenters has the opposite hypothesis, both groups will obtain results in accord with their hypotheses. The results obtained are not due to mishandling of data by biased experimenters; rather, somehow, the bias of the experimenter creates a changed environment in which subjects actually act differently. For instance, in one experiment, subjects were to assign numbers to pictures of men's faces, with high numbers representing the subject's judgment that the man in the picture was a successful person, and low numbers representing the subject's judgment that the man in the picture was an unsuccessful person. The experimenters read the same set of instructions to two groups of subjects, and were required to say nothing else than what was in the instructions. One group of experimenters was told that the subjects tended to rate the faces high; another group of experimenters was told that the subjects tended to rate the faces low. Each group of experimenters was instructed to follow precisely the same procedure: they were required to read to subjects a set of instructions, and to *say nothing else.* For the 375 subjects run, the results showed clearly that those subjects who performed the task with experimenters who expected high ratings gave high ratings, and those subjects who performed the task with experimenters who expected low ratings gave low ratings. How did this happen? The experimenters all used the same words; it was something in their conduct which made one group of subjects do one thing, and another group of subjects do another thing.

The concreteness of the changed conditions produced by expectation is a fact, a reality: even with animal subjects, in two separate studies (Rosenthal & Fode, 1960; Rosenthal & Lawson, 1961), those experimenters who were told that rats learning mazes had been especially bred for brightness obtained better learning from their rats than did experimenters believing their rats to have been bred for dullness. In a very recent study, Rosenthal & Jacobson (1968) extended their analysis to the natural classroom situation. Here, they tested a group of students and reported to the teachers that some among the students tested "showed great promise." Actually, the students so named had been selected on a random basis. Some time later, the experimenters retested the group of students: those students whose teachers had been told that they were "promising" showed real and dramatic increments in their IQ's as compared to the rest of the students. Something in the conduct of the teachers toward those who the teachers believed to be the "bright" students, made those students brighter.

Thus, even in carefully controlled experiments, and with no outward or conscious difference in behavior, the hypotheses we start with will influence enormously the behavior of another organism. These studies are extremely important when assessing the validity of psychological studies of women. Since it is beyond doubt that most of us start with notions as to the nature of men and women, the validity of a number of observations of sex differences is questionable, even when these observations have been made under carefully controlled conditions. Second, and more important, the Rosenthal experiments point quite clearly to the influence of social expectation. In some extremely important ways, people are what you expect them to be or at least they behave as you expect them to behave. Thus, if women, according to Bettelheim, want first and foremost to be good wives and mothers, it is extremely likely that this is what Bruno Bettelheim, and the rest of society, want them to be.

There is another series of brilliant social psychological experiments which point to the overwhelming effect of social context. These are the obedience experiments of Stanley Milgram (1965) in which subjects are asked to obey the orders of unknown experimenters, orders which carry with them the distinct possibility that the subject is killing somebody.

In Milgram's experiments, a subject is told that he is administering a learning experiment, and that he is to deal out shocks each time the other "subject" (in reality, a confederate of the experimenter) answers incorrectly. The equipment appears to provide graduated shocks ranging upwards from 15 volts through 450 volts; for each of four consecutive voltages there are verbal descriptions such as "mild shock," "danger, severe shock," and, finally, for the 435 and 450 volt switches, a red XXX marked over the switches. Each time the stooge answers incorrectly the subject is supposed to increase the voltage. As the voltage increases, the stooge begins to cry in pain; he demands that the experiment stop; finally, he refuses to answer at all. When he stops responding, the experimenter instructs the subject to continue increasing the voltage; for each shock administered the stooge shrieks in agony. Under these conditions, about 62.5% of the subjects administered shock that they believed to be possibly lethal.

No tested individual differences between subjects predicted how many would continue to obey, and which would break off the experiment. When forty psychiatrists predicted how many of a group of 100 subjects would go on to give the lethal shock, their predictions were orders of magnitude below the actual percentages; most expected only one-tenth of one per cent of the subjects to obey to the end.

But even though *psychiatrists* have no idea how people will behave in this situation, and even though individual differences do not predict which subjects will obey and which will not, it is easy to predict when subjects will be obedient and when they will be defiant. All the experimenter has to do is change the social situation. In a variant of Milgram's experiment, two stooges were present in addition to the "victim"; these worked along with the subject in administering electric shocks. When these two stooges refused to go on with the experiment, only ten per cent of the subjects continued to the maximum voltage. This is critical for personality theory. It says that behavior is predicted from the social situation, not from the individual history.

Finally, an ingenious experiment by Schachter and Singer (1962) showed that subjects injected with adrenalin, which produces a state of physiological arousal in all but minor respects identical to that which occurs when subjects are extremely afraid, became euphoric when they were in a room with a stooge who was acting euphoric, and became extremely angry when they were placed in a room with a stooge who was acting extremely angry.

To summarize: If subjects under quite innocuous and non-coercive social conditions can be made to kill other subjects and under other types of social conditions will positively refuse to do so; if subjects can react to a state of physiological fear by becoming euphoric because there is somebody else around who is euphoric or angry because there is somebody else around who is angry; if students become intelligent because teachers expect them to be intelligent, and rats run mazes better because experimenters are told the rats are bright, then it is obvious that a study of human behavior requires, first and foremost, a study of the social contexts within which people move, the expectations as to how they will behave, and the authority which tells them who they are and what they are supposed to do.

Biologically Based Theories

Two theories of the nature of women, which come not from psychiatric and clinical tradition, but from biology, can be disposed of now with little difficulty. The first biological theory of sex differences argues that since females and males differ in their sex hormones, and sex hormones enter the brain (Hamburg & Lunde in Maccoby, 1966), there must be innate differences in "nature." But the only thing this argument tells us is that there are differences in physiological state. The problem is whether these differences are at all relevant to behavior. Recall that Schachter and Singer (1962) have shown that a particular physiological state can itself lead to a multiplicity of felt emotional states, and outward behavior, depending on the social situation.

The second theory is a form of biological reductionism: sex-role behavior in some primate species is described, and it is concluded that this is the "natural" behavior for humans. Putting aside the not insignificant problem of observer bias (for instance, Harlow, 1962, of the University of Wisconsin, after observing differences between male and female rhesus monkeys, quotes Lawrence Sterne to the effect that women are silly and trivial, and concludes that "men and women have differed in the past and they will differ in the future"), there are a number of problems with this approach.

The most general and serious problem is that there are no grounds to assume that anything primates do is necessary, natural, or desirable in humans, for the simple reason that humans are not non-humans. For instance, it is found that male chimpanzees placed alone with infants

will not "mother" them. Jumping from hard data to ideological speculation researchers conclude from this information that *human* females are
necessary for the safe growth of human infants. It would be as reasonable to conclude, following this logic, that it is quite useless to teach
human infants to speak, since it has been tried with chimpanzees and it
does not work.

One strategy that has been used is to extrapolate from primate
behavior to "innate" human preference by noticing certain trends in
primate behavior as one moves phylogenetically closer to humans. But
there are great difficulties with this approach. When behaviors from
lower primates are directly opposite to those of higher primates, or to
those one expects of humans, they can be dismissed on evolutionary
grounds—higher primates and/or humans grew out of that kid stuff. On
the other hand, if the behavior of higher primates is counter to the
behavior considered natural for humans, while the behavior of some
lower primate is considered the natural one for humans, the higher
primate behavior can be dismissed also, on the grounds that it has
diverged from an older, prototypical pattern. So either way, one can
select those behaviors one wants to prove as innate for humans. In
addition, one does not know whether the sex-role behavior exhibited is
dependent on the phylogenetic rank, or on the environmental conditions (both physical and social) under which different species live.

Is there then any value at all in primate observations as they relate
to human females and males? There is a value but it is limited: its
function can be no more than to show some extant examples of diverse
sex-role behavior. It must be stressed, however, that this is an extremely
limited function. The extant behavior does not begin to suggest all the
possibilities, either for non-human primates or for humans. Bearing
these caveats in mind, it is nonetheless interesting that if one inspects
the limited set of existing non-human primate sex-role behaviors, one
finds, in fact, a much larger range of sex-role behavior than is commonly
believed to exist. "Biology" appears to limit very little; the fact that a
female gives birth does not mean, even in non-humans, that she necessarily cares for the infant (in marmosets, for instance, the male carries
the infant at all times except when the infant is feeding [Mitchell,
1969]); "natural" female and male behavior varies all the way from
females who are much more aggressive and competitive than males (e.g.
Tamarins, see Mitchell, 1969) and male "mothers" (e.g., Titi monkeys,
night monkeys, and marmosets, see Mitchell, 1969)[3] to submissive and
passive females and male antagonists (e.g., rhesus monkeys).

But even for the limited function that primate arguments serve, the
evidence has been misused. Invariably, only those primates have been

---

[3] All these are lower-order primates, which makes their behavior with reference
to humans unnatural, or more natural; take your choice.

cited which exhibit exactly the kind of behavior that the proponents of the biological basis of human female behavior wish were true for humans. Thus, baboons and rhesus monkeys are generally cited: males in these groups exhibit some of the most irritable and aggressive behavior found in primates, and if one wishes to argue that females are naturally passive and submissive, these groups provide vivid examples. There are abundant counter examples, such as those mentioned above (Mitchell, 1969); in fact, in general, a counter example can be found for every sex-role behavior cited, including, as mentioned in the case of marmosets, male "mothers."

But the presence of counter examples has not stopped florid and overarching theories of the natural or biological basis of male privilege from proliferating. For instance, there have been a number of theories dealing with the innate incapacity in human males for monogamy. Here, as in most of this type of theorizing, baboons are a favorite example, probably because of their fantasy value: the family unit of the hamadryas baboon, for instance, consists of a highly constant pattern of one male and a number of females and their young. And again, the counter examples, such as the invariably monogamous gibbon, are ignored.

An extreme example of this maiming and selective truncation of the evidence in the service of a plea for the maintenance of male privilege is a recent book, *Men in Groups* (1969), by a man who calls himself Tiger.[4] The central claim of this book is that females are incapable of honorable collective action because they are incapable of "bonding" as in "male bonding." What is "male bonding"? Its surface definition is simple: ". . . a particular relationship between two or more males such that they react differently to members of their bonding units as compared to individuals outside of it" (pp. 19–20). If one deletes the word male, the definition, on its face, would seem to include all organisms that have any kind of social organization. But this is not what Tiger means. For instance, Tiger asserts that females are incapable of bonding; and this alleged incapacity indicates to Tiger that females should be restricted from public life. Why is bonding an exclusively male behavior? Because, says Tiger, it is seen in male primates. All male primates? No, very few male primates. Tiger cites two examples where male bonding is seen: rhesus monkeys and baboons. Surprise, surprise. But not even all baboons: as mentioned above, the hamadryas social organization consists of one-male units; so does that of the Gelada baboon (Mitchell, 1969). And the great apes do not go in for male bonding much either. The "male bond" is hardly a serious contribution to scholarship; one reviewer for *Science* has observed that the book ". . .

---

[4] Schwarz-Belkin (1914) claims that the name was originally *Mouse*, but this may be a reference to an earlier L. Tiger (putative).

shows basically more resemblance to a partisan political tract than to a work of objective social science," with male bonding being ". . . some kind of behavioral phlogiston" (Fried, 1969, p. 884).

In short, primate arguments have generally misused the evidence; primate studies themselves have, in any case, only the very limited function of describing some possible sex-role behavior; and at present, primate observations have been sufficiently limited so that even the range of possible sex-role behavior for non-human primates is not known. This range is not known since there is only minimal observation of what happens to behavior if the physical or social environment is changed. In one study (Itani, 1963), different troops of Japanese macaques were observed. Here, there appeared to be cultural differences. Males in 3 out of the 18 troops observed differed in their amount of aggressiveness and infant-caring behavior. There could be no possibility of differential evolution here; the differences seemed largely transmitted by infant socialization. Thus, the very limited evidence points to some plasticity in the sex-role behavior of non-human primates; if we can figure out experiments which massively change the social organization of primate groups, it is possible that we might observe great changes in behavior. At present, however, we must conclude that, since non-human primates are too stupid to change their social conditions by themselves, the "innateness" and fixedness of their behavior is simply not known. Thus, even if there were some way, which there isn't, to settle on the behavior of a particular primate species as being the "natural" way for humans, we would not know whether or not this were simply some function of the present social organization of that species. And finally, once again it must be stressed that even if non-human primate behavior turned out to be relatively fixed, this would say little about our behavior. More immediate and relevant evidence, i.e. the evidence from social psychology, points to the enormous plasticity in human behavior, not only from one culture to the next, but from one experimental group to the next. One of the most salient features of human social organization is its variety; there are a number of cultures where there is at least a rough equality between men and women (Mead, 1949). In summary, primate arguments can tell us very little about our "innate" sex-role behavior; if they tell us anything at all, they tell us that there is no one biologically "natural" female or male behavior, and that sex-role behavior in non-human primates is much more varied than has previously been thought.

In brief, the uselessness of present psychology with regard to women is simply a special case of the general conclusion: one must understand social expectations about women if one is going to characterize the behavior of women.

How are women characterized in our culture, and in psychology?

They are inconsistent, emotionally unstable, lacking in a strong conscience or superego, weaker, "nurturant" rather than productive, "intuitive" rather than intelligent, and, if they are at all "normal," suited to the home and the family. In short, the list adds up to a typical minority group stereotype of inferiority (Hacker, 1951): if they know their place, which is in the home, they are really quite lovable, happy, childlike, loving creatures. In a review of the intellectual differences between little boys and little girls, Eleanor Maccoby (1966) has shown that there are no intellectual differences until about high school, or, if there are, girls are slightly ahead of boys. At high school, girls begin to do worse on a few intellectual tasks, such as arithmetic reasoning, and beyond high school, the achievement of women now measured in terms of productivity and accomplishment drops off even more rapidly. There are a number of other, non-intellectual tests which show sex differences; I chose the intellectual differences since it is seen clearly that women start becoming inferior. It is no use to talk about women being different but equal; all of the tests I can think of have a "good" outcome and a "bad" outcome. Women usually end up at the "bad" outcome. In light of social expectations about women, what is surprising is not that women end up where society expects they will; what is surprising is that little girls don't get the message that they are supposed to be stupid until high school; and what is even more remarkable is that some women resist this message even after high school, college, and graduate school.

My paper began with remarks on the task of the discovery of the limits of human potential. Psychologists must realize that it is they who are limiting discovery of human potential. They refuse to accept evidence, if they are clinical psychologists, or, if they are rigorous, they assume that people move in a context-free ether, with only their innate dispositions and their individual traits determining what they will do. Until psychologists begin to respect evidence, and until they begin looking at the social contexts within which people move, psychology will have nothing of substance to offer in this task of discovery. I don't know what immutable differences exist between men and women apart from differences in their genitals; perhaps there are some other unchangeable differences; probably there are a number of irrelevant differences. But it is clear that until social expectations for men and women are equal, until we provide equal respect for both men and women, our answers to this question will simply reflect our prejudices.

References

Astin, A. W., The functional autonomy of psychotherapy. *American Psychologist*, 1961, 16, 75–78.

Barron, F. & Leary, T. Changes in psychoneurotic patients with and without psychotherapy. *Journal of Consulting Psychology*, 1955, **19**, 239–245.

Bergin, A. E. The effects of psychotherapy: Negative results revisited. *Journal of Consulting Psychology*, 1963, **10**, 244–250.

Bettelheim, B. The commitment required of a woman entering a scientific profession in present day American society. *Woman and the Scientific Professions*, The MIT symposium on American Women in Science and Engineering, 1965.

Block, J. Some reasons for the apparent inconsistency of personality. *Psychological Bulletin*, 1968, **70**, 210–212.

Cartwright, R. D. & Vogel, J. L. A comparison of changes in psychoneurotic patients during matched periods of therapy and no-therapy. *Journal of Consulting Psychology*, 1960, **24**, 121–127.

Erikson, E. Inner and outer space: Reflections on womanhood. *Daedalus*, 1964, **93**, 582–606.

Eysenck, H. J. The effects of psychotherapy: An evaluation. *Journal of Consulting Psychology*, 1952, **16**, 319–324.

Fieldcrest—Advertisement in the *New Yorker*, 1965.

Fried, M. H. "Mankind excluding woman," review of Tiger's *Men in Groups. Science*, 1969, **165**, pp. 883–884.

Freud, S. *The sexual enlightenment of children*. Collier Books Edition, 1963.

Goldstein, A. P. & Dean, S. J. *The investigation of psychotherapy: Commentaries and readings*. New York: John Wiley & Sons, 1966.

Hacker, H. M. Women as a minority group. *Social Forces*, 1951, **30**, 60–69.

Hamburg, D. A. & Lunde, D. T. Sex hormones in the development of sex differences in human behavior. In Maccoby (Ed.), *The development of sex differences*. Stanford University Press, 1966. Pp. 1–24.

Harlow, H. F. The heterosexual affectional system in monkeys. *The American Psychologist*, 1962, **17**, 1–9.

Hooker, E. Male homosexuality in the Rorschach. *Journal of Projective Techniques*, 1957, **21**, 18–31.

Itani, J. Paternal care in the wild Japanese monkeys, *Macaca fuscata*. In C. H. Southwick (Ed.), *Primate social behavior*. Princeton: Van Nostrand, 1963.

Little, K. B. & Schneidman, E. S. Congruences among interpretations of psychological and anamestic data. *Psychological Monographs*, 1959, **73**, 1–42.

Maccoby, Eleanor E. Sex differences in intellectual functioning. In Maccoby (Ed.), *The development of sex differences*. Stanford University Press, 1966. Pp. 25–55.

Masters, W. H. & Johnson, V. E. *Human sexual response*. Boston: Little, Brown, 1966.

Mead, M. *Male and female: A study of the sexes in a changing world*. New York: William Morrow, 1949.

Milgram, S. Some conditions of obedience and disobedience to authority. *Human Relations*, 1965a, **18**, 57–76.

Milgram, S. Liberating effects of group pressure. *Journal of Personality and Social Psychology,* 1965b, **1,** 127–134.

Mitchell, G. D. Paternalistic behavior in primates. *Psychological Bulletin,* 1969, **71,** 399–417.

Powers, E. & Witmer, H. *An experiment in the prevention of delinquency.* New York: Columbia University Press, 1951.

Rheingold, J. *The fear of being a woman.* New York: Grune & Stratton, 1964.

Rosenthal, R. On the social psychology of the psychological experiment: The experimenter's hypothesis as unintended determinant of experimental results. *American Scientist,* 1963, **51,** 268–283.

Rosenthal, R. *Experimenter effects in behavioral research.* New York: Appleton-Century-Crofts, 1966.

Rosenthal, R. & Jacobson, L. *Pygmalion in the classroom: Teacher expectation and pupil's intellectual development.* New York: Holt, Rinehart & Winston, 1968.

Rosenthal, R. & Lawson, R. A longitudinal study of the effects of experimenter bias on the operant learning of laboratory rats. Unpublished manuscript, Harvard University, 1961.

Rosenthal, R. & Fode, K. L. The effect of experimenter bias on the performance of the albino rat. Unpublished manuscript, Harvard University, 1960.

Rotter, J. B. Psychotherapy. *Annual Review of Psychology,* 1960, **11,** 381–414.

Schachter, S. & Singer, J. E. Cognitive, social and physiological determinants of emotional state. *Psychological Review,* 1962, **69,** 379–399.

Schwarz-Belkin, M. "Les Fleurs de Mal," in *Festschrift for Gordon Piltdown,* Ponzi Press, New York, 1914.

Tiger, L. *Men in groups.* New York: Random House, 1969.

Truax, C. B. Effective ingredients in psychotherapy: An approach to unraveling the patient-therapist interaction. *Journal of Counseling Psychology,* 1963, **10,** 256–263.

Training the Woman to Know Her Place:
The Power of a Nonconscious Ideology

Sandra L. Bem and Daryl J. Bem[1]

Sandra L. and Daryl J. Bem are Assistant Professor and Associate Professor of Psychology, respectively, at Carnegie-Mellon University. Each holds a Ph.D. from the University of Michigan. Both Drs. Bem are members of the National Organization for Women and members of the Board of Directors of Women's Equity Action League. Sandra Bem has served before legislative committees as expert witness against the segregated want-ad policy, and she teaches courses on sex roles and the psychology of women.

In the beginning God created the heaven and the earth. . . . And God said, Let us make man in our image, after our likeness; and let them have dominion over the fish of the sea, and over the fowl of the air, and over the cattle, and over all the earth. . . . And the rib, which the Lord God had taken from man, made he a woman and brought her unto the man. . . . And the Lord God said unto the woman, What is this that thou has done? And the woman said, The serpent beguiled me, and I did eat. . . . Unto the woman He said, I will greatly multiply thy sorrow and thy conception; in sorrow thou shalt bring forth children; and thy desire shall be to thy husband, and he shall rule over thee. (Gen. 1, 2, 3)

And lest anyone fail to grasp the moral of this story, Saint Paul provides further clarification:

For a man . . . is the image and glory of God; but the woman is the glory of the man. For the man is not of the woman, but the woman of the man. Neither was the man created for the woman, but the woman for the man. (1 Cor. 11)

Let the woman learn in silence with all subjection. But I suffer not a woman to teach, nor to usurp authority over the man, but to be in silence. For Adam was first formed, then Eve. And Adam was not deceived, but the woman, being deceived, was in the transgression. Notwithstanding, she shall be saved in childbearing, if they continue in faith and charity and holiness with sobriety. (1 Tim. 2)

And lest it be thought that only Christians have this rich heritage of ideology about women, consider the morning prayer of the Orthodox Jew:

[1] Order of authorship determined by the flip of a coin.

> Blessed art Thou, oh Lord our God, King of the Universe, that I was not born a gentile.
> Blessed art Thou, oh Lord our God, King of the Universe, that I was not born a slave.
> Blessed art Thou, oh Lord our God, King of the Universe, that I was not born a woman.

Or the Koran, the sacred text of Islam:

> Men are superior to women on account of the qualities in which God has given them pre-eminence.

Because they think they sense a decline in feminine "faith, charity, and holiness with sobriety," many people today jump to the conclusion that the ideology expressed in these passages is a relic of the past. Not so. It has simply been obscured by an equalitarian veneer, and the ideology has now become nonconscious. That is, we remain unaware of it because alternative beliefs and attitudes about women go unimagined. We are like the fish who is unaware that his environment is wet. After all, what else could it be? Such is the nature of all nonconscious ideologies. Such is the nature of America's ideology about women. For even those Americans who agree that a black skin should not uniquely qualify its owner for janitorial or domestic service continue to act as if the possession of a uterus uniquely qualifies *its* owner for precisely that.

Consider, for example, the 1968 student rebellion at Columbia University. Students from the radical left took over some administration buildings in the name of equalitarian principles which they accused the university of flouting. Here were the most militant spokesmen one could hope to find in the cause of equalitarian ideals. But no sooner had they occupied the buildings than the male militants blandly turned to their sisters-in-arms and assigned them the task of preparing the food, while they—the menfolk—would presumably plan further strategy. The reply these males received was the reply they deserved, and the fact that domestic tasks behind the barricades were desegregated across the sex line that day is an everlasting tribute to the class consciousness of the ladies of the left.

But these conscious coeds are not typical, for the nonconscious assumptions about a woman's "natural" talents (or lack of them) are at least as prevalent among women as they are among men. A psychologist named Philip Goldberg (1968) demonstrated this by asking female college students to rate a number of professional articles from each of six fields. The articles were collated into two equal sets of booklets, and the names of the authors were changed so that the identical article was attributed to the male author (e.g., John T. McKay) in one set of booklets and to a female author (e.g., Joan T. McKay) in the other set.

Each student was asked to read the articles in her booklet and to rate them for value, competence, persuasiveness, writing style, and so forth.

As he had anticipated, Goldberg found that the identical article received significantly lower ratings when it was attributed to a female author than when it was attributed to a male author. He had predicted this result for articles from professional fields generally considered the province of men, like law and city planning, but to his surprise, these coeds also downgraded articles from the fields of dietetics and elementary school education when they were attributed to female authors. In other words, these students rated the male authors as better at everything, agreeing with Aristotle that "we should regard the female nature as afflicted with a natural defectiveness." We repeated this experiment informally in our own classrooms and discovered that male students show the same implicit prejudice against female authors that Goldberg's female students showed. Such is the nature of a nonconscious ideology!

It is significant that examples like these can be drawn from the college world, for today's students have challenged the established ways of looking at almost every other issue, and they have been quick to reject those practices of our society which conflict explicitly with their major values. But as the above examples suggest, they will find it far more difficult to shed the more subtle aspects of a sex-role ideology which—as we shall now attempt to demonstrate—conflicts just as surely with their existential values as any of the other societal practices to which they have so effectively raised objection. And as we shall see, there is no better way to appreciate the power of a society's nonconscious ideology than to examine it within the framework of values held by that society's avant-garde.

Individuality and Self-Fulfillment

The dominant values of today's students concern personal growth on the one hand, and interpersonal relationships on the other. The first of these emphasizes individuality and self-fulfillment; the second stresses openness, honesty, and equality in all human relationships.

The values of individuality and self-fulfillment imply that each human being, male or female, is to be encouraged to "do his own thing." Men and women are no longer to be stereotyped by society's definitions. If sensitivity, emotionality, and warmth are desirable human characteristics, then they are desirable for men as well as for women. (John Wayne is no longer an idol of the young, but their pop-art satire.) If independence, assertiveness, and serious intellectual commitment are desirable human characteristics, then they are desirable for women as well as for men. The major prescription of this college generation is that each individual should be encouraged to discover and fulfill his own unique potential and identity, unfettered by society's presumptions.

But society's presumptions enter the scene much earlier than most people suspect, for parents begin to raise their children in accord with the popular stereotypes from the very first. Boys are encouraged to be aggressive, competitive, and independent, whereas girls are rewarded for being passive and dependent (Barry, Bacon, & Child, 1957; Sears, Maccoby, & Levin, 1957). In one study, six-month-old infant girls were already being touched and spoken to more by their mothers while they were playing than were infant boys. When they were thirteen months old, these same girls were more reluctant than the boys to leave their mothers; they returned more quickly and more frequently to them; and they remained closer to them throughout the entire play period. When a physical barrier was placed between mother and child, the girls tended to cry and motion for help; the boys made more active attempts to get around the barrier (Goldberg & Lewis, 1969). No one knows to what extent these sex differences at the age of thirteen months can be attributed to the mothers' behavior at the age of six months, but it is hard to believe that the two are unconnected.

As children grow older, more explicit sex-role training is introduced. Boys are encouraged to take more of an interest in mathematics and science. Boys, not girls, are given chemistry sets and microscopes for Christmas. Moreover, all children quickly learn that mommy is proud to be a moron when it comes to mathematics and science, whereas daddy knows all about these things. When a young boy returns from school all excited about biology, he is almost certain to be encouraged to think of becoming a physician. A girl with similar enthusiasm is told that she might want to consider nurse's training later so she can have "an interesting job to fall back upon in case—God forbid—she ever needs to support herself." A very different kind of encouragement. And any girl who doggedly persists in her enthusiasm for science is likely to find her parents as horrified by the prospect of a permanent love affair with physics as they would be by the prospect of an interracial marriage.

These socialization practices quickly take their toll. By nursery school age, for example, boys are already asking more questions about how and why things work (Smith, 1933). In first and second grade, when asked to suggest ways of improving various toys, boys do better on the fire truck and girls do better on the nurse's kit, but by the third grade, boys do better regardless of the toy presented (Torrance, 1962). By the ninth grade, 25% of the boys, but only 3% of the girls, are considering careers in science or engineering (Flanagan, unpublished, cited by Kagan, 1964). When they apply for college, boys and girls are about equal on verbal aptitude tests, but boys score significantly higher on mathematical aptitude tests—about 60 points higher on the College Board examinations, for example (Brown, 1965, p. 162). Moreover, girls improve their mathematical performance if problems are reworded so that they deal with cooking and gardening, even though the abstract reasoning required for their solutions remains the same (Milton, 1958). Clearly, not just ability, but motivation too, has been affected.

But these effects in mathematics and science are only part of the story. A girl's long training in passivity and dependence appears to exact an even higher toll from her overall motivation to achieve, to search for new and independent ways of doing things, and to welcome the challenge of new and unsolved problems. In one study, for example, elementary school girls were more likely to try solving a puzzle by imitating an adult, whereas the boys were more likely to search for a novel solution not provided by the adult (McDavid, 1959). In another puzzle-solving study, young girls asked for help and approval from adults more frequently than the boys; and, when given the opportunity to return to the puzzles a second time, the girls were more likely to rework those they had already solved, whereas the boys were more likely to try puzzles they had been unable to solve previously (Crandall & Rabson, 1960). A girl's sigh of relief is almost audible when she marries and retires from the outside world of novel and unsolved problems. This, of course, is the most conspicuous outcome of all: the majority of American women become full-time homemakers. Such are the consequences of a nonconscious ideology.

But why does this process violate the values of individuality and self-fulfillment? It is *not* because some people may regard the role of homemaker as inferior to other roles. That is not the point. Rather, the point is that our society is managing to consign a large segment of its population to the role of homemaker solely on the basis of sex just as inexorably as it has in the past consigned the individual with a black skin to the role of janitor or domestic. It is not the quality of the role itself which is at issue here, but the fact that in spite of their unique identities, the majority of America's women end up in the *same* role.

Even so, however, several arguments are typically advanced to counter the claim that America's homogenization of its women subverts individuality and self-fulfillment. The three most common arguments invoke, respectively, (1) free will, (2) biology, and (3) complementarity.

1. The free will argument proposes that a 21-year-old woman is perfectly free to choose some other role if she cares to do so; no one is standing in her way. But this argument conveniently overlooks the fact that the society which has spent twenty years carefully marking the woman's ballot for her has nothing to lose in that twenty-first year by pretending to let her cast it for the alternative of her choice. Society has

controlled not her alternatives, but her motivation to choose any but one of those alternatives. The so-called freedom to choose is illusory and cannot be invoked to justify the society which controls the motivation to choose.

2. The biological argument suggests that there may really be inborn differences between men and women in, say, independence or mathematical ability. Or that there may be biological factors beyond the fact that women can become pregnant and nurse children which uniquely dictate that they, but not men, should stay home all day and shun serious outside commitment. Maybe female hormones really are responsible somehow. One difficulty with this argument, of course, is that female hormones would have to be different in the Soviet Union, where one-third of the engineers and 75% of the physicians are women. In America, women constitute less than 1% of the engineers and only 7% of the physicians (Dodge, 1966). Female physiology *is* different, and it may account for some of the psychological differences between the sexes, but America's sex-role ideology still seems primarily responsible for the fact that so few women emerge from childhood with the motivation to seek out any role beyond the one that our society dictates.

But even if there really were biological differences between the sexes along these lines, the biological argument would still be irrelevant. The reason can best be illustrated with an analogy.

Suppose that every black American boy were to be socialized to become a jazz musician on the assumption that he has a "natural" talent in that direction, or suppose that his parents should subtly discourage him from other pursuits because it is considered "inappropriate" for black men to become physicians or physicists. Most liberal Americans, we submit, would disapprove. But suppose that it *could* be demonstrated that black Americans, *on the average*, did possess an inborn better sense of rhythm than white Americans. Would *that* justify ignoring the unique characteristics of a *particular* black youngster from the very beginning and specifically socializing him to become a musician? We don't think so. Similarly, as long as a woman's socialization does not nurture her uniqueness, but treats her only as a member of a group on the basis of some assumed *average* characteristic, she will not be prepared to realize her own potential in the way that the values of individuality and self-fulfillment imply she should.

The irony of the biological argument is that it does not take biological differences seriously enough. That is, it fails to recognize the range of biological differences between individuals within the same sex. Thus, recent research has revealed that biological factors help determine many personality traits. Dominance and submissiveness, for example, have been found to have large inheritable components; in other words, biological factors *do* have the potential for partially determining how dominant or submissive an individual, male or female, will turn out to be. But the effects of this biological potential could be detected only in males (Gottesman, 1963). This implies that only the males in our culture are raised with sufficient flexibility, with sufficient latitude given to their biological differences, for their "natural" or biologically determined potential to shine through. Females, on the other hand, are subjected to a socialization which so ignores their unique attributes that even the effects of biology seem to be swamped. In sum, the biological argument for continuing America's homogenization of its women gets hoist with its own petard.

3. Many people recognize that most women do end up as full-time homemakers because of their socialization and that these women do exemplify the failure of our society to raise girls as unique individuals. But, they point out, the role of the homemaker is not inferior to the role of the professional man: it is complementary but equal.

This argument is usually bolstered by pointing to the joys and importance of taking care of small children. Indeed, mothers *and* fathers find child rearing rewarding, and it is certainly important. But this argument becomes insufficient when one considers that the average American woman now lives to age 74 and has her *last* child at about age 26; thus, by the time the woman is 33 or so, her children all have more important things to do with their daytime hours than to spend them entertaining an adult woman who has nothing to do during the second half of her life span. As for the other "joys" of homemaking, many writers (e.g., Friedan, 1963) have persuasively argued that the role of the homemaker has been glamorized far beyond its intrinsic worth. This charge becomes plausible when one considers that the average American homemaker spends the equivalent of a man's working day, 7.1 hours, in preparing meals, cleaning house, laundering, mending, shopping, and doing other household tasks. In other words, 43% of her waking time is spent in activity that would command an hourly wage on the open market well below the federally-set minimum for menial industrial work.

The point is not how little she would earn if she did these things in someone else's home, but that this use of time is virtually the same for homemakers with college degrees and for those with less than a grade school education, for women married to professional men and for women married to blue-collar workers. Talent, education, ability, interests, motivations: all are irrelevant. In our society, being female uniquely qualifies an individual for domestic work.

It is true, of course, that the American homemaker has, on the average, 5.1 hours of leisure time per day, and it is here, we are told, that each woman can express her unique identity. Thus, politically interested women can join the League of Women Voters; women with humane interests can become part-time Gray Ladies; women who love music can raise money for the symphony. Protestant women play Canasta; Jewish women play Mah-Jongg; brighter women of all denominations and faculty wives play bridge; and so forth.

But politically interested *men* serve in legislatures; *men* with humane interests become physicians or clinical psychologists; *men* who love music play in the symphony; and so forth. In other words, why should a woman's unique identity determine only the periphery of her life rather than its central core?

Again, the important point is not that the role of homemaker is necessarily inferior, but that the woman's unique identity has been rendered irrelevant. Consider the following "predictability test." When a boy is born, it is difficult to predict what he will be doing 25 years later. We cannot say whether he will be an artist, a doctor, or a college professor because he will be permitted to develop and to fulfill his own unique potential, particularly if he is white and middle class. But if the newborn child is a girl, we can usually predict with confidence how she will be spending her time 25 years later. Her individuality doesn't have to be considered; it is irrelevant.

The socialization of the American male has closed off certain options for him too. Men are discouraged from developing certain desirable traits such as tenderness and sensitivity just as surely as women are discouraged from being assertive and, alas, "too bright." Young boys are encouraged to be incompetent at cooking and child care just as surely as young girls are urged to be incompetent at mathematics and science.

Indeed, one of the errors of the early feminist movement in this country was that it assumed that men had all the goodies and that women could attain self-fulfillment merely by being like men. But that is hardly the utopia implied by the values of individuality and self-fulfillment. Rather, these values would require society to raise its children so flexibly and with sufficient respect for the integrity of individual uniqueness that some men might emerge with the motivation, the ability, and the opportunity to stay home and raise children without bearing the stigma of being peculiar. If homemaking is as glamorous as the women's magazines and television commercials portray it, then men, too, should have that option. Even if homemaking isn't all that glamorous, it would probably still be more fulfilling for some men than the jobs in which they now find themselves.

And if biological differences really do exist between men and women in "nurturance," in their inborn motivations to care for children, then this will show up automatically in the final distribution of men and women across the various roles: relatively fewer men will choose to stay at home. The values of individuality and self-fulfillment do not imply that there must be equality of outcome, an equal number of men and women in each role, but that there should be the widest possible variation in outcome consistent with the range of individual differences among people, regardless of sex. At the very least, these values imply that society should raise its males so that they could freely engage in activities that might pay less than those being pursued by their wives without feeling that they were "living off their wives." One rarely hears it said of a woman that she is "living off her husband."

Thus, it is true that a man's options are limited by our society's sex-role ideology, but as the "predictability test" reveals, it is still the woman in our society whose identity is rendered irrelevant by America's socialization practices. In 1954, the United States Supreme Court declared that a fraud and hoax lay behind the slogan "separate but equal." It is unlikely that any court will ever do the same for the more subtle motto that successfully keeps the woman in her place: "complementary but equal."

Interpersonal Equality

> Wives, submit yourselves unto your own husbands, as unto the Lord. For the husband is the head of the wife, even as Christ is the head of the church; and he is the savior of the body. Therefore, as the church is subject unto Christ, so let the wives be to their own husbands in everything. (Eph. 5)

As this passage reveals, the ideological rationalization that men and women hold complementary but equal positions is a recent invention of our modern "liberal" society, part of the equalitarian veneer which helps to keep today's version of the ideology nonconscious. Certainly those Americans who value open, honest, and equalitarian relationships generally are quick to reject this traditional view of the male-female relationship; and, an increasing number of young people even plan to enter "utopian" marriages very much like the following hypothetical example:

> Both my wife and I earned Ph.D. degrees in our respective disciplines. I turned down a superior academic post in Oregon and accepted a slightly less desirable position in New York where my wife could obtain a part-time teaching job and do research at one of the several other colleges in the area. Although I would have preferred to live in a suburb, we purchased a home near my wife's college so that she could have an office at home where she would be when the children returned from school. Because my wife earns a good salary, she can easily afford to pay a maid to do her major household chores. My wife and I share

all other tasks around the house equally. For example, she cooks the meals, but I do the laundry for her and help her with many of her other household tasks.

Without questioning the basic happiness of such a marriage or its appropriateness for many couples, we can legitimately ask if such a marriage is, in fact, an instance of interpersonal equality. Have all the hidden assumptions about the woman's "natural" role really been eliminated? Has the traditional ideology really been exorcised? There is a very simple test. If the marriage is truly equalitarian, then its description should retain the same flavor and tone even if the roles of the husband and wife were to be reversed:

> Both my husband and I earned Ph.D. degrees in our respective disciplines. I turned down a superior academic post in Oregon and accepted a slightly less desirable position in New York where my husband could obtain a part-time teaching job and do research at one of the several other colleges in the area. Although I would have preferred to live in a suburb, we purchased a home near my husband's college so that he could have an office at home where he would be when the children returned from school. Because my husband earns a good salary, he can easily afford to pay a maid to do his major household chores. My husband and I share all other tasks around the house equally. For example, he cooks the meals, but I do the laundry for him and help him with many of his other household tasks.

It seems unlikely that many men or women in our society would mistake the marriage *just* described as either equalitarian or desirable, and thus it becomes apparent that the ideology about the woman's "natural" role nonconsciously permeates the entire fabric of such "utopian" marriages. It is true that the wife gains some measure of equality when her career can influence the final place of residence, but why is it the unquestioned assumption that the husband's career solely determines the initial set of alternatives that are to be considered? Why is it the wife who automatically seeks the part-time position? Why is it *her* maid instead of *their* maid? Why *her* laundry? Why *her* household tasks? And so forth throughout the entire relationship.

The important point here is not that such marriages are bad or that their basic assumptions of inequality produce unhappy, frustrated women. Quite the contrary. It is the very happiness of the wives in such marriages that reveals society's smashing success in socializing its women. It is a measure of the distance our society must yet traverse toward the goals of self-fulfillment and interpersonal equality that such marriages are widely characterized as utopian and fully equalitarian. It is a mark of how well the woman has been kept in her place that the husband in such a marriage is often idolized by women, including his wife, for "permitting" her to squeeze a career into the interstices of their marriage as long as his own career is not unduly inconvenienced. Thus is the white man blessed for exercising his power benignly while his "natural" right to that power forever remains unquestioned.

Such is the subtlety of a nonconscious ideology!

A truly equalitarian marriage would permit both partners to pursue careers or outside commitments which carry equal weight when all important decisions are to be made. It is here, of course, that the "problem" of children arises. People often assume that the woman who seeks a role beyond home and family would not care to have children. They assume that if she wants a career or serious outside commitment, then children must be unimportant to her. But of course no one makes this assumption about her husband. No one assumes that a father's interest in his career necessarily precludes a deep and abiding affection for his children or a vital interest in their development. Once again America applies a double standard of judgment. Suppose that a father of small children suddenly lost his wife. No matter how much he loved his children, no one would expect him to sacrifice his career in order to stay home with them on a full-time basis—*even if he had an independent source of income.* No one would charge him with selfishness or lack of parental feeling if he sought professional care for his children during the day. An equalitarian marriage simply abolishes this double standard and extends the same freedom to the mother, while also providing the framework for the father to enter more fully into the pleasures and responsibilities of child rearing. In fact, it is the equalitarian marriage which has the most potential for giving children the love and concern of two parents rather than one.

But few women are prepared to make use of this freedom. Even those women who have managed to finesse society's attempt to rob them of their career motivations are likely to find themselves blocked by society's trump card: the feeling that the raising of the children is their unique responsibility and—in time of crisis—ultimately theirs alone. Such is the emotional power of a nonconscious ideology.

In addition to providing this potential for equalized child care, a truly equalitarian marriage embraces a more general division of labor which satisfies what might be called "the roommate test." That is, the labor is divided just as it is when two men or two women room together in college or set up a bachelor apartment together. Errands and domestic chores are assigned by preference, agreement, flipping a coin, given to hired help, or—as is sometimes the case—left undone.

It is significant that today's young people, many of whom live this way prior to marriage, find this kind of arrangement within marriage so foreign to their thinking. Consider an analogy. Suppose that a white male college student decided to room or set up a bachelor apartment with a black male friend. Surely the typical white student would not blithely assume that his black roommate was to handle all the domestic chores. Nor would his conscience allow him to do so even in the unlikely event that his roommate would say: "No, that's okay. I like doing housework. I'd be happy to do it." We suspect that the typical white student would still not be comfortable if he took advantage of this offer, if he took advantage of the fact that his roommate had been socialized to be "happy" with such an arrangement. But change this hypothetical black roommate to a female marriage partner, and somehow the student's conscience goes to sleep. At most it is quickly tranquilized by the thought that "she is happiest when she is ironing for her loved one." Such is the power of a nonconscious ideology.

Of course, it may well be that she *is* happiest when she is ironing for her loved one.

Such, indeed, is the power of a nonconscious ideology!

References

Barry, H., III, Bacon, M. K., & Child, I. L. A cross-cultural survey of some sex differences in socialization. *Journal of Abnormal and Social Psychology*, 1957, **55**, 327–332.

Brown, R. *Social psychology.* New York: Free Press, 1965.

Crandall, V. J. & Rabson, A. Children's repetition choices in an intellectual achievement situation following success and failure. *Journal of Genetic Psychology*, 1960, **97**, 161–168.

Dodge, N. D. *Women in the Soviet economy.* Baltimore: The Johns Hopkins Press, 1966.

Flanagan, J. C. Project talent. Unpublished manuscript.

Friedan, B. *The feminine mystique.* New York: Norton, 1963.

Goldberg, P. Are women prejudiced against women? *Transaction*, April 1968, **5**, 28–30.

Goldberg, S. & Lewis, M. Play behavior in the year-old infant: Early sex differences. *Child Development*, 1969, **40**, 21–31.

Gottesman, I. I. Heritability of personality: A demonstration. *Psychological Monographs*, 1963, **77** (Whole No. 572).

Kagan, J. Acquisition and significance of sex typing and sex role identity. In M. L. Hoffman & L. W. Hoffman (Eds.), *Review of child development research, Vol. 1.* New York: Russell Sage Foundation, 1964. Pp. 137–167.

McDavid, J. W. Imitative behavior in preschool children. *Psychological Monographs*, 1959, **73** (Whole No. 486).

Milton, G. A. Five studies of the relation between sex role identification and achievement in problem solving. Technical Report No.3, Department of Industrial Administration, Department of Psychology, Yale University, December, 1958.

Femininity and Successful Achievement:
A Basic Inconsistency

Matina S. Horner

Matina S. Horner is Assistant Professor of Personality and Development at Harvard University. She holds a Ph.D. from the University of Michigan where she became involved with the problems of motivation and the feminine personality. She is co-author of the book *Feminine Personality and Conflict*; she also teaches courses and speaks to women's groups on the same and related topics.

"Each step forward in work as a successful American regardless of sex means a step back as a woman. . . ."

> Margaret Mead
> *Male and Female*

Although Mead first made this observation in 1949, it continues to be significant in today's society. Both in theory and in practice, the role of women in American society (which is primarily an achievement-oriented system) has over the years been little understood and much ignored by psychologists. A peculiar paradox arises in the society because we have an educational system that ostensibly encourages and prepares men and women identically for careers that social and, even more importantly, internal psychological pressures really limit to men. This paradox is reflected by the feelings of the women who somehow overcome these pressures and pursue a particular career: They feel anxious, guilty, unfeminine, and selfish.

Women as well as men in this society are immersed in a culture that rewards and values achievement and that stresses self-reliance, individual freedom, self-realization, and the full development of individual resources, including one's intellectual potential. In *The Achieving Society* (1961), McClelland has carefully elaborated how these values and attitudes (which are rooted in Max Weber's "Protestant

From *Feminine Personality and Conflict* by Judith M. Bardwick, Elizabeth Douvan, Matina Horner, and David Gutmann. © 1970 by Wadsworth Publishing Company, Inc. Reprinted by permission of the publisher, Brooks/Cole Publishing Company, Belmont, California.

Ethic") effect child-rearing practices that foster the development of achievement motivation. Winterbottom's (1958) work has shown that, when early self-reliance and mastery are expected and rewarded by the parents, the child internalizes these values and is prone to develop a high achievement motive (*n* Achievement). (This behavior will not occur, however, if the parents' high standards of excellence and independence reflect authoritarianism or rejection or simply the desire to make their own burdens less.)

Despite the prevalence of these values in most middle-class American homes, femininity and individual achievement continue to be viewed as two desirable but mutually exclusive ends. The cultural attitudes toward appropriate sex roles have truly limited the horizons of women. As a result, there is a significant and increasing absence of American women in the mainstream of thought and achievement in the society. For instance, the *proportion* of women college *graduates* is smaller today than it was 30 years ago, even though in absolute numbers more women are being educated. Furthermore, although the *number* of working women is increasing, the vast majority are found in low-skilled jobs and a very small proportion are working at a level close to that reflecting their educational or professional training. Whereas the number of professional women in Europe has doubled in the past 30 years, the number in America has actually declined. There are fewer women in upper-echelon positions now than there were before World War II. Thus a great number of women have been highly educated and trained for various professions or positions of leadership but are not using their skills, even though they may be part of the labor force at some lower level. This situation reflects the greatest loss of potential.

Although the social structure decries the terrible loss of female potential in both economic and personal terms, it provides few, if any, positive incentives or sanctions for career-oriented women. This situation is particularly noticeable for women of middle- or upper-class status who want to work for reasons other than economic necessity or survival. For women the distinction between a "job" and a "career" is very important.

Recently the "intellectual community" has been exerting effort to come to some understanding of the loss of human potential and resources that is reflected in this pattern of behavior. The experimental data to be presented later in the chapter show that, despite the removal for women of many legal and educational barriers to achievement, which existed until the 20th century, there remains a *psychological barrier* that is considerably more subtle, stubborn, and difficult to overcome. I refer to this barrier as the *motive to avoid success* ($M - s$). This "fear of success" receives its impetus from the expectancy held by women that success in achievement situations will be followed by negative consequences, including social rejection and the sense of losing one's femininity.

It has been difficult to identify the nature of the psychological barrier to achievement in women. Therefore, before continuing, it would be useful to consider briefly the nature of the Expectancy-Value theory of motivation and the data that provided the background for developing this notion. In attempting to understand the motivational process, Expectancy-Value theory places equal emphasis on the significance of two elements. The first element is a stable, enduring personality characteristic called *motive* (M). The second element comprises two specific, immediate, but more transient properties of the environment that define the challenge offered by the situation: the expectancy (E) or probability of a certain outcome occurring, and the incentive value (I) or attractiveness of that outcome to the person in question. Within the theory an important distinction is made between *motive* and *motivation*. Before any motive can influence behavior, it must become motivation; that is, the motive must be aroused by one's expectancy of the consequences of his actions and by the incentive value of the expected consequences. For example, in the Theory of Achievement Motivation (Atkinson & Feather, 1966) it is assumed that the strength of one's motivation to achieve success (T_s) is determined by a multiplicative interaction between the *strength of the motive to achieve success* (M_s); *the expectancy or probability of success* (P_s) in the specific situation, which is defined by the difficulty of the task; and *the incentive value of success* (I_s), which has been shown to be inversely related to task difficulty $(I_s = 1 - P_s)$. Mathematically, then,

$$T_s = M_s \times P_s \times I_s.$$

It should be stressed that one's expectation of the consequences of his actions is an extremely important variable for determining the strength of his (achievement) motivation.

The particulars and mathematical derivations of the Theory of Achievement Motivation are presented only to clarify the distinction between motive and motivation; they need not concern us beyond that point. However, it *is* important to remember that positive motivation to do something is aroused by the expectancy that one's behavior will be followed by positive consequences. On the other hand, the expectancy or anticipation of negative consequences produces anxiety, which is a tendency to *inhibit* the activity. Once negative motivation or anxiety is aroused in a situation, it weakens the strength of all positive motivation for undertaking or persisting at the activity expected to have negative consequences.

Since the publication of *The Achievement Motive* (McClelland,

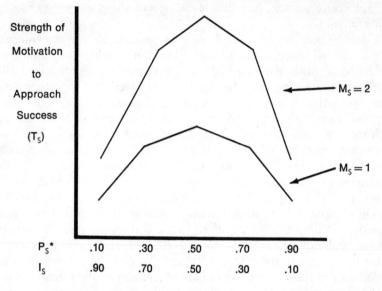

*P_S = expectancy of success

Figure 1. Tendency to approach success $= T_S \times M_S \times P_S \times I_S$ ($I_S = 1 - P_S$)

Atkinson, Clark, & Lowell, 1953) extensive research has been directed toward understanding the contemporaneous determinants of achievement-oriented behavior. As a result, there is a very impressive and theoretically consistent body of data related to achievement motivation and its sources, development, assessment, and impact on the performance of men. This evidence shows the effects of individual differences in achievement motivation on the kinds of risks preferred and taken, the levels of aspiration set, and the levels of performance and persistence shown by men in various types of achievement-oriented activity. The early work shows that male subjects who are high in achievement motivation prefer and do best at tasks of intermediate rather than extreme levels of difficulty (Atkinson & Litwin, 1960), that they set intermediate, realistic levels of aspiration (Mahone, 1958), and that they select work partners of high ability (French, 1956). In general they perform better and persist longer at all kinds of tasks in which some element of risk is involved (preferably 50–50), provided that the outcome depends on their ability rather than on chance and that the results will be made known and evaluated in terms of some standard of excellence (Atkinson, 1958).

Following these early results, the work in achievement motivation has gone mainly along two distinct lines.

McClelland has been primarily concerned with the social origins

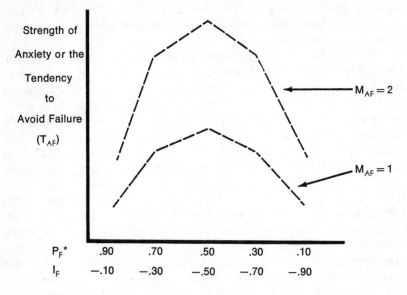

Figure 2. Tendency to avoid failure $= M_{AF} \times P_F \times I_F \times I_F = -P_S$

and molar social consequences of achievement motivation for society (McClelland, 1961). He has provided compelling evidence for his hypothesis that high achievement motivation is at least partly responsible for a high level of entrepreneurial activity, which in turn leads to the economic growth and development of a society. Particularly interesting and novel in their approach are the studies that relate the presence of achievement motivation to the economic growth and decline of certain societies in the past. This evidence is deduced from content analyses of samples of literature, such as folktales and children's readers, at critical points in these societies' histories. McClelland concludes that the risk-taking activities and new ideas tried by entrepreneurs result from a strong motive to achieve and not merely from a strong "need for money," as is more generally suspected. More recently McClelland has been involved with research in motivation training as a tool for instituting behavioral change, particularly in underdeveloped or unmotivated sectors of society. This approach raises many interesting theoretical questions.

Atkinson and his coworkers (see Atkinson & Feather, 1966) have carried on a very systematic and impressive experimental analysis of the contemporaneous determinants of achievement-oriented activities. Their work has evolved from a continuous interaction between theoretical speculation and empirical data and is a very useful and stimulating guideline for further work in the area. As a result of this work, we now have a systematic theory and a large, consistent body of data about achievement motivation in men.

Data for females, on the other hand, have been scarce. Atkinson (1958) filled more than 800 pages with a compilation of available theory and data on achievement motivation. The question of sex differences was treated only in a footnote. It is admittedly a long footnote in which he refers to the issue of sex differences as "perhaps the most persistent unresolved problem in research on *n* Achievement" (p. 33). Even more striking is the absence of any mention of achievement motivation in women by McClelland (1961). Using evidence from vases, flags, doodles, and children's books, he was able to study achievement motivation in such diverse samples as Indians, Quakers, and Ancient Greeks but not in women. This was not an oversight by either author; there are in fact not many meaningful data. The few results collected on female subjects have not been consistent with the existing theory of achievement motivation, with the findings for men, or even internally with one another. In other words, there has been neither a systematic theory nor a consistent body of data about achievement motivation in women. To add to the confusion, the sparse data that have been collected were gathered using very dissimilar methods and widely diverse samples of female subjects. As a result, it is nearly impossible to come to any meaningful conclusions.

We have not been able to explain women's inconsistent pattern of responses on the Thematic Apperception Test (TAT), which is used to assess individual differences in strength of the achievement motive, or to account for the lack of any consistent relationship between achievement motivation and performance in female subjects. Explanations offered in terms of a differential perception of what kind of striving behaviors are appropriate to their sex role have proven at best incomplete and premature.

It would be valuable now to consider briefly how achievement motivation is assessed and then to explore more carefully the nature of the sex differences that have been observed in studies of achievement motivation and behavior.

Beginning with the traditional clinical assumption that human motives are readily expressed in fantasy or imaginative behavior, and using the basic procedures developed by experimental psychologists for manipulating strength of motivation, McClelland et al. (1953) found, first with hunger and then with achievement, affiliation, and so on, that one could indeed validly and reliably assess individual differences in motive strength by analyzing fantasy or imaginative behavior. The particular criteria used for determining strength of achievement motivation were established by experimental fact, and a definitive scoring manual was developed (McClelland et al., 1953, Chap. 4; Atkinson, 1958, Chap. 12). Achievement imagery is reflected by concern with standards of excellence and with performing well, by unique accomplishments like inventions, by persistent and varying attempts to achieve, and by good or bad feelings about the consequences of the efforts. It is generally assumed that those who express the most achievement imagery under standard cues and testing procedures are the ones most highly motivated to achieve.

The major sex difference—at least the one that has received the greatest amount of attention—has been that women, unlike men, fail to show an increase in their achievement-imagery score when they are exposed to experimental conditions that arouse achievement motivation by stressing "intelligence and leadership ability" (Veroff, Wilcox, & Atkinson, 1953). Under neutral conditions the scores of women are as high or higher than those of men. McClelland points out that the two possible explanations considered, invalidity of the scoring system for women and scores too high to go higher, have been eliminated by experimental evidence. He concludes: "Apparently the usual arousal instructions simply do not increase achievement striving in women. . . ." Why is this type of arousal ineffective for women? The evidence from the more recent studies on women's motivation to avoid success provides a much clearer understanding of this problem. The earlier studies, which we shall consider only briefly, have given us a generally inconsistent pattern of results.

A study by Field (1951) suggests that achievement motivation in women can be aroused by referring to their social acceptability rather than to their "intelligence and leadership ability." On the other hand, Angelini's (1955) data on Brazilian university women argue that "intelligence and leadership" arousal *is* effective provided the sample used is made up of highly competitive women who value intellectual accomplishment. The implication is that women at large American coed universities (like that at which the previous work was done) are more socially than intellectually oriented. Lesser, Krawitz, and Packard (1963) tested Angelini's hypothesis within American society. They conducted their study at Hunter High School for girls in New York City. The school places great emphasis on the intellectual accomplishments of women. Admission is very competitive (only 150 of 4,000 highly selected candidates are admitted), and more than 99% of the graduates go on to college. A large percentage of these girls pursue professional careers. The results of the study were disappointing. Despite the fact that these girls are highly competitive and value intellectual accomplishments, no overall increase in achievement imagery was found under arousal conditions stressing intelligence and leadership ability. However, an interesting pattern of interaction was noted. The impact of the arousal condition on the TAT responses of the girls who were doing well at the school, compared with those who were not (with IQ scores matched), varied depending on whether the dominant stimulus figure on the TAT cue was male or female. The "achievers" showed an increase in achievement-motivation score under arousal conditions only to pictures of females and the "underachievers" only to pictures of males. Assuming that most of the girls who go to Hunter value achievement and see it as a relevant goal (or at least their parents do), the explanation offered for these results in terms of differential perception of social role among the girls is reasonable but not sufficient. For instance, why should the achievers—the girls who do well and presumably value achievement more than those who do not do well—show an increase in achievement motivation to female pictures, most of which depict women involved with traditional activities?

Other studies have attempted to relate such factors as individual value orientation, achievement relevance of goals, sex of the TAT stimulus figure, nature of arousal conditions (French & Lesser, 1964), and sex-role orientation (Lipinski, 1965) to achievement-motive scores and to performance. The results have been so inconsistent that, instead of resolving the problem of achievement motivation in women, they have only further emphasized the vast complexity of the issue.

The other major area of divergence between data for men and those for women has been the relationship between achievement motivation and performance. As already indicated, individual differences in strength of achievement motivation predict several types of performance for men in a theoretically consistent way but lack predictive power for women, for whom the results are both confusing and inconsistent. It is easy to see why most researchers in the area gave up on women and concentrated their efforts on the problems of achievement motivation and behavior in men. Freud (1965), in his attempts to understand women, began by pointing out that "throughout the ages the problem of women has puzzled people of every kind" (p. 154). Unsatisfied by his own efforts, he concluded that "if you want to know more about femininity, you must interrogate your own experience or turn to the poets, or else wait until science can give you more profound and more coherent information" (p. 185). But science, too, has had its problems in this area.

Some of the difficulties I have been discussing began to be clarified for me when I directed my attention beyond the achievement motive per se. Spurred on by data reporting a higher incidence of anxiety in women than in men, I became concerned with "achievement-related anxieties" that might be aroused along with the achievement motive in achievement-oriented situations.

In any achievement-oriented situation, performance is evaluated against some standard of excellence; thus the situation simultaneously offers both a chance for success and a threat of failure. The achievement motive is aroused by the expectancy that good performance will lead to a positive feeling like pride, the motive to avoid failure (test anxiety) is aroused by the expectancy that poor performance will lead to a negative feeling like shame. Measuring both types of motivation in men markedly enhances the predictive power of Atkinson's Theory of Achievement Motivation (Atkinson & Litwin, 1960; Atkinson & Feather, 1966).

Test or achievement anxiety has long been viewed primarily as motivation to avoid failure. Recently, however, I have entertained the hypothesis that women may in fact be more anxious than men in testing or achievement-oriented situations because they face negative consequences and hence anxiety not only in failing but also in succeeding. The anxiety-provoking aspects of success probably lie in the aggressive, masculine overtones that are implicit in or generally associated with successful competition in achievement situations. As I have already indicated, I refer to this disposition to become anxious in competitive achievement situations as the motive to avoid success. The anxiety is aroused whenever one expects that success will lead to negative consequences.

What exactly are the negative consequences of success in competitive achievement activity for women, and why has it taken us so long to recognize them? Perhaps part of our inability to recognize the problems results from a general lack of awareness of the extent to which we have been influenced by the image of woman and her sex role that has evolved over the centuries. Aristotle claimed that women never suffered from baldness because they never used the contents of their heads. That image of woman appears to have persisted over the centuries. Recall for a moment the misguided lamentations of the misogynic Professor Higgins in *My Fair Lady:*

> *Why Can't a Woman Be More Like a Man?*
> Women are irrational
> Their heads are full of cotton, hay, and rags.
> Why can't a woman learn to use her head?
> Why is thinking something women never do?

One wonders if this image might not be a more accurate reflection of our society's attitudes than we care to admit. While half-seriously attempting to answer Professor Higgins, we can perhaps pinpoint the source of anxiety about success: Let us consider what happens when women stray from the image and do use their heads.

If not rejected, they are praised (or castigated) for having Masculine Minds. Clare Booth Luce rejected that kind of praise from a colleague by saying: "I must refuse the compliment that I think like a man. Thought has no sex. One either thinks or one does not." Other women who are actively engaged in professional pursuits find themselves constantly trying to establish or prove their femininity, often going to great efforts and sometimes to extremes to display in dress and speech the obvious popular standards of femininity. Conrad suggested that "A woman with a masculine mind is not a being of superior efficiency; she is simply a phenomenon of imperfect differentiation—interestingly barren and without importance."

Unfortunately, many people unconsciously connect sex with certain characteristics and occupations. Although there is nothing intrinsically feminine about typing or teaching, or intrinsically masculine about medicine, physics, investment counseling, preaching, or just plain "thinking," for that matter, we have had difficulty adjusting to this idea psychologically. As a whole, society has been unable to reconcile personal ambition, accomplishment, and success with femininity. The more successful or independent a woman becomes, the more afraid society is that she has lost her femininity and therefore must be a failure as a wife and mother. She is viewed as a hostile and destructive force within the society. On the other hand, the more successful a man is in his work (as reflected in his high status, salary, and administrative powers—all of which are in keeping with his masculinity), the more attractive he becomes as a spouse and father. Whereas men are unsexed by failure (Mead, 1949), women seem to be unsexed by success.

Maccoby (1963) has pointed out that "the girl who maintains qualities of independence and active striving (achievement-orientation) necessary for intellectual mastery defies the conventions of sex appropriate behavior and must pay a price, *a price in anxiety*." This observation may help explain why, after four years at a very high-ranking women's college (during which time they became "more liberal and independent"—that is, more masculine—in their values and attitudes), girls show a higher incidence of anxiety and psychological disturbance than they did when they were freshmen (Sanford, 1961, Chap. 24).

At a symposium on the potential of women in which Mannes (1963) discussed the problems of the creative woman and described the "entrance charges" she must pay for the approval of men and other women, the point was made that "nobody objects to a woman's being a good writer or sculptor or geneticist *if*, at the same time, she manages to be a good wife, a good mother, good-looking, good-tempered, well-dressed, well-groomed, and *unaggressive*."

Most American women faced with the conflict between maintaining their feminine image and developing their ability compromise by disguising that ability and abdicating from competition in the outside world. Consider little Sally (from the *Peanuts* comic strip), who remarked, "I never said I wanted to be someone. All I want to do when I grow up is be a good wife and mother. So—why should I have to go to kindergarten?" We are all familiar with the American coed who is intelligent enough to do well but also too intelligent to get all As and thereby lose her man. She knows she will be more "desirable" if she needs the assistance of a male Galahad to help her understand her work. Women have been choosing—perhaps unconsciously—not to develop either their potential or their individuality but rather to live through and for others. This behavior is consistent with Rousseau's idea that a woman's "dignity consists in being unknown to the world; her glory is in the esteem of her husband; her pleasures in the happiness of her family."

Thus, while society has been legally opening its doors to women and decrying the loss of female potential, it has been teaching them to fail outside the home. No one ever seriously objects to a woman's education or intellectual development, provided its objective is to make her a more entertaining companion and a more enlightened, and thus better, wife and mother. Only when her objective is an independent personal career does a problem arise. Mead suggested that intense intellectual striving (of the kind necessary for the serious pursuit of a career) is viewed as "competitively aggressive behavior." The aggressive overtones of competition and success are evident in the fact that each time one person succeeds, someone else fails or is beaten. This situation may well be the basis of fear of success. It seems there is nothing more distasteful than an "uppity" woman who opts to beat a man, especially at "his own game"—be it law, medicine, physics, or rational thought. She will evoke the wrath not only of men but also of other women. Riesman (1964) points out that "women, as with many minority groups, bitterly resent and envy those among them who break out of confinement" and are frequently "shrewish and vindictive toward them."

Freud (1965) pointed out that the whole essence of femininity lies in repressing aggressiveness. A woman is threatened by success because unusual excellence in academic and intellectual areas is unconsciously equated with loss of femininity; as a result, the possibility of social rejection becomes very real. A woman who achieves success may lose her self-esteem and her sense of femininity, which is an internalized standard acquired early in the socialization process. Thus, regardless of whether anyone else finds out about her success, the inconsistency between femininity and successful achievement is so deeply embedded that most women, as Rossi (1965) has indicated, believe that even wanting something more than motherhood is unnatural and reflects emotional disturbance within them. Social rejection following success can also prevent a woman from fulfilling her other needs for affection, love, marriage, and children. Kagan and Moss (1962) summarize the problem and its consequences as follows:

> The typical female has greater anxiety over aggressiveness and competitive behavior than the male. She therefore experiences greater conflict over intellectual competition which in turn leads to inhibition of intense strivings for academic excellence.

Assuming that, for most men, active striving for success in competitive achievement activity is consistent with masculinity and self-esteem and does not give rise to the expectancy of negative consequences, it may be that the motive to avoid success is one of the major factors underlying sex differences detected in research on achievement-related motivation and performance.

Under achievement-oriented conditions that stress "leadership or intellectual ability," women may inhibit expression of their achievement motivation on the TAT because of the concurrent arousal of anxiety about failure and anxiety about success. Thus women's TAT scores may not be an accurate or valid measure of the strength of their achievement motive and cannot be expected to relate to performance in the same way that men's scores do. It would be consistent within the Expectancy-Value framework to argue that it is precisely those women who are most able or most motivated to achieve whose scores will be most adversely affected by the motive to avoid success. Only if a woman desires or is capable of attaining success in a situation can she expect the negative consequences; without this expectation, anxiety or motivation to avoid success will not be aroused.

It is evident in psychoanalytic literature that, in order to understand behavior, both anxiety and the defensive reactions against that anxiety should be considered. Under achievement arousal, women may defensively project or express their achievement motivation to TAT cues that depict women engaged in less threatening or more traditional types of activity or to pictures of men engaged in the more threatening, achievement-oriented types of activity. If less threatening cues are not available, expression of their achievement motive may be totally inhibited. These two options were available to the students in the Hunter High School study. The fact that, under arousal conditions, the "achievers" (presumably less anxious girls) showed an increase in achievement motivation to the female cues and the "underachievers" (presumably more anxious girls) to the male cues is consistent with the clinical assumption that projecting defensively to a same-sex figure engaged in less threatening activity reflects a lower level of anxiety than projecting to an opposite-sex figure engaged in the threatening activity.

I have noted that before any motive (any stable characteristic of one's personality) can influence behavior, it must become motivation; for example, it must be aroused by more specific, immediate, and transient characteristics of the environment (such as one's expectations about the consequences of his actions) and by the incentive values of the expected consequences. When the expectancies are negative, anxiety or negative inhibitory motivation results and interferes with performance. I have been suggesting that women can anticipate many negative consequences for actively seeking success in competitive achievement situations. A competitive situation is one in which performance reflecting intellectual and leadership ability is evaluated against a standard of excellence and also against the performance of one or more competitors.

Let us assume that anxiety about success—that is, anxiety about competitiveness and its masculine overtones—underlies many of the major sex differences detected in research on achievement motivation. It then follows that women should perform or behave differently in competitive and, by implication, aggressive achievement situations than in noncompetitive achievement situations. The negative incentive value of success should be greater for women if the success is attained under interpersonal competitive conditions, especially if the competitors are men and even more so if they are "important" men, such as mates or prospective boyfriends. It is in this last situation that the greatest weakening or inhibition of positive achievement motivation should occur.

Empirical Evidence

I will now present some of the empirical evidence in support of the ideas that have thus far been proposed and discussed. The first goal was to determine the extent of any sex differences in the motive to avoid success, and a measure to assess individual differences in this motive was developed (Horner, 1968). It involved a standard TAT for the achievement motive, except that four verbal, rather than pictorial, cues were used. An additional verbal lead was included that could be scored for motive to avoid success. For the 90 women in the study, the cue used was "After first-term finals, Anne finds herself at the top of her medical school class." The cue for the 88 men in the sample was "After first-term finals, John finds himself at the top of his medical school class." The subjects in this study were predominantly freshmen and sophomores at a large Midwestern coeducational university.

Precedents in the literature (Scott, 1958) show what happens in a TAT when a person is confronted with a cue or situation that represents a threat rather than a goal or that simultaneously represents a goal and a threat. These guidelines were used in developing the scoring criteria for "Fear of Success Imagery." Through a very simple present-absent system, the stories were scored for the motive to avoid success. "Fear of Success" was registered when the imagery expressed reflected serious concern about success, such as:

a. negative consequences *because of the success;*
b. anticipation of negative consequences *because of the success;*
c. negative affect *because of the success;*
d. instrumental activity away from present or future success, including leaving the field for more traditional female work such as nursing, schoolteaching, or social work;
e. any direct expression of conflict about success;
f. denial of *effort* in attaining the success (also cheating or any other attempt to deny responsibility or reject credit for the success);
g. denial of the situation described by the cue; or
h. bizarre, inappropriate, unrealistic, or nonadaptive responses to the situation described by the cue.

The subjects' responses can be readily classified into three main groups.

1. *Fear of social rejection.* This reaction appeared most frequently. The negative affect and consequences described were rooted mainly in affiliative concerns, including fear of being socially rejected and fear of losing one's friends or one's datability or marriageability. Fear of isolation or loneliness as a result of the success, as well as the desire to keep the success a secret and pretend that intelligence is not there, were also included. The following are examples of stories in this category.

> Anne has a boyfriend, Carl, in the same class, and they are quite serious. Anne met Carl at college, and they started dating about their sophomore year in undergraduate school. Anne is rather upset and so is Carl. She wants him to be higher scholastically than she is. Anne will deliberately lower her academic standing the next term, while she does all she subtly can to help Carl. His grades come up and Anne soon drops out of med school. They marry and he goes on in school while she raises their family.

> She is in a class of a great number of highly intelligent and competitive people, one of whom is her fiancé. . . . Anne is ambitious and has more innate ability than does her boyfriend. Anne is fearful that this situation will have a detrimental effect on their relationship and later on their marriage. Her superiority will mean that her eventual earning power will be greater. Although he would never let her know,

her husband would resent that. It is important that Anne marry this man because of their closeness. But Anne will *never be entirely happy* in the marriage because she must always hold back her mentality and vocational desires.

Anne is a wonderful girl who has always succeeded. She never had to work. Anne didn't really care. She went to med school because she couldn't marry. . . . She really cares nothing and wants to get married. No one will marry her. She has lots of friends but no dates. She's just another girl. She tries to pretend intelligence is not part of her. She doesn't hide it—just ignores it. She will get a great job in a marvelous hospital. I don't know if she will ever marry.

Anne doesn't want to be number one in her class. She feels she shouldn't rank so high because of social reasons. She drops down to ninth in the class and then marries the boy who graduates number one.

2. Concern about one's normality or femininity. This group comprises stories in which negative affect and consequences are free of any affiliative concern and independent of whether anyone finds out about the success. Typical reactions in this category include doubting one's femininity, feeling guilt or despair about the success, and wondering about one's normality.

Anne has planned for a long time to be a doctor. She has worked hard in her schoolwork to enable her to learn better how to fulfill her dream. Now her hard work has paid off. Unfortunately, Anne suddenly no longer feels so certain that she really wants to be a doctor. She wonders if perhaps this isn't normal. . . . Anne decides not to continue with her medical work but to continue with courses that she never allowed herself to take before but that have a deeper personal meaning for her.

Anne is completely ecstatic but at the same time feels guilty. She wishes that she could stop studying so hard, but parental and personal pressures drive her. She will finally have a nervous breakdown and quit med school and marry a successful young doctor.

Anne cannot help but be pleased; yet she is unhappy. She had not wanted to be a doctor . . . she had half hoped her grades would be too poor to continue, but she had been too proud to allow that to happen. She had worked extraordinarily hard and her grades showed it. "It is not enough," Anne thinks. "I am not happy." She is not sure what she wants—only feels the pressure to achieve something, even if it's something she doesn't want. Anne says "To hell with the whole business" and goes into social work—not hardly as glamorous, prestigious, or lucrative; but she is happy.

The great amount of confusion manifested in this last story was not uncommon.

3. *Denial.* The stories in this third group were remarkable for their psychological ingenuity. Some of the girls denied the reality or possibility of the cue by actually changing its contents, distorting it, or simply refusing to believe it. Others tried to absolve Anne of responsibility for her success—as if it were some antisocial act. Also included in this group are the stories in which the success was attributed to cheating rather than to the girl's ability. Stories involving denial of various types made up the second largest category and were particularly interesting.

> Anne is a *code* name for a nonexistent person created by a group of med students. They take turns taking exams and writing papers for Anne. . . .

> Anne is really happy she's on top, though Tom is higher than she—though that's as it should be. . . . Anne doesn't mind Tom winning.

> Anne is talking to her counselor. The counselor says she will make a fine nurse. She will continue her med school courses. She will study very hard and find she can and will become a good nurse.

> It was luck that Anne came out on top of her med class because she didn't want to go to med school anyway.

This last comment is an interesting reversal of the sour-grapes theme.

Several of the girls became very personally involved with Anne's dilemma: "I don't know. Her problem is apparently insoluble, because she is really a good student. Will she humble herself? Wait and see" or "I wonder if she will ever marry" or "The last I heard, she was still in school but had broken off her engagement." Others assumed the role of society and punished her for her accomplishment. The intensity, hostility, and symbolic quality of the language used by some of the girls was somewhat startling. They accused Anne of being a "social pariah"—someone who must "justify her existence." They attacked her physical attractiveness, her virtue, her sexuality, and sometimes even her person. For instance, in one story her classmates, "disgusted with her behavior . . . jump on her in a body and beat her. She is maimed for life." These stories in general tend to support Honoré de Balzac's contention that "A woman who is guided by the head and not the heart is a social pestilence: she has all the defects of a passionate and affectionate woman, with none of her compensations: she is without pity, without love, without virtue, without sex."

Overall, the two most common themes in the stories dealt with

Anne's physical unattractiveness and with her "lonely Friday and Saturday nights." This result receives further support from some recent data gathered at an outstanding Eastern women's college. In an interview, the girls were told: "Anne is at the top of her med school class. Describe her." More than 70% of them described Anne as having an unattractive face, figure, or manners. Interestingly enough, more than 50% described her as "tall" (perhaps reducing the number of men who would find her attractive). The following are a few descriptions of Anne gathered from the interviews:

1. Snotty, conniving, goody-goody, conceited, brainy, tall.
2. Hard-working, devoted. Wears long skirts. Not feminine; tall, straight. Doesn't go out.
3. Masculine looking. Has short hair. Straight—doesn't smoke dope. Very smart, very competitive with men, not unattractive. Dates but not a steady boyfriend.
4. Quiet, until you get her going; meticulous—goes overboard in this way, not terribly concerned about her appearance. If she does go out, she probably goes out with older men or else she doesn't go out. Med students may be friends but only that. Not more intelligent than boys in her class but more willing to "grub" and do work. Driven person; maybe a liberal but not radical. Don't think she's examined whether it's all worthwhile.
5. Worked hard, but more than a machine. Really cool. Sincerely interested. Doesn't have to try hard. Bright, attractive, feminine. Surprises everyone.

This last description is an optimistic note from which to turn to the question of sex differences in the motive to avoid success. The sheer magnitude of the differences in the kind of responses made to the TAT cues by men and women in the first study was very striking. As had been hypothesized, the women did in fact show significantly more evidence of

Table 1. Sex Differences in the Motive to Avoid Success

Motive to Avoid Success	Males	Females	x^2	p
High	8	59	58.055	0.0005
Low	80	31		

motive to avoid success than did the men. Only 8 out of 88, or less than 10%, of the men, compared with 59 out of 90, or more than 65%, of the women, wrote stories high in fear of success imagery. The percentage of white women showing fear of success imagery in response to this cue has been consistently between 62% and 75% in all the subsequent studies.

Perhaps the best way to understand the sex differences found is to consider a few of the typical stories written by men.

> John is a conscientious young man who worked hard. He is pleased with himself. John has always wanted to go into medicine and is very dedicated. His hard work has paid off. He is thinking that he must not let up now, but must work even harder than he did before. His good marks have encouraged him (he may even consider going into research now). While others with good first-term marks sluff off, John continues working hard and eventually graduates at the top of his class.

The positive affect, increased striving, and heightened level of aspiration following success that are found in this and many of the other male stories are strikingly different from the typical female responses. The following story clarifies the positive impact that successful achievement has on the social relationships of men.

> John is very pleased with himself, and he realizes that all his efforts have been rewarded: He has finally made the top of his class. John has worked hard, and his long hours of study have paid off. He spent hour after hour in preparation for finals. He is thinking of his girl, Cheri, whom he will marry at the end of med school. He realizes he can give her all the things she desires after he becomes established. He will go on in med school making good grades and be successful in the long run.

We have observed great differences in the presence of fear of success imagery in men and women based on differences in the expected consequences of successful achievement. It is reasonable therefore to speculate that the motive to avoid success is in fact a major variable underlying previously unresolved sex differences in studies of achievement motivation.

The next issue to consider is how—if at all—individual differences in the motive to avoid success affect behavior in achievement-oriented situations. Inasmuch as motives affect performance only when they are aroused, we should expect to see the behavioral manifestations of motivation to avoid success only in competitive achievement conditions in which success implies aggressiveness and behavior unbecoming to a "lady." Anxiety aroused by the expectancy of negative consequences of successful competition and by its aggressive overtones is assumed to be most prevalent in the most able or highly motivated women who are competing against men, particularly if they are doing so in male-dominated fields.

In the study designed to explore some of these hypotheses (Horner, 1968), each girl was administered a number of tasks in a large mixed-sex competitive condition (not unlike a large classroom or lecture situation). The girls were then randomly assigned to three other experimental conditions. Some were placed in a strictly noncompetitive (NC) situation in which they worked on a number of tasks guided only by tape-recorded instructions. The rest of the girls were divided at random between two competitive situations in which they worked on the same tasks and followed the same instructions as did those girls in the NC situation. In one of these two groups each girl competed against one male and in the other group against one female. None of the girls knew or had previous contact with the competitors. Performance in the initial large group condition was most highly related to that in the two-person, opposite-sex competitive condition. This result is reasonable, since the large group also involved members of both sexes. Only the 30 subjects in the NC condition worked in both a competitive and a noncompetitive situation.

It was important to exert some control over initial ability differences between the subjects; otherwise, I could not have determined how much of the difference in performance stemmed from motivation and how much from initial ability differences. In this study the best control possible was letting each subject act as her own control—that is, perform in both the competitive and noncompetitive setting. Thus the performance of the 30 women in the NC situation was compared with their own previous performance in the large mixed-sex situation. The tasks involved were two standard, similar, and highly correlated verbal tasks.

Table 2. The motive to avoid success and performance in competitive and noncompetitive achievement situations

Motive to Avoid Success	Performed Better in Noncompetitive Situation	Performed Better in Competitive Situation
High	13	4
Low	1	12
	$x^2 = 11.374$	$p < 0.005$

The results from this part of the study are shown in Table 2. Clearly, the women who score high in fear of success imagery do better working alone than they do in the competitive condition, whereas those who score low in fear of success imagery do better in the competitive condition. The performance of this latter group of women resembles that of the men, who are generally low in fear of success imagery and two-thirds of whom do better in the competitive than in the noncompetitive situation.

On a questionnaire following performance, the high-fear-of-success women who worked in the competitive situations reported that it was significantly less important for them to do well on their tasks than it was for the women working alone in the noncompetitive condition. In other words, high-fear-of-success women working alone consider it more important to do well and probably try harder than do high-fear-of-success women working against a competitor. There are no differences in reported level of importance between the conditions for women low in fear of success imagery. Overall, subjects with high-fear-of-success imagery report a lower level of importance for doing well than do those

Table 3. Mean level of "importance" reported by women in response to the question "How important was it for you to do well on tests in this part of the experiment?" as a function of individual differences in fear of success imagery and experimental condition

Fear of Success Imagery	Noncompetitive Condition NC			Competitive Condition Mixed Sex FM			Competitive Condition Same Sex FF		
	N	M	σ	N	M	σ	N	M	σ
High	(17)	55.6	9.2	(19)	45.7	19.4	(20)	44.7	24.4
Low	(13)	66.5	24.0	(11)	61.1	27.1	(10)	56.5	12.3
	$t = 1.56; p < .10$			$t = 1.66; p < .05$			$t = 1.75; p < .05$		

For subjects with:
    High Fear of Success Imagery   NC vs. FM $t = 1.99; p < .05$
    Low Fear of Success Imagery   NC vs. FF $t = 1.85; p < .05$
                                    No Significant Differences

with low-fear-of-success imagery. The responses on the questionnaire are consistent with the performance data in suggesting that women—especially those high in motive to avoid success—will not fully explore their intellectual potential when they are in a competitive setting, especially when they are competing against men. Optimal performance for most women high in fear of success can be obtained only if they work in achievement settings that are noncompetitive. In the absence of interpersonal competition and its aggressive overtones, whereby the tendency to avoid success (T_{-s}) is minimally, if at all, aroused, these women will perform efficiently.

This study, as an exciting first step toward understanding the behavior of women in achievement situations, has raised many interesting and challenging questions. However, further explorations are needed. For instance, we will have to probe into the nature of both the personal and the situational factors that arouse motivation to avoid success as well as those that minimize its influence on performance. Particularly important and interesting will be studies on the developmental issues involved with respect to the motive to avoid success.

Some recent data (that are still being analyzed) show a very marked and progressive increase—both quantitative and qualitative—in fear of success imagery in two groups of girls: one from junior high to senior high and the other from the freshman to senior years in college. The increment is reflected in the increasing percentage of girls expressing fear of success imagery as well as in the increasing mean score of motive to avoid success in each group. The motive-to-avoid-success score for the girls in this study was based on responses to two cues, one of which was highly competitive and threatening and the other less so. The threatening cue involved successful competition against men in a male-dominated field like medicine or law. The second cue involved success in what we believed to be a less directly competitive, less masculine area such as the writing of a novel in one's spare time. The older girls responded with more fear of success imagery than did the younger group to the less threatening cue.

It is easy to conjecture why a senior, particularly in the college group, would show higher motivation to avoid success. As Sanford (1961) has indicated, the senior year in college is critical, especially for those girls who have not as yet become engaged. Most of the girls are convinced that it is more important to *be* a woman than to *become* some kind of specialist. It is very clear to them that the brighter they are, and the more fully they extend and fulfill their potential, the more they restrict their choices or possibilities for marriage. Riesman (1964, pp. 731–732) has made the following observation on the subject:

> Just as girls six feet tall complain of the still taller men who marry girls who are five feet two, since there are not enough really tall men to go around, so girls who are six feet tall in intellect and drive realize that many men of comparable power will marry very low-pressure, eye-fluttering girls, and that there will not be enough secure, nondependent men left for the women who could grow and develop in marriage to such men. Hence girls who feel that if they do not marry early . . . they may not marry at all are prepared unconsciously if not consciously to surrender chances for personal distinction in order to be fairly sure of pleasing a larger range of men.

Thus for the girl who is a senior in college the conflict of marriage vs. career becomes very intense. The decision to pursue a higher level of education or a career as opposed to marriage and/or a job is usually made then and requires some degree of commitment. After all, a woman does not usually get a Ph.D. in biology, physics, or some other field to be a more entertaining companion or a more enlightened wife and mother. (These reasons are frequently given to "justify" college education for women.)

An important question that must now be considered is at what point and *why* motivation to avoid success becomes a significant factor in achievement-related behavior in women. What exactly are the major determinants of its arousal in the "real world"? In the early school years girls outperform boys, but at about the time of puberty—and perhaps coincidental with dating interests—the advantage is significantly reversed, particularly in nonverbal areas such as mathematics and science, which are traditionally viewed as "masculine." Interestingly enough, girls who are either engaged or married to "brilliant, successful, secure young men" have little difficulty maintaining their standing. No problem arises for them as long as he is viewed as the "smarter" or "more intelligent" of the two and the one against whom "competition would be hopeless."

There is increasing evidence that, in the course of their college experience, most capable young women change their plans toward a less ambitious, more traditionally feminine direction—that is, away from "role innovation" (Tangri, 1969; Schwenn, 1970). We can now only speculate as to how much of this trend can be attributed to the arousal of the motive to avoid success and the fear of social rejection as a result of success. We must come to some understanding of what it is in the college experience that influences otherwise achievement-oriented, capable girls to change their plans. Komarovsky (1959) reports evidence of a sudden shift or reversal of parental pressures and approval for academic success. Whereas parents (and society) encourage girls to go to college and reward their good performance up to that point, they suddenly begin to evaluate their daughters "in terms of some abstract standard of femininity with an emphasis on marriage as the appropriate goal for girls of this age."

How important are these pressures, and are they reinforced by the girls' peers, both male and female? A long-term study would be valuable, especially if it followed young girls through adolescence, college, marriage, and career choice (if any). It should consider how both the development and expression of motivation to avoid success are influenced by parental and peer attitudes (as well as attitudes of "significant men" in the girls' lives) toward the role of women in contemporary life. A pilot study at an Eastern college on highly motivated or intelligent girls (the grades were all above B—) showed that the major role in the *arousal* of the motive to avoid success is played by the girls' male peers (Schwenn, 1970). A very interesting and suggestive pattern emerges from this study. The girls who showed evidence of motivation to avoid success or of anxiety about social rejection were those who either did not date at all (all had A averages) or who dated men who disapproved of "career women." They manifested their anxieties by refusing to divulge that they were doing well or had received an A (preferring to make their failures known) and by changing their future plans toward a more traditional, less ambitious career (or none at all) or even by deciding to drop out of school altogether. When asked how the boys in their lives responded to their aspirations—even the less ambitious ones—the girls frequently answered, "They laugh." Other replies included, "He thinks it's ridiculous for me to go to graduate school or law school. He says I can be happy as a housewife and I just need to get a liberal arts education" or "He wants a wife who will be a mother full-time until the kids are grown" or "I am turning more and more to the traditional role because of the attitudes of my boyfriend and his roommates. I am concerned about what they think." This result is consistent with the finding that women are dependent on others for their self-esteem. Independence itself is inconsistent with the female image.

On the other hand, the girls who were not fearful of making their success known and who continued to strive for innovative careers were engaged to or seriously dating men who were not threatened by the girls' success. In fact, those men actively encouraged and expected the girls to do well. The girls indicated the support they received in such statements as:

> "He wants me to be intelligent. It is a source of pride to him that I do so well."

> "I would have to explain myself if I got a C. I want him to think I'm as bright as he is."

> "He thinks it would be a good idea for me to go to law school."

> "He feels very strongly that I should go to graduate school to get a master's degree. He does not want to feel that he has denied me a complete education."

One of the factors distinguishing the couples in the second group from those in the first is a mutual understanding that the boy is the more intelligent of the two. In the first group a tension is rooted between them in the fear that she is the more intelligent one. Other important factors stem from how threatening the boyfriend considers her present and future success: If they are in the same school, or taking the same courses, or planning to go to the same graduate school or have the same career, he will very likely feel threatened and resentful. Clearly the problems of achievement motivation in women involve more than a traditional view of the female role.

It would not be unreasonable at this point for us to speculate that what we have observed in the laboratory does in fact extend into and influence the intellectual and professional lives of women in our society.

The arousal of motivation to avoid success may very well account for a major part of the withdrawal of so many trained American women from the mainstream of thought and achievement. We have already noted the great loss in human and economic resources that this withdrawal reflects.

The evidence presented here raises many questions about our educational system. For instance, is attendance at a same-sex educational institution more effective than attendance at a coed institution in reducing the impact of the motive to avoid success in girls? In the absence of competition against men, can the women develop their interests and explore their intellectual potential more fully? Many persons believe that they can. Recently Wellesley considered admitting men to the school, but several coeds protested, saying:

> How can a girl maintain her role as a woman when she is in intense academic competition with men, especially if she is excelling? Many capable girls have faced the frustration of accusations of aggressiveness, lack of femininity, and a desire to "beat the boys" when they were in high school and college . . . (*Harvard Crimson*, 1969).

The next question is whether the influence and support received at a same-sex institution continue after the women leave its protective atmosphere and again enter the "real world" of mixed-sex competition. The issue of competition being unfeminine is not especially relevant at an all-girls school. On the other hand, these girls do not have the opportunity presented to those at coeducational institutions to confront the problem and find ways to resolve it. These issues are presented rather clearly in comments made by two of the girls in the Radcliffe sample.

A girl who had attended an all-girls high school remarked:

> It had never entered my mind before I got here that I would be competing with boys. . . . You see the aggressive girls when you get here and you know it's the last thing in the world you want to be.

The other girl, who had attended a coed high school, observed:

> I used to feel self-conscious about being smart and getting good grades, but by my junior year in high school I had gotten over that . . . because I was a student leader and a cheerleader, too.

This last comment suggests that one way in which women who are successful in competitive achievement activities can resolve their anxiety about being unfeminine is to be equally successful in feminine tasks appropriate to their ages: cheerleading and dating in high school and later sexual attractiveness, cooking, motherhood, and so on.

It is clear that a psychological barrier exists in otherwise achievement-motivated and able women that prevents them from exercising their rights and fulfilling their potential. Even when legal and educational barriers to achievement are removed, the motive to avoid success will continue to inhibit women from doing "too well"—thereby risking the possibility of being socially rejected as "unfeminine" or "castrating." Unless we can find ways to prevent the motive from being aroused, our society will continue to suffer a great loss in both human and economic resources.

The negative feelings and consequences of a girl beating a boy in intellectual competition are poetically summarized by Whittier in his poem "In School Days." Having outperformed the boy in a spelling match, the girl says:

"I'm sorry that I spelt the word:
I hate to go above you,
Because,"—the brown eyes lower fell—
"Because, you see, I love you."

At the end, despite her regrets, she too is "socially" rejected:

Dear girl! The grasses on her grave
Have forty years been growing!

References

Angelini, A. L. Un novo método para avaliar a motivação humano ("A new method of evaluating human motivation"). Unpublished doctoral dissertation, Universidade de São Paulo, Brazil, 1955. (Results summarized in Atkinson, 1958.)

Atkinson, J. W. (Ed.) *Motives in fantasy, action, and society.* Princeton, N.J.: Van Nostrand, 1958.

Atkinson, J. W., & Feather, N. T. *A theory of achievement motivation.* New York: Wiley, 1966.

Atkinson, J. W., & Litwin, G. H. Achievement motive and test anxiety conceived as motive to approach success and motive to avoid failure. *Journal of Abnormal and Social Psychology,* 1960, 60, 52–63.

Field, W. F. The effects of thematic apperception on certain experimentally aroused needs. Unpublished doctoral dissertation, University of Maryland, 1951.

French, E. G. Motivation as a variable in work partner selection. *Journal of Abnormal and Social Psychology,* 1956, 53, 96–99.

French, E. G. The interaction of achievement motivation and ability in problem solving success. *Journal of Abnormal and Social Psychology,* 1958, 57, 306–309.

French, E. G., & Lesser, G. S. Some characteristics of the achievement motive in women. *Journal of Abnormal and Social Psychology*, 1964, **68**, 119–128.

Freud, S. *New introductory lectures on psychoanalysis.* New York: Norton, 1965. Lecture XXXIII.

Harvard Crimson, The. "Must Wellesley go coed to survive?" Dec. 16, 1969, p. 3.

Horner, M. Sex differences in achievement motivation and performance in competitive and noncompetitive situations. Unpublished doctoral dissertation, University of Michigan, 1968.

Kagan, J., & Moss, H. A. *Birth to maturity.* New York: Wiley, 1962.

Komarovsky, M. Functional analysis of sex roles. *American Sociological Review*, 1959, **15**, 508–516.

Lesser, G. S., Krawitz, R., & Packard, R. Experimental arousal of achievement motivation in adolescent girls. *Journal of Abnormal and Social Psychology*, 1963, **66**, 59–66.

Lipinski, B. G. Sex-role conflict and achievement motivation in college women. Unpublished doctoral dissertation, University of Cincinnati, 1965.

Maccoby, E. E. Woman's intellect. In S. M. Farber & R. H. L. Wilson (Eds.), *The potential of woman.* New York: McGraw-Hill, 1963. Pp. 24–39.

Mahone, C. Fear of failure and unrealistic vocational aspiration. Unpublished doctoral dissertation, University of Michigan, 1958.

Mannes, M. The problems of creative women. In S. M. Farber & R. H. L. Wilson (Eds.), *The potential of woman.* New York: McGraw-Hill, 1963. Pp. 116–130.

McClelland, D. C., Atkinson, J. W., Clark, R. A., & Lowell, E. L. *The achievement motive.* New York: Appleton, 1953.

McClelland, D. C. *The achieving society.* Princeton, N.J.: Van Nostrand, 1961.

Mead, M. *Male and female.* New York: Morrow, 1949. Also New York: Dell (Laurel Ed.), 1968.

Riesman, D. Two generations. *Daedalus*, 1964, **93**, 711–735.

Rossi, A. The case against full-time motherhood. *Redbook Magazine*, March 1965.

Sanford, N. (Ed.) *The American college.* New York: Wiley, 1961.

Schwenn, M. Arousal of the motive to avoid success. Unpublished junior honors paper, Harvard University, 1970.

Scott, W. A. The avoidance of threatening material in imaginative behavior. In J. W. Atkinson (Ed.), *Motives in fantasy, action, and society.* Princeton, N.J.: Van Nostrand, 1958. Chap. 40.

Tangri, S. Role-innovation in occupational choice. Unpublished doctoral dissertation, University of Michigan, 1969.

Veroff, J., Wilcox, S., & Atkinson, J. The achievement motive in high school and college-age women. *Journal of Abnormal and Social Psychology*, 1953, **48**, 103–119.

Winterbottom, M. R. The relation of need for achievement to learning experiences in independence and mastery. In J. W. Atkinson (Ed.), *Motives in fantasy, action, and society.* Princeton, N.J.: Van Nostrand, 1958. Chap. 33.

The Social Construction of the Second Sex

Jo Freeman

Jo Freeman is a graduate student in political science at the University of Chicago and a free-lance writer/photographer. Much of her free-lance work has been about women. In addition, she has organized women's liberation groups in Chicago and was founder and editor of the first women's liberation national newsletter.

> The passivity that is the essential characteristic of the "feminine" woman is a trait that develops in her from the earliest years. But it is wrong to assert a biological datum is concerned; it is in fact a destiny imposed upon her by her teachers and by society.
>
> Simone de Beauvoir

During the last thirty years social science has paid scant attention to women, confining its explorations of humanity to the male. Research has generally reinforced the sex stereotypes of popular mythology that women are essentially nurturant/expressive/passive and men instrumental/active/aggressive. Social scientists have tended to justify these stereotypes rather than analyze their origins, their value, or their effect.

In part this is due to the general conservatism and reluctance to question the status quo which has characterized the social sciences during this era of the feminine mystique. In part it is attributable to the "pervasive permeation of psychoanalytic thinking throughout American society."[1] The result has been a social science which is more a mechanism of social control than of social inquiry. Rather than trying to analyze why, it has only described what. Rather than exploring how men and women came to be the way they are, it has taken their condition as an irremediable given and sought to justify it on the basis of "biological" differences.

Nonetheless, the assumption that psychology recapitulates physiology has begun to crack. Masters and Johnson shattered the myth of woman's natural sexual passivity—on which her psychological passivity was claimed to rest. Research is just beginning into the other areas. Even without this new research new interpretations of the old data are being explored. What these new interpretations say is that women are the way they are because they've been trained to be that way. As the Bems put it: "We overlook the fact that the society that has spent twenty years carefully marking the women's ballot for her has nothing to lose in that twenty-first year by pretending to let her cast it for the alternative of her choice. Society has controlled not her alternatives, but her motivation to choose any but the one of those alternatives."[2]

This motivation is controlled through the socialization process. Women are raised to want to fill the social roles in which society needs them. They are trained to model themselves after the accepted image and to meet as individuals the expectations that are held for women as a group. Therefore, to understand how most women are socialized we must first understand how they see themselves and are seen by others. Several studies have been done on this. Quoting from one of them, McClelland stated that "the female image is characterized as small, weak, soft and light. In the United States it is also dull, peaceful, relaxed, cold, rounded, passive and slow."[3] A more thorough study which asked men and women to choose out of a long list of adjectives those which most closely applied to themselves showed that women strongly felt themselves to be uncertain, anxious, nervous, hasty, careless, fearful, dull, childish, helpless, sorry, timid, clumsy, stupid, silly, and domestic. On a more positive side, women felt that they were understanding, tender, sympathetic, pure, generous, affectionate, loving, moral, kind, grateful, and patient.[4]

This is not a very favorable self-image but it does correspond fairly well with the social myths about what women are like. The image has some nice qualities, but they are not the ones normally required for that kind of achievement to which society gives its highest social rewards. Now one can justifiably question both the idea of achievement and the qualities necessary for it, but this is not the place to do so. Rather, because the current standards are the ones which women have been told they do not meet, the purpose here will be to look at the socialization process as a mechanism to keep them from doing so. We will also need to analyze some of the social expectations about women and about what they define as a successful *woman* (not a successful person) because they are inextricably bound up with the socialization process. All people are socialized to meet the social expectations held for them, and it is only when this process fails to do so (as is currently happening on several fronts) that it is at all questioned.

Let us further examine the effects on women of minority group status. Here, an interesting parallel emerges, but it is one fraught with much heresy. When we look at the *results* of female socialization we find a strong similarity between what our society labels, even extols, as the typical "feminine" character structure and that of oppressed peoples in this country and elsewhere.

In his classic study on *The Nature of Prejudice,* Allport devotes a chapter to "Traits Due to Victimization." Included are such personality characteristics as sensitivity, submission, fantasies of power, desire for protection, indirectness, ingratiation, petty revenge and sabotage, sympathy, extremes of both self and group hatred and self and group glorification, display of flashy status symbols, compassion for the underprivileged, identification with the dominant group's norms, and passivity.[5] Allport was primarily concerned with Jews and Negroes, but compare his characterization with the very thorough review of the literature on sex differences among young children made by Terman and Tyler. For girls, they listed such traits as sensitivity, conformity to social pressures, response to environment, ease of social control, ingratiation, sympathy, low levels of aspiration, compassion for the underprivileged, and anxiety. They found that girls compared to boys were more nervous, unstable, neurotic, socially dependent, submissive, had less self-confidence, lower opinions of themselves and of girls in general, and were more timid, emotional, ministrative, fearful, and passive.[6]

Girls' perceptions of themselves were also distorted. Although girls make consistently better school grades than boys until late high school, their opinion of themselves grows progressively worse with age and their opinion of boys and boys' abilities grows better. Boys, however, have an increasingly better opinion of themselves and worse opinion of girls as they grow older.[7]

These distortions become so gross that, according to Goldberg, by the time girls reach college they have become prejudiced against women. He gave college girls sets of booklets containing six identical professional articles in traditional male, female, and neutral fields. The articles were identical, but the names of the authors were not. For example, an article in one set would bear the name John T. McKay and in another set the same article would be authored by Joan T. McKay. Each booklet contained three articles by "women" and three by "men." Questions at the end of each article asked the students to rate the articles on value, persuasiveness and profundity and the authors on writing style and competence. The male authors fared better in every field, even such "feminine" areas as Art History and Dietetics. Goldberg concluded that "Women are prejudiced against female professionals and, regardless of the actual accomplishments of these professionals, will firmly refuse to recognize them as the equals of their male colleagues."[8]

This combination of group self-hate and distortion of perceptions to justify that group self-hate are precisely the traits typical of a "minority group character structure."[9] It has been noted time and time again. The Clarks' finding of this pattern in Negro children in segregated schools contributed to the 1954 Supreme Court decision that outlawed such schools. These traits, as well as the others typical of the "feminine" stereotype, have been found in the Indians under British rule,[10] in the Algerians under the French,[11] and in black Americans.[12] There seems to be a correlation between being "feminine" and experiencing status deprivation.

This pattern repeats itself even within cultures. In giving TATs to women in Japanese villages, De Vos discovered that those from fishing villages where the status position of women was higher than in farming communities were more assertive, not as guilt-ridden and were more willing to ignore the traditional pattern of arranged marriages in favor of love marriages.[13]

In Terman's famous 50-year study of the gifted, a comparison in adulthood of those men who conspicuously failed to fulfill their early promise with those who did fulfill it showed that the successful had more self-confidence, fewer background disabilities, and were less nervous and emotionally unstable. But, they concluded "the disadvantages associated with lower social and home status appeared to present the outstanding handicap."[14]

The fact that women do have lower social status than men in our society and that both sexes tend to value men and male characteristics, values, and activities more highly than those of women has been noted by many authorities.[15] What has not been done is to make the connection between this status and its accompanying personality.

The failure to extensively analyze the effects and the causes of lower social status is surprising in light of the many efforts that have been made to uncover distinct psychological differences between men and women to account for the tremendous disparity in their social production and creativity. The Goldberg study implies that even if women did achieve on a par with men it would not be perceived or accepted as such and that a woman's work must be of a much higher quality than that of a man to be given the same recognition. But these circumstances alone, or the fact that it is the male definition of achievement which is applied, are not sufficient to account for the lack of social production. So research has turned to male/female differences.

Most of this research, in the Freudian tradition, has focused on finding the psychological and developmental differences supposedly inherent in feminine nature and function. Despite all these efforts, the general findings of psychological testing indicate that: (1) Individual differences are greater than sex differences; i.e. sex is just one of the many characteristics which define a human being. (2) Most differences in ability in any field do not appear until elementary school age or later. "Sex differences become more apparent with increasing education even if it is co-education."[16]

An examination of the literature of intellectual differences between the sexes discloses some interesting patterns. First, the statistics themselves show some regularity. Most conclusions of what is typical of one sex or the other are founded upon the performances of two thirds of the subjects. For example, two thirds of all boys do better on the math section of the College Board Exam than the verbal, and two thirds of the girls do better on the verbal than the math. Bales' studies show a similar distribution when he concludes that in small groups men are the task-oriented leaders and women are the social-emotional leaders.[17] Not all tests show this two-thirds differential, but it is the mean about which most results of the ability test cluster. Sex is an easily visible, differentiable and testable criterion on which to draw conclusions; but it doesn't explain the one third that doesn't fit. The only characteristic virtually all women seem to have in common, besides their anatomy, is their lower social status.

Second, girls get off to a very good start. They begin speaking, reading, and counting sooner. They articulate more clearly and put words into sentences earlier. They have fewer reading and stuttering problems. Girls are even better in math in the early school years. Consistent sex differences in favor of boys do not appear until high-school age.[18] Here another pattern begins to develop.

During high school, girls' performance in school and on ability tests begins to drop, sometimes drastically. Although well over half of all high-school graduates are girls, significantly less than half of all college students are girls. Presumably, this should mean that a higher percentage of the better female students go on to higher education, but their performance *vis-à-vis* boys' continues to decline.

Girls start off better than boys and end up worse. This change in their performance occurs at a very significant point in time. It occurs when their status changes, or to be more precise, when girls become aware of what their adult status is supposed to be. It is during adolescence that peer-group pressures to be "feminine" or "masculine" increase and the conceptions of what is "feminine" and "masculine" become more narrow.[19] It is also at this time that there is a personal drive for conformity.[20]

One of the norms of our culture to which a girl learns to conform is that only men excel. This was evident in Lipinski's study of "Sex-Role Conflict and Achievement Motivation in College Women," which showed that thematic pictures depicting males as central characters elicited significantly more achievement imagery than female pictures.[21] One need only recall Asch's experiments to see how peer-group pressures, armed only with our rigid ideas about "femininity" and "masculinity" could lead to a decline in girls' performance. Asch found that some 33 percent of his subjects would go contrary to the evidence of their own senses about something as tangible as the comparative length of two lines when their judgments were at variance with those made by the other group members.[22] All but a handful of the other 67 percent experienced tremendous trauma in trying to stick to their correct perceptions.

When we move to something as intangible as sex-role behavior and to social sanctions far greater than the displeasure of a group of unknown experimental stooges, we can get an idea of how stifling social expectations can be. It is not surprising, in light of our cultural norm that a girl should not appear too smart or surpass boys in anything, that those pressures to conform, so prevalent in adolescence, should prompt girls to believe that the development of their minds will have only negative results. The lowered self-esteem and the denigration of their own sex noted by Smith[23] and Goldberg[24] are a logical consequence. These pressures even affect the supposedly unchangeable IQ scores. Corresponding with the drive for social acceptance, girls' IQs drop below those of boys during high school, rise slightly if they go to college, and go into a steady and consistent decline when and if they become full-time housewives.[25]

These are not the only consequences. Negative self-conceptions have negative effects in a manner that can only be called a self-fulfilling prophecy. They stifle motivation and channel energies into those areas that are likely to get some positive social rewards. Then those subject to these pressures are condemned for not having strived for the highest social rewards society has to offer.

A good example of this double bind is what psychologists call the "need for achievement." Achievement motivation in male college sophomores has been studied extensively. In women it has barely been looked at; women didn't fit the model social scientists set up to explain achievement in men. Girls do not seem to demonstrate the same consistent correlation between achievement and scores on achievement tests that boys do. For example, Stivers found that "non-motivated for college" girls scored higher on achievement motivation exams than "well-motivated for college" girls.[26] There has been little inquiry as to why this is so. The general policy followed by the researchers was that if girls didn't fit, leave them out. Nonetheless some theories have been put forward.

Pierce postulated that part of the confusion resulted from using the same criteria of achievement for girls that were used for boys—achievement in school. Therefore, he did a study of marriage vs. career orientation in high-school girls which did show a small but consistent correlation between high achievement motivation scores and marriage orientation.[27] In 1961 he did another study which showed a very strong correlation between high achievement scores and actual achievement of marriage within a year of high-school graduation. Those who went on to college and/or did not get married had low achievement scores.[28]

Although he unfortunately did not describe the class origins and other relevant characteristics of his study it does seem clear that the real situation is not that women do not have achievement motivation but that this motivation is directed differently from that of men. In fact, the achievement orientation of both sexes goes precisely where it is socially directed—educational achievement for boys and marriage achievement for girls. Pierce suggested that "achievement motivation in girls attaches itself not to academic performance, but rather to more immediate adult status goals. This would be a logical assumption in that academic success is much less important to achievement status as a woman than it is for a man."[29]

He goes on to say that "girls see that to achieve in life as adult females they need to achieve in non-academic ways, that is, attaining the social graces, achieving beauty in person and dress, finding a desirable social status, marrying the right man. This is the successful adult woman. . . . Their achievement motivations are directed toward realizing personal goals through their relationship with men. . . . Girls who are following the normal course of development are most likely to seek adult status through marriage at an early age."[30]

Achievement for women is adult status through marriage, not success in the usual use of the word. One might postulate that both kinds of success might be possible, particularly for the highly achievement-oriented woman. But in fact the two are more often perceived as contradictory; success in one is seen to preclude success in the other.

Horner just completed a study at the University of Michigan from which she postulated a psychological barrier to achievement in women. She administered a TAT word item to undergraduates that said "After first term finals Anne finds herself at the top of her medical school class." A similar one for a male control group used a masculine name. The results were scored for imagery of fear of success and Horner found that 65% of the women and only 10% of the men demonstrated a definite "motive to avoid success." She explained the results by hypothesizing that the prospect of success, or situations in which success or failure is a relevant dimension, are perceived as having, and in fact do have, negative consequences for women. Success in the normal sense is threatening to women. Further research confirmed that fear of social rejection and role conflict did generate a "motive to avoid success."[31]

Ability differences correlate strongly with interest differences [32] and women have a definite interest in avoiding success. This is reinforced by peer and cultural pressures. However, many sex differences appear too early to be much affected by peer groups and are not directly related to sex-role attributes.

One such sex difference is spatial perception, or the ability to visualize objects out of their context. This is a test in which boys do better, though differences are usually not discernible before the early school years.[33] Other tests, such as the Embedded Figures and the Rod and Frame Tests, likewise favor boys. They indicate that boys perceive more analytically, while girls are more contextual. This ability to "break set" or be "field independent" also does not seem to appear until after the fourth or fifth year.[34]

According to Maccoby, this contextual mode of perception common to women is a distinct disadvantage for scientific production. "Girls on the average develop a somewhat different way of handling incoming information—their thinking is less analytic, more global, and more preservative—and this kind of thinking may serve very well for many kinds of functioning but it is not the kind of thinking most conducive to high-level intellectual productivity, especially in science."[35]

Several social psychologists have postulated that the key developmental characteristic of analytic thinking is what is called early "independence and mastery training," or "whether and how soon a child is encouraged to assume initiative, to take responsibility for himself, and to solve problems by himself, rather than rely on others for the direction of his activities."[36] In other words, analytically inclined children are those who have not been subject to what Bronfenbrenner calls "oversocialization,"[37] and there is a good deal of indirect evidence that such is the case. Levy has observed that "overprotected" boys tend to develop intellectually like girls.[38] Bing found that those girls who were good at spatial tasks were those whose mothers left them alone to solve the problems by themselves, while the mothers of verbally inclined daughters insisted on helping them.[39] Witkin similarly found that mothers of analytic children had encouraged their initiative, while mothers of nonanalytic children had encouraged dependence and discouraged self-assertion.[40] One writer commented on these studies that "this is to be expected, for the independent child is less likely to accept superficial appearances of objects without exploring them for himself, while the dependent child will be afraid to reach out on his own, and will accept appearances without question. In other words, the independent child is likely to be more *active*, not only psychologically but physically, and the physically active child will naturally have more kinesthetic experience with spatial relationships in his environment."[41]

The qualities associated with independence training also have an effect on IQ. Sontag did a longitudinal study in which he compared children whose IQs had improved with those whose IQs had declined with age. He discovered that the child with increasing IQ was competitive, self-assertive, independent, and dominant in interaction with other children. Children with declining IQs were passive, shy, and dependent.[42]

Maccoby commented on this study that "the characteristics associated with a rising IQ are not very feminine characteristics. When one of the people working on it was asked about what kind of developmental history was necessary to make a girl into an intellectual person, he replied, 'The simplest way to put it is that she must be a tomboy at some point in her childhood.' "[43]

Likewise Kagan and Moss noted that "females who perform well on problems requiring analysis and complex reasoning tend to reject a traditional feminine identification."[44] They also observed that among the children involved in the Fels study "protection of girls was associated with the adoption of feminine interests during childhood and adulthood. Maternal protection apparently 'feminized' both the boys and the girls."[45]

However, analytic abilities are not the only ones that are valued in our society. Being person-oriented and contextual in perception are very valuable attributes for many fields where, nevertheless, very few women are found. Such characteristics are also valuable in the arts and some of the social sciences. But while women do succeed here more than in the sciences, their achievement is still not equivalent to that of men. One explanation of this, of course, is the Horner study that established a "motive to avoid success." But when one looks further it appears that there is an earlier cause here as well.

The very same early independence and mastery training that has such a beneficial effect on analytic thinking also determines the extent of one's achievement orientation.[46]

Although comparative studies of parental treatment of boys and girls are not extensive, those that have been made indicate that the traditional practices applied to girls are very different from those applied to boys. Girls receive more affection, more protectiveness, more control and more restrictions. Boys are subjected to more achievement demands and higher expectations.[47] In short, while girls are not always encouraged to be dependent *per se*, they are usually not encouraged to be *independent* and physically active. "Such findings indicate that the differential treatment of the two sexes reflects in part a difference in goals. With sons, socialization seems to focus primarily on directing and constraining the boys' impact on the environment. With daughters, the aim is rather to protect the girl from the impact of environment. The boy is being prepared to mold his world, the girl to be molded by it."[48] The pattern is typical of girls, Bronfenbrenner maintains, and involves the risk of "oversocialization."

He doesn't discuss the possible negative effects such oversocialization has on girls, but he does express his concern about what would happen to the "qualities of independence, initiative, and self-sufficiency" of boys if such training were applied to them. "While an affectional context is important for the socialization of boys, it must evidently be accompanied by and be compatible with a strong component of parental discipline. Otherwise, the boy finds himself in the same situation as the girl, who, having received greater affection, is more sensitive to its withdrawal, with the result that a little discipline goes a long way and strong authority is constricting rather than constructive."[49]

That these variations in socialization result in variations in personality is corroborated by Schachter's studies of first and later-born children. Like girls, first children tend to be better socialized but also more anxious and dependent, whereas second children, like boys, are more aggressive and self-confident.[50]

Bronfenbrenner concludes that the crucial variable is the differential treatment by the father and "in fact, it is the father who is especially likely to treat children of the two sexes differently." His extremes of affection, and of authority, are both deleterious. Not only do his high degrees of nurturance and protectiveness toward girls result in "oversocialization," but "the presence of strong paternal power is particularly debilitating. In short, boys thrive in a patriarchal context, girls in a matriarchal one."[51]

His observations receive indirect support from Douvan who noted that "part-time jobs of mothers have a beneficial effect on adolescent children, particularly daughters. This reflects the fact that adolescents may receive too much mothering."[52]

The importance of mothers, as well as mothering, was pointed out by Kagan and Moss. In looking at the kinds of role models that mothers provide for developing daughters, they discovered that it is those women who are looked upon as unfeminine whose daughters tend to achieve intellectually. These mothers are "aggressive and competitive women who were critical of their daughters and presented themselves to their daughters as intellectually competitive and aggressive role models. It is reasonable to assume that the girls identified with these intellectually aggressive women who valued mastery behavior."[53]

There seems to be some evidence that the sexes have been differentially socialized with different training practices, for different goals, and with different results. If McClelland is right in all the relationships he finds between child-rearing practices (in particular independence and mastery training), achievement-motivation scores of individuals tested, actual achievement of individuals, and indeed, the economic growth of whole societies,[54] there is no longer much question as to why the historical achievement of women has been so low. In fact, with the dependency training they receive so early in life, the wonder is that they have achieved so much.

But this is not the whole story. Maccoby, in her discussion of the relationship of independence training to analytic abilities, notes that the girl who does not succumb to overprotection and develop the appropriate personality and behavior for her sex has a major price to pay: a price in anxiety. Or, as other observers have noted: "The universe of appropriate behavior for males and females is delineated early in development and it is difficult for the child to cross these culturally given frontiers without considerable conflict and tension."[55]

Some anxiety is beneficial to creative thinking, but high or sustained levels of it are damaging, "for it narrows the range of solution efforts, interferes with breaking set, and prevents scanning of the whole range of elements open to perception."[56] This anxiety is particularly manifest in college women,[57] and of course they are the ones who experience the most conflict between their current—intellectual—activities, and expectations about behavior in their future—unintellectual—careers.

Maccoby feels that "it is this anxiety which helps to account for the lack of productivity among those women who do make intellectual careers." The combination of social pressures, role-expectations and parental training together tell "something of a horror story. It would appear that even when a woman is suitably endowed intellectually and develops the right temperament and habits of thought to make use of her endowment, she must be fleet of foot indeed to scale the hurdles society has erected for her and to remain a whole and happy person while continuing to follow her intellectual bent."[58]

The reasons for this horror story must by now be clearly evident. Traditionally, women have been defined as passive creatures, sexually, physically, and mentally. Their roles have been limited to the passive, dependent, auxiliary ones, and they have been trained from birth to fit these roles. However, those qualities by which one succeeds in this society are active ones. Achievement orientation, intellectuality, and analytic ability all require a certain amount of aggression.

As long as women were convinced that these qualities were beyond them, that they were inferior in their exercise and much happier if they stayed in their place, they remained quiescent under the paternalistic system of Western civilization. Paternalism was a pre-industrial scheme of life, and its yoke was partially broken by the industrial revolution.[59] With this loosening up of the social order, the talents of women began to appear.

In the 18th Century it was held that no woman had ever produced anything worthwhile in literature with the possible exception of Sappho. But in the first half of the 19th Century, feminine writers of genius flooded the literary scene.[60] It wasn't until the end of the 19th Century that women scientists of note appeared, and it was still later that women philosophers were found.

Only since the industrial revolution shook the whole social order have women been able to break some of the traditional bounds of society. In pre-industrial societies, the family was the basic unit of social and economic organization, and women held a significant and functional role within it. This, coupled with the high birth and death rates of those times, gave women more than enough to do within the home. It was the center of production and women could be both at home and in the world at the same time. But the industrial revolution, along with decreased infant mortality, increased life-span and changes in economic organization, have all but destroyed the family as the economic unit. Technological advances have taken men out of the home, and now those functions traditionally defined as female are being taken out also.[61] For the first time in human history women have had to devote themselves to being full-time mothers in order to have enough to do.[62]

Conceptions of society have also changed. At one time, authoritarian hierarchies were the norm and paternalism was reflective of a general social authoritarian attitude. While it is impossible to do retroactive studies on feudalistic society, we do know that authoritarianism as a personality trait does correlate strongly with a rigid conception of sex roles, and with ethnocentrism.[63] We also know from ethnological data that there is a "parallel between family relationships and the larger social hierarchy. Autocratic societies have autocratic families. As the king rules his subjects and the nobles subjugate and exploit the commoners, so does husband tend to lord it over wife, father rule over son."[64]

According to D'Andrade, "another variable that appears to affect the distribution of authority and deference between the sexes is the degree to which men rather than women control and mediate property."[65] He presented data which showed a direct correlation between the extent to which inheritance, succession, and descent-group membership were patrilineal and the degree of subjection of women.

Even today, the equality of the sexes in the family is often reflective of the economic equality of the partners. In a Detroit sample, Blood and Wolfe found that the relative power of the wife was low if she did not work and increased with her economic contribution to the family.[66] "The employment of women affects the power structure of the family by equalizing the resources of husband and wife. A working wife's husband listens to her more, and she listens to herself more. She expresses herself and has more opinions. Instead of looking up into her husband's eyes and worshipping him, she levels with him, compromising on the issues at hand. Thus her power increases and, relatively speaking, the husband's falls."[67]

Goode also noted this pattern but said it varied inversely with class status. Toward the upper strata, wives are not only less likely to work but when they do they contribute a smaller percentage of the total family income than is true in the lower classes.[68] Hill went so far as to say "Money is a source of power that supports male dominance in the family. . . . Money belongs to him who earns it, not to her who spends it, since he who earns it may withhold it."[69] Hallenbeck feels more than just economic resources are involved but does conclude that there is a balance of power in every family which affects "every other aspect of the marriage—division of labor, amount of adaptation necessary for either spouse, methods used to resolve conflicts, and so forth."[70] Blood feels the economic situation affects the whole family structure. "Daughters of working mothers are more independent, more self-reliant, more aggressive, more dominant, and more disobedient. Such girls are no longer meek, mild, submissive, and feminine like 'little ladies' ought to be. They are rough and tough, actively express their ideas, and refuse to take anything from anybody else. . . . Because their mothers have set an example, the daughters get up the courage and the desire to earn money as well. They take more part-time jobs after school and more jobs during summer vacation."[71]

Barry, Bacon and Child did an ethnohistoriographic analysis that provides some further insights into the origins of male dominance. After examining the ethnographic reports of 110 cultures, they concluded that large sexual differentiation and male superiority occur concurrently and in "an economy that places a high premium on the superior strength and superior development of motor skills requiring strength, which characterize the male."[72] It is those societies in which great physical strength and mobility are required for survival, in which hunting and herding, or warfare, play an important role, that the male, as the physically stronger and more mobile sex, tends to dominate. This is supported by Spiro's analysis of sex roles in an Israeli kibbutz. There, the economy was largely unmechanized and the superior average strength of the men was needed on many jobs. Thus, despite a conscious attempt to break down traditional sex-roles, they began reasserting themselves, as women were assigned to the less strenuous jobs.[73]

Although there are a few tasks which virtually every society assigns only to men or women, there is a great deal of overlap for most jobs. Virtually every task, even in the most primitive societies, can be performed by either men or women. Equally important, what is defined as a man's task in one society may well be classified as a woman's job in another.[74] Nonetheless, the sexual division of labor is much more narrow than dictated by physical limitations, and what any one culture defines as a woman's job will seldom be performed by a man and vice versa. It seems that what originated as a division of labor based upon the necessities of survival has spilled over into many other areas and lasted long past the time of its social value. Where male strength and mobility has been crucial to social survival, male dominance and the aura of male superiority has been the strongest. The latter has been incorporated into the value structure and attained an existence of its own.

Thus, male superiority has not ceased with an end to the need for male strength. As Goode pointed out, there is one consistent element in the assignment of jobs to the sexes, even in modern societies: "Whatever the strictly male tasks are, they are defined as *more honorific* (emphasis his). . . . Moreover, the tasks of control, management, decision, appeals to the gods—in short the higher level jobs that typically do *not* require strength, speed or traveling far from home—are male jobs."[75]

He goes on to comment that "this element suggests that the sexual division of labor within family and society comes perilously close to the racial or caste restrictions in some modern countries. That is, the low-ranking race, caste, or sex is defined as not being *able* to do certain types of prestigious work, but it is also considered a violation of propriety if they do it. Obviously, if women really cannot do various kinds of male tasks, no moral or ethical prohibition would be necessary to keep them from it."[76]

Sex roles originated in economic necessities but the value attached to any one role has become a factor of sex alone. Even cross-culturally, these roles, and the attitudes associated with them, are ingrained by common socialization practices. Barry, Bacon, and Child discovered that "pressure toward nurturance, obedience and responsibility is most often stronger for girls, whereas pressure toward achievement and self-reliance is most often stronger for boys."[77] These are the same socialization practices traditionally found in Western society. As the Barry, Bacon, and Child study showed, these socializations serve to prepare children for roles as adults that require women to stay near the home and men to go out and achieve. The greater emphasis a society places on physical strength, the greater the sex-role differentiation and the sex differences in socialization.

These sex-role differences may have served a natural function at one time, but it is doubtful that they still do so. The characteristics we observe in women and men today are a result of socialization practices that were developed for survival of a primitive society. The value structure of male superiority is a reflection of the primitive orientations and values. But social and economic conditions have changed drastically since these values were developed. Technology has reduced to almost nothing the importance of muscular strength. In fact, the warlike attitude which goes along with an idealization of physical strength and dominance is proving to be positively destructive. The value of large families has also become a negative one. Now we are concerned with the population explosion and prefer that our society produce children of quality rather than quantity. The result of all these changes is that the traditional sex-roles and the traditional family structures have become dysfunctional.

To some extent, patterns of child-rearing have also changed. Bronfenbrenner reports that at least middle-class parents are raising both boys and girls much the same. He noted that over a 50-year period middle-class parents have been developing a "more acceptant, equalitarian relationship with their children."[78] With an increase in the family's social position, the patterns of parental treatment of children begin to converge.[79] He likewise noted that a similar phenomenon is beginning to develop in lower-class parents and that equality of treatment is slowly working its way down the social ladder.

These changes in patterns of child-rearing correlate with changes in relationships within the family. Both are moving toward a less hierarchical and more egalitarian pattern of living.

As Blood has pointed out, "today we may be on the verge of a new phase in American family history, when the companionship family is beginning to manifest itself. One distinguishing characteristic of this family is the dual employment of husband and wife. . . . Employment emancipates women from domination by their husbands and, secondarily, raises their daughters from inferiority to their brothers. . . . The classic differences between masculinity and femininity are disappearing as both sexes in the adult generation take on the same roles in the labor market. . . . The roles of men and women are converging for both adults and children. As a result the family will be far less segregated internally, far less stratified into different age generations and different sexes. The old asymmetry of male-dominated, female-serviced family life is being replaced by a new symmetry."[80]

All these data indicate that several trends are converging at about the same time. Our value structure has changed from an authoritarian one to a more democratic one, though our social structure has not yet caught up. Social attitudes begin in the family; only a democratic family can raise children to be citizens in a democratic society. The social and economic organization of society which kept women in the home has likewise changed. The home is no longer the center of society. The primary male and female functions have left it and there is no longer any major reason for maintaining the large sex-role differentiations which it supported. The value placed on physical strength which reinforced the dominance of men, and the male superiority attitudes that this generated, have also become dysfunctional. It is the mind, not the body, which must now prevail, and woman's mind is the equal of man's. The "pill" has liberated women from the uncertainty of childbearing, and with it the necessity of being attached to a man for economic support. But our attitudes toward women, and toward the family, have not changed concomitantly with the other developments. There is a distinct "cultural lag." Definitions of the family, conceptions of women and ideas about social function are left over from an era when they were necessary for social survival. They have persisted into an era in which they are no longer viable. The result can only be called severe role dysfunctionality for women.

The necessary relief for this dysfunctionality must come through changes in the social and economic organization of society and in social attitudes which will permit women to play a full and equal part in the social order. With this must come changes in the family, so that men and women are not only equal, but can raise their children in a democratic atmosphere. These changes will not come easily, nor will they come through the simple evolution of social trends. Trends do not move all in the same direction or at the same rate. To the extent that changes are dysfunctional with each other they create problems. These problems must be solved not by complacency but by conscious human direction. Only in this way can we have a real say in the shape of our future and the shape of our lives.

Footnotes

1. Rossi, A. Equality between the sexes: An immodest proposal. In Robert J. Lifton (Ed.), *The woman in America*. Boston: Beacon Press, 1965. Pp. 102–103.
2. Bem, S. & Bem, D. We're all nonconscious sexists. *Psychology Today*, 1970, 4(6), 26.
3. McClelland, D. Wanted: A new self-image for women. In Robert J. Lifton (Ed.), *The woman in America*. Boston: Beacon Press, 1965. P. 173.
4. Bennett, E. M. & Cohen, L. R. Men and women: Personality patterns and contrasts. *Genetic Psychology Monographs*, 1959, 59, 101–155.
5. Allport, G. *The nature of prejudice*. Reading, Mass.: Addison-Wesley, 1954. Pp. 142–161.
6. Terman, L. M. & Tyler, L. Psychological sex differences. In Leonard Carmichael (Ed.), *Manual of child psychology*. New York: Wiley & Sons, 1954. Pp. 1080–1100.
7. Smith, S. Age and sex differences in children's opinion concerning sex differences. *Journal of Genetic Psychology*, 1939, 54, 17–25.
8. Goldberg, P. Are women prejudiced against women? *Transaction*, April 1969, 28.
9. Clark, K. & Clark, M. Racial identification and preference in Negro children. In T. M. Newcomb and E. L. Hartley (Eds.), *Readings in social psychology*. New York: Holt, Rinehart & Winston, 1947.
10. Fisher, L. *Gandhi*. New York: Signet Key, 1954.
11. Fanon, F. *The wretched of the earth*. New York: Grove Press, 1963.
12. Myrdal, G. *An American dilemma*. New York: Harper, 1944.

13. De Vos, G. The relation of guilt toward parents to achievement and arranged marriage among the Japanese. *Psychiatry*, 1960, **23**, 287–301.
14. Miles, C. C. Gifted children. In Carmichael, *op. cit.*, p. 1045.
15. See: Brown, R. *Social psychology*. New York: The Free Press. P. 162; Reuben Hill and Howard Becker (Eds.), *Family, marriage and parenthood*. Boston: D. C. Heath, 1955. P. 790; Goldberg, *op. cit.*, p. 28; Myrdal, *op. cit.*, Appendix V; and Goode, W. J., *The family*. Englewood Cliffs, New Jersey: Prentice-Hall, 1965. P. 70.
16. Tyler, L. Sex differences. Under "Individual differences" in the *International encyclopedia of the social sciences*, Vol. 7, 1968, New York: The Macmillan Co. Pp. 207–213.
17. Bales, R. F. Task roles and social roles in problem-solving groups. In T. M. Newcomb, E. Maccoby, and E. L. Hartly (Eds.), *Readings in social psychology* (3rd ed.). New York: Holt, Rinehart & Winston, 1958.
18. Maccoby, E. Sex differences in intellectual functioning. In E. Maccoby (Ed.), *The development of sex differences*. Stanford: Stanford University Press, 1966. Pp. 26 ff.
19. Neiman, L. J. The influence of peer groups upon attitudes toward the feminine role. *Social Problems*, 1954, **2**, 104–111.
20. Milner, E. Effects of sex-role and social status on the early adolescent personality. *Genetic Psychological Monographs*, **40**, 231–325.
21. Lipinski, B. *Sex-role conflict and achievement motivation in college women*. Unpublished doctoral dissertation, University of Cincinnati, 1965.
22. Asch, S. E. Studies of independence and conformity. A minority of one against a unanimous majority. *Psychological Monographs*, 1956, **70**, No. 9.
23. Smith, *op. cit.*
24. Goldberg, *op. cit.*
25. Bradway, K. P. & Thompson, C. W. Intelligence at adulthood: A twenty-five year followup. *Journal of Educational Psychology*, 1962, **53**, 1–14.
26. Stivers, E. N. *Motivation for college of high school boys and girls*. Unpublished doctoral dissertation, University of Chicago, 1959.
27. Pierce, J. V. & Bowman, P. H.: The educational motivation patterns of superior students who do and do not achieve in high school. U.S. Office of Education Project #208, *Co-operative Research Monograph No. 2*, U.S. Printing Office, Washington, 1960, 33–66.
28. Pierce, J. V. Sex differences in achievement motivation of able high school students, *Co-operative Research Project No. 1097*, University of Chicago, December 1961.
29. *Ibid.*, p. 23.
30. *Ibid.*, p. 42.
31. Horner, M. Femininity and successful achievement: A basic inconsistency. In Bardwick, et al., *Feminine personality and conflict*. Belmont: Brooks/Cole, 1970. See also pp. 97–122 in this text.
32. Terman & Tyler, *op. cit.*, p. 1104.

33. Maccoby, 1966, *op. cit.*, p. 26.
34. *Ibid.*, p. 27.
35. Maccoby, E. Woman's intellect. In Farber & Wilson (Eds.), *The potential of women*. New York: McGraw-Hill, 1963. P. 30.
36. *Ibid.*, p. 31. See also: Sherman, J. A. Problems of sex differences in space perception and aspects of intellectual functioning. *Psychological Review*, July 1967, **74**, No. 4, 290–299; and Vernon, P. E. Ability factors and environmental influences. *American Psychologist*, Sept. 1965, **20**, No. 9, 723–733.
37. Bronfenbrenner, U. Some familial antecedents of responsibility and leadership in adolescents. In Luigi Petrullo and Bernard M. Bass (Eds.), *Leadership and interpersonal behavior*. New York: Holt, Rinehart, & Winston, 1961. P. 260.
38. Levy, D. M. *Maternal overprotection*. New York: Columbia University Press, 1943.
39. Maccoby, 1963, *op. cit.*, p. 31.
40. Witkin, H. A., Dyk, R. B., Paterson, H. E., Goodenough, D. R., & Karp, S. A. *Psychological differentiation*. New York: Wiley, 1962.
41. Clapp, J. *Sex differences in mathematical reasoning ability*. Unpublished paper, 1968.
42. Sontag, I. W., Baker, C. T., & Nelson, V. A. Mental growth and personality development: A longitudinal study. *Monographs of the Society for Research in Child Development*, 1953, **23**, No. 68.
43. Maccoby, 1963, *op. cit.*, p. 33.
44. Kagan, J. & Moss, H. A. *Birth to maturity: A study in psychological development*. New York and London: John Wiley and Sons, 1962. P. 275.
45. *Ibid.*, p. 225.
46. Winterbottom, M. The relation of need for achievement to learning experiences in independence and mastery. In Harold Proshansky and Bernard Seidenberg (Eds.), *Basic studies in social psychology*. New York: Holt, Rinehart & Winston, 1965. Pp. 294–307.
47. Sears, R. R., Maccoby, E., & Levin, H. *Patterns of child rearing*. Evanston, Ill.: Row, Peterson, 1957.
48. Bronfenbrenner, *op. cit.*, p. 260.
49. *Ibid.*
50. Schachter, S. *The psychology of affiliation*. Stanford: Stanford University Press, 1959.
51. Bronfenbrenner, *op. cit.*, p. 267.
52. Douvan, E. Employment and the adolescent. In F. Ivan Nye and Lois W. Hoffman (Eds.), *The employed mother in America*. Chicago: Rand McNally, 1963.
53. Kagan and Moss, *op. cit.*, p. 222.
54. McClelland, D. C. *The achieving society*. Princeton: Van Nostrand, 1961.
55. Kagan and Moss, *op. cit.*, p. 270.
56. Maccoby, 1963, *op. cit.*, p. 37.

57. Sinick, D. Two anxiety scales correlated and examined for sex differences. *Journal of Clinical Psychology*, 1956, **12**, 394–395.
58. Maccoby, 1963, *op. cit.*, p. 37.
59. Myrdal, *op. cit.*, p. 1077.
60. Montagu, A. Anti-feminism and race prejudice. *Psychiatry*, 1946, **9**, 69–71.
61. Keniston, E. & Keniston, K. An American anachronism: The image of women and work. *American Scholar*, Summer 1964, **33**, No. 3, 355–375.
62. Rossi, *op. cit.*
63. Adorno, T. W., et al., *The authoritarian personality*. New York: Harper, 1950.
64. Stephens, W. N. *The family in cross-cultural perspective*. New York: Holt, Rinehart & Winston, 1963.
65. D'Andrade, R. Sex differences and cultural institutions. In Maccoby (Ed.), 1966, *op. cit.*, p. 189.
66. Blood, R. O., & Wolfe, D. M. *Husbands and wives*. Glencoe: The Free Press, 1960.
67. Blood, R. O. Long-range causes and consequences of the employment of married women. *Journal of Marriage and the Family*, 1965, **27**, No. 1, 46.
68. Goode, *op. cit.*, p. 76.
69. Hill and Becker, *op. cit.*, p. 790.
70. Hallenbeck, P. N. An analysis of power dynamics in marriage. *Journal of Marriage and the Family*, May 1966, **28**, No. 2, 203.
71. Blood, *op. cit.*, p. 47.
72. Barry, H., Bacon, M. K., & Child, I. L. A cross-cultural survey of some sex differences in socialization. *Journal of Abnormal and Social Psychology*, 1957, **55**, 330.
73. Spiro, M. E. *Kibbutz: Venture in utopia*. Cambridge: Harvard University Press, 1956.
74. D'Andrade, *op. cit.*, p. 191.
75. Goode, *op. cit.*, p. 70.
76. *Ibid.*
77. Barry, Bacon, & Child, *op. cit.*, p. 328.
78. Bronfenbrenner, U. Socialization and social class through time and space. In Maccoby, Newcomb and Hartly, *op. cit.*
79. Bronfenbrenner, U. The effects of social and cultural change on personality. *Journal of Social Issues*, 1969, **17**, No. 1, 6–18.
80. Blood, *op. cit.*, p. 47.

Section Three

Toward the Liberation
of Women

Hopefully, the first two sections of this book have made several facts more readily apparent than they may have been before. First, women do not have equal opportunity at home, in school, or on the job; most roles in this society are clearly sex-typed. Second, despite what we have been taught to believe, women's "place" is not only different from men's but it is inferior to men's. Even the same work when done by a woman is valued less than when done by a man. Third, there is no scientific evidence that innate sex differences biologically determine the differences that we see between the sexes in this society. Instead, there is a good deal of evidence that sex roles are determined by social and economic factors rather than physiology.

These facts and their implications have led to the enormous growth of the women's liberation movement. Many early feminists thought that the vote and specific law changes would lead to generalized emancipation, but new groups have learned from past failures and are expanding their focus to concepts of identity, social roles, and the very basis of the political and economic structures. Their basic goal is liberation—liberation from the inhuman structuring of life alternatives. They believe that individuals must be encouraged by society to develop and to contribute according to their fullest human potential, not according to their sex (or skin color, or class background). Different groups within the movement see the possibility of obtaining such societal change in different perspective. Some are limiting their work to attempts to change discriminatory laws, to reform hiring practices, and to eliminate graduate-school sex quotas. Others are learning self-defense, auto mechanics, and a variety of traditionally male skills in an effort to become self-sufficient. Many are seeking communal solutions for what formerly were considered to be the individual problems of home and child care. Communal, noncompetitive sharing of responsibilities and resources can reduce manyfold the number of child-care, shopping, and cooking hours and result in many free hours for creative activity.

Other women consider individual liberation to be impossible unless women as an exploited group are liberated through basic changes in the economic system under which they live. They see the subjugation of women to be an integral part of a capitalist society. Therefore, socialism is to them a necessary condition for women's liberation.

The articles in this section reflect several different levels of thinking about women's liberation. The approaches are not contradictory, but rather complementary, developing from different perspectives. The first article, an excerpt from "Equality Between the Sexes: An Immodest Proposal," by Alice S. Rossi, suggests three institutional changes that would basically alter the inequality now existing between the sexes. In the second article, Marlene Dixon presents her views on "Why Women's Liberation" is necessary. The third article, "I Am Furious (Female)," by Ellen Cantarow, Elizabeth Diggs, Katherine Ellis, Janet Marx, Lillian Robinson, and Muriel Schien, explains why the authors feel a socialist revolution is a means of liberating women. The fourth article, "The Political Economy of Women's Liberation," by Margaret Benston, discusses the economic changes she feels are necessary for "woman's work" to become worthy of value by the society.

Equality Between the Sexes:
An Immodest Proposal

Alice S. Rossi

Alice S. Rossi, Associate Professor of Sociology at Goucher College, holds a Ph.D. from Columbia University. She has been active from the early 1960s in abortion reform and repeal, and she is a charter member of the National Organization for Women and a member of its Board of Directors for the years 1966–1970. More recently she has been involved as advisor to the Committee of the National Conference of Commissioners of Uniform State Laws in drawing up a model marriage and divorce statute. She has also participated in women's liberation groups and was the organizer of the Women's Caucus of the American Sociological Association.

Institutional Levers for Achieving Sex Equality

In turning to the problem of how equality between the sexes may be implemented as a societal goal, I shall concentrate on the three major areas of child care, residence and education. Institutional change in these areas in no sense exhausts the possible spheres in which institutional change could be effected to facilitate the goal of sex equality. Clearly government and industry, for example, could effect highly significant changes in the relations between the sexes. But one must begin somewhere, and I have chosen these three topics, for they all involve questions of critical significance to the goal of equality between men and women.

1. It is widely assumed that rearing children and maintaining a career is so difficult a combination that except for those few women with an extraordinary amount of physical strength, emotional endurance and a dedicated sense of calling to their work, it is unwise for women to attempt the combination. Women who have successfully combined child-rearing and careers are considered out of the ordinary, although many men with far heavier work responsibilities who yet spend willing loving hours as fathers, and who also contribute to home maintenance, are cause for little comment. We should be wary of the assumption that home and work combinations are necessarily difficult. The simplified contemporary home and smaller sized family of a working mother today

Reprinted from *Daedalus*, Journal of the American Academy of Arts and Sciences, Boston, Massachusetts, Volume 93, Number 2. By permission of the publisher and the author.

probably represent a lesser burden of responsibility than that shouldered by her grandmother.

This does not mean that we should overlook the real difficulties that are involved for women who attempt this combination. Working mothers do have primary responsibility for the hundreds of details involved in home maintenance, as planners and managers, even if they have household help to do the actual work. No one could suggest that child-rearing and a career are easy to combine, or even that this is some royal road to greater happiness, but only that the combination would give innumerable intelligent and creative women a degree of satisfaction and fulfillment that they cannot obtain in any other way. Certainly many things have to "give" if a woman works when she also has young children at home. Volunteer and social activities, gardening and entertaining may all have to be curtailed. The important point to recognize is that as children get older, it is far easier to resume these social activities than it is to resume an interrupted career. The major difficulty, and the one most in need of social innovation, is the problem of providing adequate care for the children of working mothers.

If a significant number of American middle-class women wish to work while their children are still young and in need of care and supervision, who are these mother-substitutes to be? In the American experience to date, they have been either relatives or paid domestic helpers. A study conducted by the Children's Bureau in 1958 outlines the types of child-care arrangements made by women working full time who had children under twelve years of age. The study showed that the majority of these children (57 per cent) were cared for by relatives: fathers, older siblings, grandparents and others. About 21 per cent were cared for by nonrelatives, including neighbors as well as domestic helpers. Only 2 per cent of the children were receiving group care—in day nurseries, day-care centers, settlement houses, nursery schools and the like. Of the remainder, 8 per cent were expected to take care of themselves, the majority being the "latchkey" youngsters of ten and twelve years of age about whom we have heard a good deal in the press in recent years.

These figures refer to a national sample of employed mothers and concern women in blue collar jobs and predominantly low-skill white collar jobs. Presumably the proportion of middle-class working mothers who can rely on either relatives or their husbands would be drastically lower than this national average, and will probably decline even further in future years. Many of today's, and more of tomorrow's American grandmothers are going to be wage earners themselves and not baby-sitters for their grandchildren. In addition, as middle-class women enter the occupational world, they will experience less of a tug to remain close to the kinswomen of their childhood, and hence may contribute further to the pattern of geographic and social separation between young couples and both sets of their parents. Nor can many middle-class husbands care for their children, for their work hours are typically the same as those of their working wives: there can be little dovetailing of the work schedules of wives and husbands in the middle class as there can be in the working class.

At present, the major child-care arrangement for the middle-class woman who plans a return to work has to be hired household help. In the 1920's the professional and business wife-mother had little difficulty securing such domestic help, for there were thousands of first generation immigrant girls and women in our large cities whose first jobs in America were as domestic servants.[1] In the 1960's, the situation is quite different: the major source of domestic help in our large cities is Negro and Puerto Rican women. Assuming the continuation of economic affluence and further success in the American Negro's struggle for equal opportunity in education, jobs and housing, this reservoir will be further diminished in coming decades. The daughters of many present-day Negro domestic servants will be able to secure far better paying and more prestigeful jobs than their mothers can obtain in 1964. There will be increasing difficulty of finding adequate child-care help in future years as a result.

The problem is not merely that there may be decreasing numbers of domestic helpers available at the same time more women require their aid. There is an even more important question involved: are domestic helpers the best qualified persons to leave in charge of young children? Most middle-class families have exacting standards for the kind of teachers and the kind of schools they would like their children to have. But a working mother who searches for a competent woman to leave in charge of her home has to adjust to considerably lower standards than she would tolerate in any nursery school program in which she placed her young son or daughter, either because such competent help is scarce, or because the margin of salary left after paying for good child care and the other expenses associated with employment is very slight.

One solution to the problem of adequate child care would be an attempt to upgrade the status of child-care jobs. I think one productive way would be to develop a course of study which would yield a certificate for practical mothering, along the lines that such courses and certificates have been developed for practical nursing. There would be

---

[1] In one study conducted for the Bureau of Vocational Information in 1925, Collier found that 42% of the one hundred professional and business mothers she interviewed had two or more full-time domestic servants to maintain their homes and care for their children during the day; only 9 of these 100 women had no full-time servants, five of whom had their mothers living with them. Virginia MacMakin Collier, *Marriage and Careers: A Study of One Hundred Women Who Are Wives, Mothers, Homemakers and Professional Women* (New York: The Channel Bookshop, 1926), pp. 59 and 74.

several important advantages to such a program. There are many older women in American communities whose lives seem empty because their children are grown and their grandchildren far away, yet who have no interest in factory or sales work, for they are deeply committed to life and work within the context of a home. Indeed, there are many older women who now work in factories or as cashiers or salesclerks who would be much more satisfied with child-care jobs, if the status and pay for such jobs were upgraded. These are the women, sometimes painfully lonely for contact with children, who stop young mothers to comment on the baby in the carriage, to talk with the three-year-old and to discuss their own distant grandchildren. I think many of these women would be attracted by a program of "refresher" courses in first aid, child development, books and crafts appropriate for children of various ages, and the special problems of the mother substitute-child relationship. Such a program would build upon their own experiences as mothers but would update and broaden their knowledge, bringing it closer to the values and practices of the middle-class woman who is seeking a practical mother for her family. Substitute motherhood for which she earns a wage, following active motherhood of her own, could provide continuity, meaning and variety to the life-span of those American women who are committed to the traditional conception of woman's role. Such a course of study might be developed in a number of school contexts—a branch of a college department of education, an adult education extension program or a school of nursing.

A longer-range solution to the problem of child care will involve the establishment of a network of child-care centers.[2] Most of the detailed plans for such centers must be left for future discussion, but there are several important advantages to professionally run child-care centers which should be noted. Most important, better care could be provided by such centers than any individual mother can provide by hiring a mother's helper, housekeeper or even the practical mother I have just proposed. In a child-care center, there can be greater specialization of skills, better facilities and equipment, and play groups for the children.

---

[2] Child-care centers would not be an entirely new phenomenon in the United States, for there were a number of municipal day-care centers established during World War II when the need for womanpower in factories engaged in war production made them necessary to free women to accept employment. There have also been continuing debates about the provision of child-care centers for other mothers, such as the ADC mother, the problem revolving about whether such women should be given sufficient money from municipal funds to stay at home and care for her children, or to establish child-care centers and thus enable such women to hold down jobs and at least partially support their children. In either case, the focus has been upon working-class women. Child-care centers as an institutional device to facilitate the combination of job and family by women in professional and technical occupations in the middle class are very rare, and are largely confined to small private ventures in the large metropoli.

Second, a child-care center would mean less expense for the individual working mother, and both higher wages and shorter hours for the staff of the center. Third, these centers could operate on a full-time, year-round schedule, something of particular importance for women trained in professional or technical fields, the majority of which can be handled only on a full-time basis. Except for the teaching fields, such women must provide for the afternoon care of their nursery school and kindergarten-age children, after-school hours for older children and three summer months for all their children. Fourth, a child-care center could develop a roster of home-duty practical mothers or practical nurses to care for the ill or convalescent child at home, in much the way school systems now call upon substitute teachers to cover the classes of absent regular teachers.

A major practical problem is where to locate such child-care centers. During the years of experimentation which would follow acceptance of this idea, they might be in a variety of places, under a variety of organizational auspices, as a service facility offered by an industrial firm, a large insurance company, a university, the federal or a state government. Community groups of women interested in such service might organize small centers of their own much as they have informal pooled baby-sitting services and cooperatively run nursery schools at the present time.

I believe that one of the most likely contexts for early experimentation with such child-care centers is the large urban university. As these universities continue to expand in future years, in terms of the size of the student body, the varied research institutes associated with the university and the expansion of administrative, technical and counseling personnel, there will be increasing opportunity and increasing need for the employment of women. A child-care center established under the auspices of a major university would facilitate the return for training of older women to complete or refresh advanced training, forestall the dropping out of younger graduate married women with infants and young children to care for, and attract competent professional women to administrative, teaching or research positions, who would otherwise withdraw from their fields for the child-rearing years. It would also be an excellent context within which to innovate a program of child care, for the university has the specialists in psychology, education and human development on whom to call for the planning, research and evaluation that the establishment of child-care centers would require. If a university-sponsored child-care program were successful and widely publicized, it would then constitute an encouragement and a challenge to extend child-care centers from the auspices of specific organizations to a more inclusive community basis. A logical location for community child-care centers may be as wings of the elementary schools, which have precisely the geographic distribution throughout a city to make for easy access between the homes of very young children and the centers for their daytime care. Since school and center would share a location, it would also facilitate easy supervision of older children during the after-school hours. The costs of such care would also be considerably reduced if the facilities of the school were available for the older children during after-school hours, under the supervision of the staff of the child-care center. There are, of course, numerous problems to be solved in working out the details of any such program under a local educational system, but assuming widespread support for the desirability of community facilities for child care, these are technical and administrative problems well within the competence of school and political officials in our communities.

I have begun this discussion of the institutional changes needed to effect equality between the sexes with the question of child-care provision because it is of central importance in permitting women to enter and remain in the professional, technical and administrative occupations in which they are presently so underrepresented. Unless provision for child care is made, women will continue to find it necessary to withdraw from active occupational involvement during the child-rearing years. However, the professional and scientific fields are all growing in knowledge and skill, and even a practitioner who remains in the field often has difficulty keeping abreast of new developments. A woman who withdraws for a number of years from a professional field has an exceedingly difficult time catching up. The more exacting the occupation, then, the shorter the period of withdrawal should probably be from active participation in the labor force. If a reserve of trained practical mothers were available, a professional woman could return to her field a few months after the birth of a child, leaving the infant under the care of a practical mother until he or she reached the age of two years, at about which age the child could enter a child-care center for daytime care. Assuming a two-child family, this could mean not more than one year of withdrawal from her professional field for the working mother.

2. The preferred residential pattern of the American middle class in the postwar decades has been suburban. In many sections of the country it is difficult to tell where one municipality ends and another begins, for the farm, forest and waste land between towns and cities have been built up with one housing development after another. The American family portrayed in the mass media typically occupies a house in this sprawling suburbia, and here too are the American women, and sometimes men, whose problems are aired and analyzed with such frequency. We know a good deal about the characteristics and quality of social life in the American suburb and the problems of the men and women who live in them. We hear about the changing political

complexion of the American suburbs, the struggle of residents to provide sufficient community facilities to meet their growing needs. But the social and personal difficulties of suburban women are more likely to be attributed to their early family relationships or to the contradictory nature of the socialization of girls in our society than to any characteristic of the environment in which they now live. My focus will be somewhat different: I shall examine the suburban residence pattern for the limitations it imposes on the utilization of women's creative work abilities and the participation of men in family life. Both limitations have important implications for the lives of boys and girls growing up in the suburban home.

The geographic distance between home and work has a number of implications for the role of the father-husband in the family. It reduces the hours of possible contact between children and their fathers. The hour or more men spend in cars, buses or trains may serve a useful decompression function by providing time in which to sort out and assess the experiences at home and the events of the work day, but it is questionable whether this outweighs the disadvantage of severely curtailing the early morning and late afternoon hours during which men could be with their children.

The geographic distance also imposes a rigid exclusion of the father from the events which highlight the children's lives. Commuting fathers can rarely participate in any special daytime activities at home or at school, whether a party, a play the child performs in or a conference with a teacher. It is far less rewarding to a child to report to his father at night about such a party or part in a play than to have his father present at these events. If the husband-father must work late or attend an evening function in the city, he cannot sandwich in a few family hours but must remain in the city. This is the pattern which prompted Margaret Mead to characterize the American middle-class father as the "children's mother's husband," and partly why mother looms so oversized in the lives of suburban children.

Any social mixing of family-neighborhood and job associates is reduced or made quite formal: a work colleague cannot drop in for an after-work drink or a Saturday brunch when an hour or more separates the two men and their families. The father-husband's office and work associates have a quality of unreality to both wife and children. All these things sharpen the differences between the lives of men and women— fewer mutual acquaintances, less sharing of the day's events, and perhaps most importantly, less simultaneous filling of their complementary parent roles. The image of parenthood to the child is mostly motherhood, a bit of fatherhood and practically no parenthood as a joint enterprise shared at the same time by father and mother. Many suburban parents, I suspect, spend more time together as verbal parents—discussing their children in the children's absence—than they do actively interacting with their children, the togetherness cult notwithstanding. For couples whose relationship in courtship and early marriage was equalitarian, the pressures are strong in the suburban setting for parenthood to be highly differentiated and skewed to an ascendant position of the mother. Women dominate the family, men the job world.

The geographic distance between home and the center of the city restricts the world of the wife-mother in a complementary fashion. Not only does she have to do and be more things to her children, but she is confined to the limitations of the suburban community for a great many of her extrafamilial experiences. That suburban children are restricted in their social exposure to other young children and relatively young adults, mostly women and all of the same social class, has often been noted. I think the social restriction of the young wife to women of her own age and class is of equal importance: with very few older persons in her immediate environment, she has little first-hand exposure to the problems attending the empty-nest stage of life which lies ahead for herself. It is easy for her to continue to be satisfied to live each day as it comes, with little thought of preparing for the thirty-odd years when her children are no longer dependent upon her. If the surburban wife-mother had more opportunity to become acquainted with older widows and grandmothers, this would be pressed home to her in a way that might encourage a change in her unrealistic expectations of the future, with some preparation for that stage of life while she is young.[3]

3 George Gallup and Evan Hill, "The American Woman," *The Saturday Evening Post*, December 22, 1962. One must read this survey very carefully to get behind the gloss of the authors' rosy perspective. Gallup reports that almost half of the married women in the sample claimed that childbirth was the "most thrilling event" in their lives. He gives two quotes to illustrate why these women were so fascinated by childbirth: one stresses the point that it was "the one time in my life when everything was right"; the other points out "you've done something that's recognized as a good thing to do, and you're the center of attention." If these are truly typical, it tells us a good deal about the underlying attitude toward the thousands of days on which no child is born: things are *not* all right, and there must be some sense of being on the sidelines, of having a low level of self-esteem, if childbirth is important because "society views it as good" and it is the only time in her life that she is the important center of attention. In other parts of the article, which generally stresses the central importance of children to women, and their high satisfaction with marriage, we learn that a large proportion of American women wish the schools would do more of the socializing of these children—teach them good citizenship, how to drive, sex education; and if these women were so satisfied with their lives, why does only 10% of the sample want their daughters to live the same lives they have? Instead, these women say they want their daughters to get more education and to marry later than they did. If marriage is the perfect female state, then why wish to postpone it, unless there are unexpressed sides of the self which have not been fulfilled?

The only strong critical point made is the following: "with early weddings and extended longevity, marriage is now a part-time career for women, and unless they

If and when the suburban woman awakens from this short-range perspective and wants either to work or to prepare for a return to work when her children are older, how is she to do this, given the suburban pattern of residence? It is all very well to urge that school systems should extend adult education, that colleges and universities must make it possible for older women to complete education interrupted ten or more years previously or to be retrained for new fields; but this is a difficult program for the suburban wife to participate in. She lives far from the center of most large cities, where the educational facilities tend to be concentrated, in a predominantly middle-class community, where domestic help is often difficult to arrange and transportation often erratic during the hours she would be using it.

It is for these reasons that I believe any attempt to draw a significant portion of married women into the mainstream of occupational life must involve a reconsideration of the suburban pattern of living. Decentralization of business and industry has only partly alleviated the problem: a growing proportion of the husbands living in the suburbs also work in the suburbs. There are numerous shops and service businesses providing job opportunities for the suburban wife. Most such jobs, however, are at skill levels far below the ability potential and social status of the suburban middle-class wife. Opportunities for the more exacting professional, welfare and business jobs are still predominantly in the central sections of the city. In addition, since so many young wives and mothers in this generation married very young, before their formal education was completed, they will need more schooling before they can hope to enter the fields in which their talents can be most fruitfully exercised, in jobs which will not be either dull or a status embarrassment to themselves and their husbands. Numerous retail stores have opened suburban branches; colleges and universities have yet to do so. A woman can spend in the suburb, but she can neither learn nor earn.

That some outward expansion of American cities has been necessary is clear, given the population increase in our middle- to large-sized cities. But there are many tracts in American cities between the business center and the outlying suburbs which imaginative planning and architectural design could transform and which would attract the men and women who realize the drawbacks of a suburban residence. Unless there is a shift in this direction in American housing, I do not think there

---

prepare now for the freer years, this period will be a loss. American society will hardly accept millions of ladies of leisure, or female drones, in their 40's" (p. 32). But only 31% of the sample reported they are "taking courses or following a plan to improve themselves," a third of these involving improvement of their physical shape or appearance. The photographs accompanying this article reveal the authors' own focus on the years of youth rather than of maturity: of 29 women appearing in these pictures, only 2 are clearly of women over 45 years of age.

can be any marked increase in the proportion of married middle-class women who will enter the labor force. That Swedish women find work and home easier to combine than American women is closely related to the fact that Sweden avoided the sprawling suburban development in its postwar housing expansion. The emphasis in Swedish housing has been on inner-city housing improvement. With home close to diversified services for schooling, child care, household help and places of work, it has been much easier in Sweden than in the United States to draw married women into the labor force and keep them there.

In contrast, the policy guiding the American federal agencies which affect the housing field, such as the FHA, have stressed the individual home, with the result that mortgage money was readily available to encourage builders to develop the sprawling peripheries of American cities. Luxury high-rise dwellings at the hub of the city and individual homes at the periphery have therefore been the pattern of middle-class housing development in the past twenty years. A shift in policy on the part of the federal government which would embrace buildings with three and four dwelling units and middle-income high-rise apartment buildings in the in-between zones of the city could go a long way to counteract this trend toward greater and greater distance between home and job. Not everyone can or will want to live close to the hub of the city. From spring through early fall, it is undoubtedly easier to rear very young children in a suburban setting with back yards for the exercise of healthy lungs and bodies. But this is at the expense of increased dependence of children on their mothers, of minimization of fathers' time with their youngsters, of restriction of the social environment of women, of drastic separation of family and job worlds and of less opportunity for even part-time schooling or work for married women.

3. Men and women must not only be able to participate equally; they must want to do so. It is necessary, therefore, to look more closely into their motivations, and the early experiences which mold their self-images and life expectations. A prime example of this point can be seen in the question of occupational choice. The goal of sex equality calls for not only an increase in the extent of women's participation in the occupational system, but a more equitable distribution of men and women in all the occupations which comprise that system. This means more women doctors, lawyers and scientists, more men social workers and school teachers. To change the sex ratio within occupations can only be achieved by altering the sex-typing of such occupations long before young people make a career decision.[4] Many men and women

---

[4] The extent of this sex-typing of occupations is shown dramatically in a study of the June, 1961 college graduates conducted by the National Opinion Research Center at the University of Chicago. Although the women in this sample of college graduates showed a superior academic performance during the college years—only

change their career plans during college, but this is usually within a narrow range of relatively homogeneous fields: a student may shift from medicine to a basic science, from journalism to teaching English. Radical shifts such as from nursing to medicine, from kindergarten teaching to the law, are rare indeed. Thus while the problem could be attacked at the college level, any significant change in the career choices men and women make must be attempted when they are young boys and girls. It is during the early years of elementary school education that young people develop their basic views of appropriate characteristics, activities and goals for their sex. It is for this reason that I shall give primary attention to the sources of sex-role stereotypes and what the elementary school system could do to eradicate these stereotypes and to help instead in the development of a more androgynous conception of sex role.[5]

The all-female social atmosphere of the American child has been frequently noted by social scientists, but it has been seen as a problem only in its effect upon boys. It has been claimed, for example, that the American boy must fight against a feminine identification this atmosphere encourages, with the result that he becomes overly aggressive, loudly asserting his maleness. In contrast, it is claimed that the American girl has an easy socialization, for she has an extensive number of

---

36% of the women in contrast to 50% of the men were in the "bottom half" of their class—their career aspirations differed markedly from those of men. Of those who were going on to graduate and professional schools in the fall of 1961, only 6% of those aspiring to careers in medicine were women; 7% in physics, 7% in pharmacology, 10% in business and administration, 28% in the social sciences. In contrast, women predominated in the following fields: 51% in humanities, 59% in elementary and secondary education, 68% in social work, 78% in health fields such as nursing, medical technology, physical and occupational therapy. In a sample of 33,782 college graduates, there were 11,000 women who expected to follow careers in elementary and secondary education, but only 285 women who hoped to enter the combined fields of medicine, law and engineering. See James A. Davis and Norman Bradburn, "Great Aspirations: Career Plans of America's June 1961 College Graduates," National Opinion Research Center Report No. 82, September, 1961 (mimeographed). Davis and Bradburn report that some 40% of the graduates had changed their career plans during their college years (p. 40).

[5] My attention in this section will be largely on the early years of schooling. There is a great need, however, for a return of the spirit that characterized high school and college educators of women in the 1930's. It has seemed to me that there is an insidious trend at this level of education toward discouraging women from aspiring to the most demanding and rewarding fields of work and thought. Dr. Mary Bunting, noteworthy for the imaginative Radcliffe Institute for Independent Study, now urges women to work on the "fringes" of the occupational system, away from the most competitive intellectual market places. In her first public address upon assuming the presidency of Barnard College, Dr. Rosemary Park stated that in her view college education of women in the United States should have as its goal the creation of "enlightened laymen." High school and college counselors give hearty approval if women students show talent and interest in elementary school teaching, nursing, social work; their approval is all too often very lukewarm if not discouraging, if women students show interest in physics, medicine or law.

feminine models in her environment to facilitate her identification as a female.

There are several important factors which this analysis overlooks. To begin with the boy: while it is certainly true that much of his primary group world is controlled by women, this does not mean that he has no image of the male social and job world as well. The content of the boy's image of man's work has a very special quality to it, however. Although an increasingly smaller proportion of occupations in a complex industrial society relies on sheer physical strength, the young boy's exposure to the work of men remains largely the occupations which do require physical strength. The jobs he can see are those which are socially visible, and these are jobs in which men are reshaping and repairing the physical environment. The young boy sees working class men operating trucks, bulldozers, cranes; paving roads; building houses; planting trees; delivering groceries. This image is further reinforced by his television viewing: the gun-toting cowboy, the bat-swinging ball-player, the arrow-slinging Indian. Space operas suggest not scientific exploration but military combat, the collision and collusion of other worlds. In short, even if the boy sees little of his father and knows next to nothing of what his father does away from home, there is some content to his image of men's work in the larger society. At least some part of his aggressive active play may be as much acting out similar male roles in response to the cultural cues provided by his environment as it is an over-reaction to his feminine environment or an identification with an aggressor-father.

And what of the girl? What image of the female role is she acquiring during her early years? In her primary group environment, she sees women largely in roles defined in terms that relate to her as a child—as mother, aunt, grandmother, baby-sitter—or in roles relating to the house—the cleaning, cooking, mending activities of mother and domestic helpers. Many mothers work outside the home, but the daughter often knows as little of that work as she does of her father's. Even if her own mother works, the reasons for such working that are given to the child are most often couched in terms of the mother or housewife role. Thus, a girl is seldom told that her mother works because she enjoys it or finds it very important to her own satisfaction in life, but because the money she earns will help pay for the house, a car, the daughter's clothes, dancing lessons or school tuition.[6] In other words, working is

6 Although her sample was upper-middle-class mothers of girls in progressive schools in New York City, Ruth Hartley reports that the working mothers in her sample told their children they were working out of the home because of financial need: "They express guilt about their working and appear to hold quite traditional concepts of appropriate 'feminine' behavior which they feel they are violating." An example is provided by a well-to-do working mother who obviously loves her work but told her daughter that she works because of financial necessity. When asked

something mothers sometimes have to do as mothers, not something mothers do as adult women. This is as misleading and distorted an image of the meaning of work as the father who tells his child he works "to take care of mummy and you" and neglects to mention that he also works because he finds personal satisfaction in doing so, or that he is contributing to knowledge, peace or the comfort of others in the society.

The young girl also learns that it is only in the family that women seem to have an important superordinate position. However high her father's occupational status outside the home, when he returns at night, he is likely to remove his white shirt and become a blue collar Mr. Fixit or mother's helper. The traditional woman's self-esteem would be seriously threatened if her husband were to play a role equal to her own in the lives and affections of her children or in the creative or managerial aspect of home management, precisely because her major sphere in which to acquire the sense of personal worth is her home and children.[7] The lesson is surely not lost on her daughter, who learns that at home father does not know best, though outside the home men are the bosses over women, as she can see only too well in the nurse-doctor, secretary-boss, salesclerk-store manager, space Jane-space John relationships that she has an opportunity to observe.

The view that the socialization of the girl is an easy one compared with the boy depends on the kind of woman one has in mind as an end-product of socialization. Only if the woman is to be the traditional wife-mother is present-day socialization of young girls adequate, for from this point of view the confinement to the kinds of feminine models noted above and the superordinate position of the mother in the family facilitate an easy identification. If a girl sees that women reign only at home or in a history book, whereas outside the home they are Girl Fridays to men, then clearly for many young girls the wife-mother role may appear the best possible goal to have. It should be noted, however, that identification has been viewed primarily as an either-or process—the child identifies either with the mother or the father—and not as a process in which there is a fusion of the two parent models such that identification involves a modeling of the self after mother in some respects, father in others. It is possible that those women who have led

---

why she doesn't let her daughter know she enjoys her work, she answered, "well, then what excuse would I have for working?" Ruth Hartley and A. Klein, "Sex Role Concepts among Elementary School-Age Girls," *Marriage and Family Living,* 21 (February, 1959), 59–64.

[7] Women enhance their own self-esteem when they urge their children to "be good when father gets home" because he is tired and needs to rest. They are not only portraying an image of the father as a fragile person, a "Dresden cup" as Irene Joselyn expresses it, but by expanding their maternalism to include the father, they are symbolically relegating him to the subordinate position of the child in the family structure. See Irene Joselyn, "Cultural Forces, Motherliness and Fatherliness," *American Journal of Orthopsychiatry,* 26 (1956), 264–271.

exciting, intellectually assertive and creative lives did not identify exclusively with their traditional mothers, but crossed the sex line and looked to their fathers as model sources for ideas and life commitments of their own. This is to suggest that an exclusively same-sex identification between parent and child is no necessary conditon for either mentally healthy or creative adults.

If I am correct about the significance of the father in the childhoods of those women who later led creative adult lives, then an increased accessibility of the middle-class father to his daughters and greater sharing of his ideas and interests could help to counteract the narrow confines of the feminine models daughters have. Beyond this, young girls need exposure to female models in professional and scientific occupations and to women with drive and dedication who are playing innovative volunteer roles in community organizations; they need an encouragement to emulate them and a preparation for an equalitarian rather than a dominant role in parenthood. Only if a woman's self-esteem is rooted in an independent life outside her family as well as her roles within the home can she freely welcome her husband to share on an equal basis the most rewarding tasks involved in child-rearing and home maintenance.

What happens when youngsters enter school? Instead of broadening the base on which they are forming their image of male and female roles, the school perpetuates the image children bring from home and their observations in the community. It has been mother who guided their preschool training; now in school it is almost exclusively women teachers who guide their first serious learning experiences. In the boy's first readers, men work at the same jobs with the same tools he has observed in his neighborhood—"T" for truck, "B" for bus, "W" for wagon. His teachers expect him to be rugged, physically strong and aggressive. After a few years he moves into separate classes for gym, woodworking and machine shop. For the girl, women are again the ones in charge of children. Her first readers portray women in aprons, brooms in their hands or babies in their arms. Teachers expect her to be quiet, dependent, with feminine interests in doll and house play and dressing up. In a few years she moves into separate classes for child care, cooking and practical nursing. In excursions into the community, elementary school boys and girls visit airports, bus terminals, construction sites, factories and farms.

What can the schools do to counteract these tendencies to either outmoded or traditional images of the roles of men and women? For one, class excursions into the community are no longer needed to introduce American children to building construction, airports or zoos. Except for those in the most underprivileged areas of our cities, American children have ample exposure to such things with their car- and plane-riding families. There are, after all, only a limited number of such excursions possible in the course of a school year. I think visits to a publishing house, research laboratory, computer firm or art studio would be more enriching than airports and zoos.

Going out into the community in this way, youngsters would observe men and women in their present occupational distribution. By a program of bringing representatives of occupations into the classroom and auditorium, however, the school could broaden the spectrum of occupations young children may link to their own abilities and interests regardless of the present sex-typing of occupations, by making a point of having children see and hear a woman scientist or doctor; a man dancer or artist; both women and men who are business executives, writers and architects.[8]

Another way in which the elementary schools could help is making a concerted effort to attract male teachers to work in the lower grades. This would add a rare and important man to the primary group environment of both boys and girls. This might seem a forlorn hope to some, since elementary school teaching has been such a predominantly feminine field, and it may be harder to attract men to it than to attract women to fields presently considered masculine. It may well be that in the next decade or so the schools could not attract and keep such men as teachers. But it should be possible for graduate schools of education and also school systems to devise ways of incorporating more men teachers in the lower grades, either as part of their teacher training requirements or in the capacity of specialized teachers: the science, art or music teacher who works with children at many grade levels rather than just one or two contiguous grade levels.[9] His presence in the lives of very young children could help dispel their expectation that only women are in charge of children, that nurturance is a female attribute or that strength and an aggressive assault on the physical environment is the predominant attribute of man's work.

The suggestions made thus far relate to a change in the sex-linking

[8] In a large metropolis, resource persons could be invited through the city business and professional organizations, the Chamber of Commerce, art, music and dancing schools, etc. This could constitute a challenging program for PTA groups to handle; or a Community Resources Pool could be formed similar to that the New World Foundation has supported in New York City whereby people from business, the arts and sciences and the professions work with the public schools. Many educators and teachers might hesitate to try such a project in anticipation of parent-resistance. But parent-resistance could be a good opportunity for parent-education, if teachers and school officials were firm and informed about what they are trying to do.

[9] Though predominantly a feminine field, there is one man to approximately every two women planning careers in teaching. In the "Great Aspirations" study, there were 11,388 women students planning to teach in elementary and secondary schools, but also 5038 men. The problem may therefore not be as great as it seems at first: schools of education could surely do more to encourage some of these men to work in the lower grades, in part or for part of their teaching careers.

of occupations. There is one crucial way in which the schools could effect a change in the traditional division of labor by sex within the family sphere. The claim that boys and girls are reared in their early years without any differentiation by sex is only partially true. There are classes in all elementary schools which boys and girls take separately or which are offered only to one sex. These are precisely the courses most directly relevant to adult family roles: courses in sex and family living (where communities are brave enough to hold them) are typically offered in separate classes for boys and for girls, or for girls only. Courses in shop and craft work are scheduled for boys only; courses in child care, nursing and cooking are for girls only. In departing from completely coeducational programs, the schools are reinforcing the traditional division of labor by sex which most children observe in their homes. Fifteen years later, these girls find that they cannot fix a broken plug, set a furnace pilot light or repair a broken high chair or favorite toy. These things await the return of the child's father and family handyman in the evening. When a child is sick in the middle of the night, his mother takes over; father is only her assistant or helper.

These may seem like minor matters, but I do not think they are. They unwittingly communicate to and reinforce in the child a rigid differentiation of role between men and women in family life. If first aid, the rudiments of child care and of cooking have no place in their early years as sons, brothers and schoolboys, then it is little wonder that as husbands and fathers American men learn these things under their wives' tutelage. Even assuming these wives were actively involved in occupations of their own and hence free of the psychological pressure to assert their ascendancy in the family, it would be far better for all concerned—the married pair and the children as well—if men brought such skills with them to marriage.

This is the point where the schools could effect a change: if boys and girls took child care, nursing, cooking, shop and craft classes together, they would have an opportunity to acquire comparable skills and pave the way for true parental substitutability as adults. They would also be learning something about how to complement each other, not just how to compete with each other.[10] Teamwork should be taught in school in the subjects relevant to adult family roles, not just within each sex on the playground or in the gymnasium. In addition to encouraging more equality in the parental role, such preparation as school children

[10] Bruno Bettelheim makes the point that American boys and girls learn to compete with each other, but not how to complement each other. He sees this lack of experience in complementarity as part of the difficulty in achieving a satisfactory sexual adjustment in marriage: the girl is used to "performing with males on equal -grounds, but she has little sense of how to complement them. She cannot suddenly learn this in bed." See Bruno Bettelheim, "Growing Up Female," *Harper's*, November, 1962, p. 125.

could ease their adjustment to the crises of adult life; illness, separation due to the demands of a job or military service, divorce or death would have far less trauma and panic for the one-parent family—whether mother or father—if such equivalence and substitutability were a part of the general definition of the parental role.

A school curriculum which brought boys and girls into the same classes and trained them in social poise, the healing skills, care of children, handling of interpersonal difficulties and related subjects would also encourage the development of skills which are increasingly needed in our complex economy. Whether the adult job is to be that of a worker in an automated industry, a professional man in law, medicine or scholarship, or an executive in a large bureaucratic organization, the skills which are needed are not physical strength and ruggedness in interpersonal combat but understanding in human dealings, social poise and persuasive skill in interpersonal relations.[11] All too often, neither the family nor the school encourages the development of these skills in boys. Hundreds of large business firms look for these qualities in young male applicants but often end up trying to develop them in their young executives through on-the-job training programs.

I have suggested a number of ways in which the educational system could serve as an important catalyst for change toward sex equality. The schools could reduce sex-role stereotypes of appropriate male and female attributes and activities by broadening the spectrum of occupations youngsters may consider for themselves irrespective of present sex-linked notions of man's work and woman's work, and by providing boys as well as girls with training in the tasks they will have as parents and spouses. The specific suggestions for achieving these ends which I have made should be viewed more as illustrative than as definitive, for educators themselves may have far better suggestions for how to implement the goal in the nation's classrooms than I have offered in these pages. Equality between the sexes cannot be achieved by proclamation or decree but only through a multitude of concrete steps, each of which may seem insignificant by itself, but all of which add up to the social blueprint for attaining the general goal.

Summary Profile

In the course of this essay I have suggested a number of institutional innovations in education, residence and child care which would facilitate equality between the sexes. Instead of a more conventional

---

[11] These are the same skills which, when found in women, go by the names of charm, tact, intuition. See Helen Mayer Hacker, "The New Burdens of Masculinity," *Marriage and Family Living,* **19** (August, 1957), 227–233.

kind of summary, I shall describe a hypothetical case of a woman who is reared and lives out her life under the changed social conditions proposed in this essay.

She will be reared, as her brother will be reared, with a combination of loving warmth, firm discipline, household responsibility and encouragement of independence and self-reliance. She will not be pampered and indulged, subtly taught to achieve her ends through coquetry and tears, as so many girls are taught today. She will view domestic skills as useful tools to acquire, some of which, like fine cooking or needlework, having their own intrinsic pleasures but most of which are necessary repetitive work best gotten done as quickly and efficiently as possible. She will be able to handle minor mechanical breakdowns in the home as well as her brother can, and he will be able to tend a child, press, sew, and cook with the same easy skills and comfortable feeling his sister has.

During their school years, both sister and brother will increasingly assume responsibility for their own decisions, freely experiment with numerous possible fields of study, gradually narrowing to a choice that best suits their interests and abilities rather than what is considered appropriate or prestigeful work for men and women. They will be encouraged by parents and teachers alike to think ahead to a whole life span, viewing marriage and parenthood as one strand among many which will constitute their lives. The girl will not feel the pressure to belittle her accomplishments, lower her aspirations, learn to be a receptive listener in her relations with boys, but will be as true to her growing sense of self as her brother and male friends are. She will not marry before her adolescence and schooling are completed, but will be willing and able to view the college years as a "moratorium" from deeply intense cross-sex commitments, a period of life during which her identity can be "at large and open and various." Her intellectual aggressiveness as well as her brother's tender sentiments will be welcomed and accepted as *human* characteristics, without the self-questioning doubt of latent homosexuality that troubles many college-age men and women in our era when these qualities are sex-linked.[12] She will not cling to her parents, nor they to her, but will establish an increasingly larger sphere of her own independent world in which she moves and works, loves and thinks, as a maturing young person. She will learn to take pleasure in her own body and a man's body and to view sex as a good and wonderful experience, but not as an exclusive basis for an ultimate commitment

[12] David Riesman has observed that this latent fear of homosexuality haunts the Ivy League campuses, putting pressure on many young men to be guarded in their relations with each other and their male teachers, reflecting in part the lag in the cultural image of appropriate sex characteristics. See David Riesman, "Permissiveness and Sex Roles," *Marriage and Family Living*, 21 (August, 1959), 211–217.

to another person, and not as a test of her competence as a female or her partner's competence as a male. Because she will have a many-faceted conception of her self and its worth, she will be free to merge and lose herself in the sex act with a lover or a husband.[13]

Marriage for our hypothetical woman will not mark a withdrawal from the life and work pattern that she has established, just as there will be no sharp discontinuity between her early childhood and youthful adult years. Marriage will be an enlargement of her life experiences, the addition of a new dimension to an already established pattern, rather than an abrupt withdrawal to the home and a turning in upon the marital relationship. Marriage will be a "looking outward in the same direction" for both the woman and her husband. She will marry and bear children only if she deeply desires a mate and children, and will not be judged a failure as a person if she decides against either. She will have few children if she does have them, and will view her pregnancies, childbirth and early months of motherhood as one among many equally important highlights in her life, experienced intensely and

---

[13] It goes beyond the intended scope of this essay to discuss the effects of a social pattern of equality between men and women upon their sexual relationship. A few words are, however, necessary, since the defenders of traditional sex roles often claim that full equality would so feminize men and masculinize women that satisfactory sexual adjustments would be impossible and homosexuality would probably increase. If the view of the sex act presupposes a dominant male actor and a passive female subject, then it is indeed the case that full sex equality would probably be the death knell of this traditional sexual relationship. Men and women who participate as equals in their parental and occupational and social roles will complement each other sexually in the same way, as essentially equal partners, and not as an ascendant male and a submissive female. This does mean, however, that equality in non-sexual roles necessarily de-eroticizes the sexual one. The enlarged base of shared experience can, if anything, heighten the salience of sex *qua* sex. In Sweden, where men and women approach equality more than perhaps any other western society, visitors are struck by the erotic atmosphere of that society. Sexually men and women do after all each lack what the other has and wishes for completion of the self; the salience of sex may be enhanced precisely in the situation of the diminished significance of sex as a differentiating factor in all other areas of life. It has always seemed paradoxical to me that so many psychoanalysts defend the traditional sex roles and warn that drastic warping of the sexual impulses may flow from full sex equality; surely they are underestimating the power and force of the very drive which is in so central a position in their theoretical framework. Maslow is one of the few psychologists who has explored the connections between sex experience and the conception of self among women. With a sample of one hundred and thirty college-educated women in their twenties, he found, contrary to traditional notions of femininity and psychoanalytic theories, that the more "dominant" the woman, the greater her enjoyment of sexuality, the greater her ability to give herself freely in love. Women with dominance feelings were free to be completely themselves, and this was crucial for their full expression in sex. They were not feminine in the traditional sense, but enjoyed sexual fulfillment to a much greater degree than the conventionally feminine woman he studied. See A. H. Maslow, "Dominance, Personality and Social Behavior in Women," *Journal of Social Psychology*, 10 (1939), 3–39; and "Self-Esteem (Dominance Feeling) and Sexuality in Women," *Journal of Social Psychology*, 16 (1942), 259–294; or a review of Maslow's studies in Betty Friedan, *The Feminine Mystique*, pp. 316–326.

with joy but not as the exclusive basis for a sense of self-fulfillment and purpose in life. With planning and foresight, her early years of child bearing and rearing can fit a long-range view of all sides of herself. If her children are not to suffer from "paternal deprivation," her husband will also anticipate that the assumption of parenthood will involve a weeding out of nonessential activities either in work, civic or social participation. Both the woman and the man will feel that unless a man can make room in his life for parenthood, he should not become a father. The woman will make sure, even if she remains at home during her child's infancy, that he has ample experience of being with and cared for by other adults besides herself, so that her return to a full-time position in her field will not constitute a drastic change in the life of the child, but a gradual pattern of increasing supplementation by others of the mother. The children will have a less intense involvement with their mother, and she with them, and they will all be the better for it. When they are grown and establish adult lives of their own, our woman will face no retirement twenty years before her husband, for her own independent activities will continue and expand. She will be neither an embittered wife, an interfering mother-in-law nor an idle parasite, but together with her husband she will be able to live an independent, purposeful and satisfying third act in life.

Why Women's Liberation

Marlene Dixon

Marlene Dixon is Assistant Professor of Sociology at McGill University where she teaches courses in the sociology of women and radical sociology. She is a well-known activist in the women's liberation movement.

The 1960's has been a decade of liberation; women have been swept up by that ferment along with blacks, Latins, American Indians and poor whites—the whole soft underbelly of this society. As each oppressed group in turn discovered the nature of its oppression in American society, so women have discovered that they too thirst for free and fully human lives. The result has been the growth of a new women's movement, whose base encompasses poor black and poor white women on relief, working women exploited in the labor force, middle class women incarcerated in the split level dream house, college girls awakening to the fact that sexiness is not the crowning achievement in life, and movement women who have discovered that in a freedom movement they themselves are not free. In less than four years women have created a variety of organizations, from the nationally-based middle class National Organization of Women (NOW) to local radical and radical feminist groups in every major city in North America. The new movement includes caucuses within nearly every New Left group and within most professional associations in the social sciences. Ranging in politics from reform to revolution, it has produced critiques of almost every segment of American society and constructed an ideology that rejects every hallowed cultural assumption about the nature and role of women.

As is typical of a young movement, much of its growth has been underground. The papers and manifestos written and circulated would surely comprise two very large volumes if published, but this literature is almost unknown outside of women's liberation. Nevertheless, where even a year ago organizing was slow and painful, with small cells of six or ten women, high turnover, and an uphill struggle against fear and resistance, in 1969 all that has changed. Groups are growing up everywhere with women eager to hear a hard line, to articulate and express their own rage and bitterness. Moving about the country, I have found an electric atmosphere of excitement and responsiveness. Everywhere there are doubts, stirrings, a desire to listen, to find out what it's all about. The extent to which groups have become politically radical is astounding. A year ago the movement stressed male chauvinism and psychological oppression; now the emphasis is on understanding the economic and social roots of women's oppression, and the analyses range from social democracy to Marxism. But the most striking change of all in the last year has been the loss of fear. Women are no longer afraid that their rebellion will threaten their very identity as women. They are not frightened by their own militancy, but liberated by it. Women's Liberation is an idea whose time has come.

The old women's movement burned itself out in the frantic decade of the 1920's. After a hundred years of struggle, women won a battle, only to lose the campaign: the vote was obtained, but the new millennium did not arrive. Women got the vote and achieved a measure of legal emancipation, but the real social and cultural barriers to full equality for women remained untouched.

For over 30 years the movement remained buried in its own ashes. Women were born and grew to maturity virtually ignorant of their own history of rebellion, aware only of a caricature of blue stockings and suffragettes. Even as increasing numbers of women were being driven into the labor force by the brutal conditions of the 1930's and by the massive drain of men into the military in the 1940's, the old ideal remained: a woman's place was in the home and behind her man. As the war ended and men returned to resume their jobs in factories and offices, women were forced back to the kitchen and nursery with a vengeance. This story has been repeated after each war and the reason is clear: women form a flexible, cheap labor pool which is essential to a capitalist system. When labor is scarce, they are forced onto the labor market. When labor is plentiful, they are forced out. Women and blacks have provided a reserve army of unemployed workers, benefiting capitalists and the stable male white working class alike. Yet the system imposes untold suffering on the victims, blacks and women, through low wages and chronic unemployment.

With the end of the war the average age at marriage declined, the average size of families went up, and the suburban migration began in earnest. The political conservatism of the '50s was echoed in a social conservatism which stressed a Victorian ideal of the woman's life: a full womb and selfless devotion to husband and children.

As the bleak decade played itself out, however, three important social developments emerged which were to make a rebirth of the women's struggle inevitable. First, women came to make up more than a third of the labor force, the number of working women being twice the prewar figure. Yet the marked increase in female employment did nothing to better the position of women, who were more occupationally disadvantaged in the 1960's than they had been 25 years earlier. Rather than moving equally into all sectors of the occupational structure, they were being forced into the low paying service, clerical and semi-skilled categories. In 1940, women had held 45 per cent of all professional and technical positions; in 1967, they held only 37 per cent. The proportion of women in service jobs meanwhile rose from 50 to 55 per cent.

Second, the intoxicating wine of marriage and suburban life was turning sour; a generation of women woke up to find their children grown and a life (roughly 30 more productive years) of housework and bridge parties stretching out before them like a wasteland. For many younger women, the empty drudgery they saw in the suburban life was a sobering contradiction to adolescent dreams of romantic love and the fulfilling role of woman as wife and mother.

Third, a growing civil rights movement was sweeping thousands of young men and women into a moral crusade—a crusade which harsh political experience was to transmute into the New Left. The American Dream was riven and tattered in Mississippi and finally napalmed in Viet-Nam. Young Americans were drawn not to Levittown, but to Berkeley, the Haight-Ashbury and the East Village. Traditional political ideologies and cultural myths, sexual mores and sex roles with them, began to disintegrate in an explosion of rebellion and protest.

The three major groups which make up the new women's movement—working women, middle class married women and students—bring very different kinds of interests and objectives to women's liberation. Working women are most concerned with the economic issues of guaranteed employment, fair wages, job discrimination and child care. Their most immediate oppression is rooted in industrial capitalism and felt directly through the vicissitudes of an exploitative labor market.

Middle class women, oppressed by the psychological mutilation and injustice of institutionalized segregation, discrimination and imposed inferiority, are most sensitive to the dehumanizing consequences of severely limited lives. Usually well educated and capable, these women are rebelling against being forced to trivialize their lives, to live vicariously through husbands and children.

Students, as unmarried middle class girls, have been most sensitized to the sexual exploitation of women. They have experienced the frustration of one-way relationships in which the girl is forced into a "wife" and companion role with none of the supposed benefits of marriage. Young women have increasingly rebelled not only against passivity and dependency in their relationships but also against the notion that they must function as sexual objects, being defined in purely sexual rather than human terms, and being forced to package and sell themselves as commodities on the sex market.

Each group represents an independent aspect of the total institutionalized oppression of women. Their differences are those of emphasis and immediate interest rather than of fundamental goals. All women suffer from economic exploitation, from psychological deprivation, and from exploitive sexuality. Within women's liberation there is a growing understanding that the common oppression of women provides the basis for uniting across class and race lines to form a powerful and radical movement.

Racism and Male Supremacy

Clearly, for the liberation of women to become a reality it is necessary to destroy the ideology of male supremacy which asserts the biological and social inferiority of women in order to justify massive institutionalized oppression. Yet we all know that many women are as loud in their disavowal of this oppression as are the men who chant the litany of "a woman's place is in the home and behind her man." In fact, women are as trapped in their false consciousness as were the mass of blacks 20 years ago, and for much the same reason.

As blacks were defined and limited socially by their color, so women are defined and limited by their sex. While blacks, it was argued, were preordained by God or nature, or both, to be hewers of wood and drawers of water, so women are destined to bear and rear children, and to sustain their husbands with obedience and compassion. The Sky-God tramples through the heavens and the Earth/Mother-Goddess is always flat on her back with legs spread, putting out for one and all.

Indeed, the phenomenon of male chauvinism can only be understood when it is perceived as a form of racism, based on stereotypes drawn from a deep belief in the biological inferiority of women. The so-called "black analogy" is no analogy at all; it is the same social process that is at work, a process which both justifies and helps perpetuate the exploitation of one group of human beings by another.

The very stereotypes that express the society's belief in the biological inferiority of women recall the images used to justify the oppression of blacks. The nature of women, like that of slaves, is depicted as dependent, incapable of reasoned thought, childlike in its simplicity and warmth, martyred in the role of mother, and mystical in the role of sexual partner. In its benevolent form, the inferior position of women results in paternalism; in its malevolent form, a domestic tyranny which can be unbelievably brutal.

It has taken over 50 years to discredit the scientific and social "proof" which once gave legitimacy to the myths of black racial inferiority. Today most people can see that the theory of the genetic inferiority of blacks is absurd. Yet few are shocked by the fact that scientists are still busy "proving" the biological inferiority of women.

In recent years, in which blacks have led the struggle for liberation, the emphasis on racism has focused only upon racism against blacks. The fact that "racism" has been practiced against many groups other than blacks has been pushed into the background. Indeed, a less forceful but more accurate term for the phenomenon would be "social Darwinism." It was the opinion of the social Darwinists that in the natural course of things the "fit" succeed (i.e. oppress) and the "unfit" (i.e. the biologically inferior) sink to the bottom. According to this view, the very fact of a group's oppression proves its inferiority and the inevitable correctness of its low position. In this way each successive immigrant group coming to America was decked out in the garments of "racial" or biological inferiority until the group was sufficiently assimilated, whereupon Anglo-Saxon venom would turn on a new group filling up the space at the bottom. Now two groups remain, neither of which has been assimilated according to the classic American pattern: the "visibles"—blacks and women. It is equally true for both: "it won't wear off."

Yet the greatest obstacle facing those who would organize women remains women's belief in their own inferiority. Just as all subject populations are controlled by their acceptance of the rightness of their own status, so women remain subject because they believe in the rightness of their own oppression. This dilemma is not a fortuitous one, for the entire society is geared to socialize women to believe in and adopt as immutable necessity their traditional and inferior role. From earliest training to the grave, women are constrained and propagandized. Spend an evening at the movies or watching television, and you will see a grotesque figure called woman presented in a hundred variations upon the themes of "children, church, kitchen" or "the chick sexpot."

For those who believe in the "rights of mankind," the "dignity of man," consider that to make a woman a person, a human being in her own right, you would have to change her sex: imagine Stokely Carmichael "prone and silent"; imagine Mark Rudd as a Laugh-In-girl; picture Rennie Davis as Miss America. Such contradictions as these show how pervasive and deep-rooted is the cultural contempt for women, how difficult it is to imagine a woman as a serious human being, or conversely, how empty and degrading is the image of woman that floods the culture.

Countless studies have shown that black acceptance of white stereotypes leads to mutilated identity, to alienation, to rage and self-hatred. Human beings cannot bear in their own hearts the contradictions of those who hold them in contempt. The ideology of male supremacy and its effect upon women merits as serious study as has been given to the effects of prejudice upon Jews, blacks, and immigrant groups.

It is customary to shame those who would draw the parallel between women and blacks by a great show of concern and chest beating over the suffering of black people. Yet this response itself reveals a refined combination of white middle class guilt and male chauvinism, for it overlooks several essential facts. For example, the most oppressed group within the feminine population is made up of black women, many of whom take a dim view of the black male intellectual's adoption of white male attitudes of sexual superiority (an irony too cruel to require comment). Neither are those who make this pious objection to the racial parallel addressing themselves very adequately to the millions of white working class women living at the poverty level, who are not likely to be moved by this middle class guilt-ridden one-upmanship while having to deal with the boss, the factory, or the welfare worker day after day. They are already dangerously resentful of the gains made by blacks, and much of their "racist backlash" stems from the fact that they have been forgotten in the push for social change. Emphasis on the real mechanisms of oppression—on the commonality of the process—is essential lest groups such as these, which would work in alliance, become divided against one another.

White middle class males already struggling with the acknowledgment of their own racism do not relish an added burden of recognition: that to white guilt must soon be added "male." It is therefore understandable that they should refuse to see the harshness of the lives of most women—to honestly face the facts of massive institutionalized discrimination against women. Witness the performance to date: "Take her down off the platform and give her a good f--k," "Petty Bourgeois Revisionist Running Dogs," or in the classic words of a Berkeley male "leader," "Let them eat c--k."

Among whites, women remain the most oppressed—and the most unorganized—group. Although they constitute a potential mass base for the radical movement, in terms of movement priorities they are ignored; indeed they might as well be invisible. Far from being an accident, this omission is a direct outgrowth of the solid male supremist beliefs of white radical and left-liberal men. Even now, faced with both fact and agitation, leftist men find the idea of placing any serious priority upon women so outrageous, such a degrading notion, that they respond with a virulence far out of proportion to the modest requests of movement women. This only shows that women must stop wasting their time worrying about the chauvinism of men in the movement and focus instead on their real priority: organizing women.

Marriage: Genesis of Women's Rebellion

The institution of marriage is the chief vehicle for the perpetuation of the oppression of women; it is through the role of wife that the subjugation of women is maintained. In a very real way the role of wife has been the genesis of women's rebellion throughout history.

Looking at marriage from a detached point of view one may well ask why anyone gets married, much less women. One answer lies in the economics of women's position, for women are so occupationally limited that drudgery in the home is considered to be infinitely superior to drudgery in the factory. Secondly, women themselves have no independent social status. Indeed, there is no clearer index of the social worth of a woman in this society than the fact that she has none in her own right. A woman is first defined by the man to whom she is attached, but more particularly by the man she marries, and secondly by the children she bears and rears—hence the anxiety over sexual attractiveness, the frantic scramble for boyfriends and husbands. Having obtained and married a man the race is then on to have children, in order that their attractiveness and accomplishments may add more social worth. In a woman, not having children is seen as an incapacity somewhat akin to impotence in a man.

Beneath all of the pressures of the sexual marketplace and the marital status game, however, there is a far more sinister organization of economic exploitation and psychological mutilation. The housewife role, usually defined in terms of the biological duty of a woman to reproduce and her "innate" suitability for a nurturant and companionship role, is actually crucial to industrial capitalism in an advanced state of technological development. In fact, the housewife (some 44 million women of all classes, ethnic groups and races) provides, unpaid, absolutely essential services and labor. In turn, her assumption of all household duties makes it possible for the man to spend the majority of his time at the workplace.

It is important to understand the social and economic exploitation of the married woman, since the real productivity of her labor is denied by the commonly held assumption that she is dependent on her husband, exchanging her keep for emotional and nurturant services. Margaret Benston, a radical women's liberation leader, points out: "In sheer quantity, household labor, including child care, constitutes a huge amount of socially necessary production. Nevertheless, in a society based on commodity production, it is not usually considered even as 'real work' since it is outside of trade and the marketplace. This assignment of household work as the function of a special category 'women' means that this group *does* stand in a different relationship to production. . . . The material basis for the inferior status of women is to be found in just this definition of women. In a society in which money determines value, women are a group who work outside the money economy. Their work is not worth money, is therefore valueless, is therefore not even real work. And women themselves, who do this valueless work, can hardly be expected to be worth as much as men, who work for money."

Women are essential to the economy not only as free labor, but also as consumers. The American system of capitalism depends for its survival on the consumption of vast amounts of socially wasteful goods, and a prime target for the unloading of this waste is the housewife. She is the purchasing agent for the family, but beyond that she is eager to buy because her own identity depends on her accomplishments as a consumer and her ability to satisfy the wants of her husband and children. This is not, of course, to say that she has any power in the economy. Although she spends the wealth, she does not own or control it—it simply passes through her hands.

In addition to their role as housewives and consumers, increasing numbers of women are taking outside employment. These women leave the home to join an exploited labor force, only to return at night to assume the double burden of housework on top of wage work—that is, they are forced to work at two full-time jobs. No man is required or expected to take on such a burden. The result: two workers from one household in the labor force with no cutback in essential female functions—three for the price of two, quite a bargain.

Friedrich Engels, now widely read in women's liberation, argues that, regardless of her status in the larger society, within the context of the family the woman's relationship to the man is one of proletariat to bourgeoisie. One consequence of this class division in the family is to weaken the capacity of men and women oppressed by the society to struggle together against it.

In all classes and groups, the institution of marriage functions to a greater or lesser degree to oppress women; the unity of women of different classes hinges upon our understanding of that common oppression. The 19th century women's movement refused to deal with marriage and sexuality, and chose instead to fight for the vote and elevate the feminine mystique to a political ideology. That decision retarded the movement for decades. But 1969 is not 1889. For one thing, there now exist alternatives to marriage. The most original and creative politics of the women's movement has come from a direct confrontation with the issue of marriage and sexuality. The cultural revolution—experimentation with life-styles, communal living, collective child-rearing—have all come from the rebellion against dehumanized sexual relationships, against the notion of women as sexual commodities, against the constriction and spiritual strangulation inherent in the role of wife.

Lessons have been learned from the failures of the earlier movement as well. The feminine mystique is no longer mistaken for politics, nor gaining the vote for winning human rights. Women are now all together at the bottom of the work world, and the basis exists for a common focus of struggle for all women in American society. It remains for the movement to understand this, to avoid the mistakes of the past, to respond creatively to the possibilities of the present.

Women's oppression, although rooted in the institution of marriage, does not stop at the kitchen or the bedroom door. Indeed, the economic exploitation of women in the workplace is the most commonly recognized aspect of the oppression of women.

Most women who enter the labor force do not work for "pin money" or "self-fulfillment." Sixty-two per cent of all women working in 1967 were doing so out of economic need (i.e., were either alone or with husbands earning less than $5000 a year). In 1963, 36 per cent of American families had an income of less than $5000 a year. Women from these families work because they must; they contribute 35 to 40 per cent of the family's total income when working full-time, and 15 to 20 per cent when working part-time.

Despite their need, however, women have always represented the most exploited sector of the industrial labor force. Child and female labor were introduced during the early stages of industrial capitalism, at a time when most men were gainfully employed in crafts. As industrialization developed and craft jobs were eliminated, men entered the industrial labor force, driving women and children into the lowest categories of work and pay. Indeed, the position of women and children industrial workers was so pitiful, and their wages so small, that the craft unions refused to organize them. Even when women organized themselves and engaged in militant strikes and labor agitation—from the shoemakers of Lynn, Massachusetts, to the International Ladies' Garment Workers and their great strike of 1909—male unionists continued to ignore their needs. As a result of this male supremacy in the unions, women remain essentially unorganized, despite the fact that they are becoming an ever larger part of the labor force.

The trend is clearly toward increasing numbers of women entering the work force: women represented 55 per cent of the growth of the total labor force in 1962, and the number of working women rose from 16.9 million in 1957 to 24 million in 1962. There is every indication that the number of women in the labor force will continue to grow as rapidly in the future.

Job discrimination against women exists in all sectors of work, even in occupations which are predominantly made up of women. This discrimination is reinforced in the field of education, where women are being short-changed at a time when the job market demands higher educational levels. In 1962, for example, while women constituted 53 per cent of the graduating high school class, only 42 per cent of the entering college class were women. Only one in three people who received a B.A. or M.A. in that year was a woman, and only one in ten who received a Ph.D was a woman. These figures represent a decline in educational achievement for women since the 1930's, when women received two out of five of the B.A. and M.A. degrees given, and one out .

of seven of the Ph.Ds. While there has been a dramatic increase in the number of people, including women, who go to college, women have not kept pace with men in terms of educational achievement. Furthermore, women have lost ground in professional employment. In 1960 only 22 per cent of the faculty and other professional staff at colleges and universities were women—down from 28 per cent in 1949, 27 per cent in 1930, 26 per cent in 1920. 1960 does beat 1919 with only 20 per cent—"you've come a long way, baby"—right back to where you started! In other professional categories: 10 per cent of all scientists are women, 7 per cent of all physicians, 3 per cent of all lawyers, and 1 per cent of all engineers.

Chart A. Comparative Statistics for Men and Women in the Labor Force, 1960

Occupation	Percentage of working women in each occupational category	Income of year round full time workers		Numbers of workers in millions	
		Women	Men	Women	Men
Professional	13%	$4358	$7115	3	5
Managers, officials and proprietors	5	3514	7241	1	5
Clerical	31	3586	5247	7	3
Operatives	15	2970	4977	4	9
Sales	7	2389	5842	2	3
Service	15	2340	4089	3	3
Private household	10	1156	—	2	—

Sources: U.S. Department of Commerce, Bureau of the Census: "Current Population Reports," P-60, No. 37, and U.S. Department of Labor, Bureau of Labor Statistics and U.S. Department of Commerce, Bureau of the Census.

Even when women do obtain an education, in many cases it does them little good. Women, whatever their educational level, are concentrated in the lower paying occupations. The figures in Chart A tell a story that most women know and few men will admit: most women are forced to work at clerical jobs, for which they are paid, on the average, $1600 less per year than men doing the same work. Working class women in the service and operative (semi-skilled) categories, making up 30 per cent of working women, are paid $1900 less per year on the average than are men. Of all working women, only 13 per cent are professionals (including low-pay and low-status work such as teaching, nursing and social work), and they earn $2600 less per year than do professional men. Household workers, the lowest category of all, are predominantly women (over 2 million) and predominantly black and third world, earning for their labor barely over $1000 per year.

Not only are women forced onto the lowest rungs of the occupational ladder, they are in the lowest income levels as well. The most constant and bitter injustice experienced by all women is the income differential. While women might passively accept low status jobs, limited opportunities for advancement, and discrimination in the factory, office and university, they choke finally on the daily fact that the male worker next to them earns more, and usually does less. In 1965 the median wage or salary income of year-round full-time women workers was only 60 per cent that of men, a 4 per cent loss since 1955. Twenty-nine per cent of working women earned less than $3000 a year as compared with 11 per cent of the men; 43 per cent of the women earned from $3000 to $5000 a year as compared with 19 per cent of the men; and 9 per cent of the women earned $7000 or more as compared with 43 per cent of the men.

What most people do not know is that in certain respects, women suffer more than do non-white men, and that black and third world women suffer most of all.

Chart B. Median Annual Wages for Men and Women by Race, 1960

	Median Annual Wage
Males, white	$5137
Males, non-white	$3075
Females, white	$2537
Females, non-white	$1276

Sources: U.S. Department of Commerce, Bureau of the Census. Also see: President's Commission on the Status of Women, 1963.

Women, regardless of race, are more disadvantaged than are men, including non-white men. White women earn $2600 less than white men and $1500 less than non-white men. The brunt of the inequality is carried by 2.5 million non-white women, 94 per cent of whom are black. They earn $3800 less than white men, $1900 less than non-white men, and $1200 less than white women.

There is no more bitter paradox in the racism of this country than that the white man, articulating the male supremacy of the white male middle class, should provide the rationale for the oppression of black women by black men. Black women constitute the largest minority in the United States, and they are the most disadvantaged group in the labor force. The further oppression of black women will not liberate

black men, for black women were never the oppressors of their men—
that is a myth of the liberal white man. The oppression of black men
comes from institutionalized racism and economic exploitation: from
the world of the white man. Consider the following facts and figures.

The percentage of black working women has always been propor-
tionately greater than that of white women. In 1900, 41 per cent of
black women were employed, as compared to 17 per cent for white
women. In 1963, the proportion of black women employed was still a
fourth greater than that of whites. In 1960, 44 per cent of black married
women with children under six years were in the labor force, in contrast
to 29 per cent for white women. While job competition requires ever
higher levels of education, the bulk of illiterate women are black. On
the whole, black women—who often have the greatest need for employment—are the most discriminated against in terms of opportunity.
Forced by an oppressive and racist society to carry unbelievably heavy
economic and social burdens, black women stand at the bottom of that
society, doubly marked by the caste signs of color and sex.

The rise of new agitation for the occupational equality of women
also coincided with the re-entry of the "lost generation"—the housewives of the 1950's—into the job market. Women from middle class
backgrounds, faced with an "empty nest" (children grown or in school)
and a widowed or divorced rate of one-fourth to one-third of all marriages, returned to the workplace in large numbers. But once there they
discovered that women, middle class or otherwise, are the last hired, the
lowest paid, the least often promoted, and the first fired. Furthermore,
women are more likely to suffer job discrimination on the basis of age,
so the widowed and divorced suffer particularly, even though their
economic need to work is often urgent. Age discrimination also means
that the option of work after child-rearing is limited. Even highly
qualified older women find themselves forced into low-paid, unskilled or
semi-skilled work—if they are lucky enough to find a job in the first
place.

The realities of the work world for most middle class women—that
they become members of the working class, like it or not—are under-
standably distant to many young men and women in college who have
never had to work, and who tend to think of the industrial "proletariat"
as a revolutionary force, to the exclusion of "bourgeois" working
women. Their image of the "pampered middle class woman" is factually
incorrect and politically naive. It is middle class women forced into
working class life who are often the first to become conscious of the
contradiction between the "American Dream" and their daily experience.

Faced with discrimination on the job—after being forced into the
lower levels of the occupational structure—millions of women are

inescapably presented with the fundamental contradictions in their unequal treatment and their massive exploitation. The rapid growth of women's liberation as a movement is related in part to the exploitation of working women in all occupational categories.

Male supremacy, marriage, and the structure of wage labor—each of these aspects of women's oppression has been crucial to the resurgence of the women's struggle. It must be abundantly clear that radical social change must occur before there can be significant improvement in the social position of women. Some form of socialism is a minimum requirement, considering the changes that must come in the institutions of marriage and the family alone. The intrinsic radicalism of the struggle for women's liberation necessarily links women with all other oppressed groups.

The heart of the movement, as in all freedom movements, rests in women's knowledge, whether articulated or still only an illness without a name, that they are not inferior—not chicks, nor bunnies, nor quail, nor cows, nor bitches, nor ass, nor meat. Women hear the litany of their own dehumanization each day. Yet all the same, women know that male supremacy is a lie. They know they are not animals or sexual objects or commodities. They know their lives are mutilated, because they see within themselves a promise of creativity and personal integration. Feeling the contradiction between the essentially creative and self-actualizing human being within her, and the cruel and degrading less-than-human role she is compelled to play, a woman begins to perceive the falseness of what her society has forced her to be. And once she perceives this, she knows that she must fight.

Women must learn the meaning of rage, the violence that liberates the human spirit. The rhetoric of invective is an equally essential stage, for in discovering and venting their rage against the enemy—and the enemy in everyday life is men—women also experience the justice of their own violence. They learn the first lessons in their own latent strength. Women must learn to know themselves as revolutionaries. They must become hard and strong in their determination, while retaining their humanity and tenderness.

There is a rage that impels women into a total commitment to women's liberation. That ferocity stems from a denial of mutilation; it is a cry for life, a cry for the liberation of the spirit. Roxanne Dunbar, surely one of the most impressive women in the movement, conveys the feelings of many: "We are damaged—we women, we oppressed, we disinherited. There are very few who are not damaged, and they rule. . . . The oppressed trust those who rule more than they trust themselves, because self-contempt emerges from powerlessness. Anyway, few oppressed people believe that life could be much different. . . . We are damaged and we have the right to hate and have contempt and to kill and to scream. But for what? . . . Do we want the oppressor to admit he is wrong, to withdraw his misuse of us? He is only too happy to admit guilt—then do nothing but try to absorb and exorcize the new thought. . . . That does not make up for what I have lost, what I never had, and what all those others who are worse off than I never had. . . . Nothing will compensate for the irreparable harm it has done to my sisters. . . . How could we possibly settle for anything remotely less, even take a crumb in the meantime less, than total annihilation of a system which systematically destroys half its people. . . ."

I Am Furious (Female)

Ellen Cantarow, Elizabeth Diggs, Katherine Ellis, Janet Marx, Lillian Robinson, and Muriel Schien

In 1969, when this paper was written, Elizabeth Diggs, Katherine Ellis, Janet Marx, Lillian Robinson, and Muriel Schien were members of the Women's Caucus of the Columbia University chapter of the New University Conference (NUC). All were graduate students and/or teachers at Columbia. Ellen Cantarow, an NUC member from Harvard University and a participant in Bread and Roses (a Boston women's liberation group) was invited to join in this attempt to formulate a women's perspective for NUC. Now, Ellen and Lillian are with Bread and Roses, Kate and Liz are working with the women's unions in New York, and Janet is in a commune in British Columbia.

. . . . though both
Not equal, as their sex not equal seemed;
For contemplation he, and valour formed,
For softness she and sweet attractive grace;
He for God only, she for God in him.

      Milton, *Paradise Lost,* IV (295 *ff*)

The ultimate goal of a radical women's movement must be revolution. This is because the condition of female oppression does not "depend on," is not "the product of," is not "integral to" the structure of society; it *is* that structure. The oppression of women, though similar to that of blacks, differs from it in that it depends not on class division of labor premised on private property and resulting in the family as primary unit for the functioning of the economy. "The modern family," says Marx, "contains in embryo not only slavery . . . but serfdom also, since from the very beginning it is connected with agricultural services. It contains within itself in miniature all the antagonisms which later develop on a wide scale within society and its state." (Quoted in Engels, *The Origin of the Family, Private Property, and the State.*)

Engels, moreover, explains that "the word familia did not originally signify the ideal of our modern philistine, which is a compound of sentimentality and domestic discord."

Among the early Romans it referred to the totality of slaves

This essay began as an attempt to formulate perspectives for the Women's Caucus of the New University Conference.

belonging to one individual and then became incorporated in a legal term to describe "a new social organism, the head of which had under him wife and children and a number of slaves." (Ibid.) Engels notes as well that the shift of inheritance from female to male lineage among the Shawnees, Miami and Delaware Indians, involved a mere semantic change in legal phraseology.

We begin with such allusions because they illustrate that the enslavement of women, like any social phenomenon, is a cultural and not a divinely arbitrated fact, proceeding by small, mundane human acts. The beginning of radical consciousness is recognizing cultural development for what it is. That it is the product of human history and not of cataclysm or immutable law means that it is within our power to understand it without bowing meekly before it. It is the revolutionary's task to seize those realities he has understood as oppressive, and to dare to change them.

Labor and Work—The American Way

The conditions of female servitude prevail today, and remain, in miniature, the basis for, if not the exact embodiment of, the contradictions that divide all of us in order to preserve the smooth functioning of the system. IBM, General Motors, and our corporate universities depend on a highly mobile and docile labor force for their perpetuation and furthering. They own men—that is, they set down rules regulating men's labor and thereby the structure of their lives. In turn the structure of men's lives determines what women's lives will be. A woman, once married, goes where her husband goes. Whether or not she herself holds a job, it is understood that her real and legitimate vocation is child-rearing. The mythology that society has constructed to make female subjection a positive good is massive and profoundly rooted. In America, this has been carried to the point of cultural hyperbole; for the first time in human history motherhood has become a full-time, 12 to 14 hour a day occupation. This development is in fact extremely recent, having occurred only since the Second World War.

According to Marx, there are two modes of productivity: labor and work. Labor is activity that renews itself cyclically—daily, monthly, or yearly. All janitorial, maintenance, secretarial and assembly-line work is included here. In a capitalist society, labor is always alienated. Work, by contrast, is activity that involves mental creation. Its results are public, whereas those of labor are private. The work of politics, art, and science involves the public employment of the mind's resources. Since it is an individual expression, work fulfills individual identity, but its ultimate use is public. Labor is needed for survival, and physical survival depends on essentially private activity. One must care for one's body, wash, comb it, feed it, wipe it, if one is to survive.

In capitalist society, the activities considered to be woman's realm fall into the sphere of labor. Woman is seen as the modern "expert" in matters having to do with caring for children and servicing the family's environment. She is increasingly denied existence in the realm of work, for she is chained to male preconceptions of her being as essentially physical. Man conceives of woman primarily as a sexual object: she is the means by which the species reproduces itself. Therefore it is her *a priori* duty to subjugate all impulses towards public action to the interests of private labor in the home.

Marx observes that "the proletarians, if they are to achieve recognition as persons, will be obliged to abolish their own former conditions of existence, which are at the same time those of society as a whole, that is, to abolish labour. They are consequently in direct opposition to the State as their collective expression, and in order to develop as persons they must overthrow the State." (*German Ideology*). This analysis is particularly relevant to women because we are oppressed in two ways, according to class, and according to sex. In order to abolish the conditions of our existence which oppress us (and prevent us from developing as persons) we must recognize specific institutions and prejudices that must be overcome.

The Angel in the House

The division of labor between male and female, food-getting versus housekeeping and childcare, is nearly universal and has appeared in all cultures and all ages. This traditional division of labor was based on biological differences between males and females. Pregnancy and nursing made the female ill-adapted for the hardships of the food-quest. Since children depend on adults for education and sustenance for at least thirteen years, it was efficient for the female to take care of them. Further, primitive technology and the difficulties of food-preparation made household chores a full-time activity.

This is not to say that females have never participated in food-getting or males in childcare. There are many societies in which women till fields and men take part in child-rearing. However, the ideals of behavior and the value-systems still tend to uphold the primal separation of functions, whatever the social realities. They do this in the form of archetypes of masculinity and femininity which say that females should not have to work and are better suited to stay at home, and that males should not have to stay at home and are better suited to work outside the home. The reality is that in the United States the traditional division of labor is an anachronism. Pregnancy no longer means that the female is exceptionally vulnerable and unable to work. From the age of six on, children are now cared for and socialized by formal educational institutions. Changes in the technology of housekeeping and in the transportation and preparation of food mean that household care is no longer a time-consuming task.

As long as a woman's time is subject to the demands of others, she is not free even in the most minimal sense. A man's time is not entirely his own either, since eight hours belong to his employer, but however degrading his servitude may be, it ends after eight hours. For a woman, on the other hand, the demands of others define her every waking moment. Her energy is channeled into a narrow round of activities which must be endlessly repeated in order to produce no change whatsoever.

The effectiveness of this full-time conditioning is difficult to exaggerate. Years of preparation have preceded it. From puberty on, girls are encouraged to make use of the "freedom" they have in order to prepare themselves for a future in which they will no longer want it. A woman who cannot or will not make this surrender of her time and energy forfeits the right of her caste and becomes, quite literally, untouchable. This is the price she pays for being an "unproductive" member of society, a fact which makes it clear that, despite the prevalence of Virginia Slims and other signs of the times, the realm of female productivity is limited to the most socially useful product of all.

Yet society provides women with many socially acceptable means of self-fulfillment. Achievement in any of these activities is enthusiastically praised and a woman who seeks self-realization through them is complacently patronized as "creative," "enterprising," "vital." These acceptable activities include all kinds of work that can be done in isolation, such as writing, painting, and music, as well as the "arts and crafts" activities such as potting, weaving, sewing and making hand-printed place mats and Christmas cards. It becomes obvious at once that these occupations have several things in common: 1) they are solitary, and can therefore be performed in the home; 2) they are recognized as being activities that release frustrations by channeling the human need to be productive and creative; 3) they fall within the framework of traditionally "feminine" activities because they imply and affirm sensitivity, introspection, and emotional expression rather than the rationality, intellectual rigor, and the precision implied by traditionally "male" activities.

What is the larger social function of these activities? Most important, they perpetuate the status quo by stabilizing the function and position of woman in society. Any frustrations she may feel are co-opted if she can express them in these accepted ways. The heretical alternative is for woman to assert herself in the male world, the public world, in which fulfillment involves communication, social inter-change, self-assertion (i.e. aggression, undoubtedly the most unacceptable trait in a female), and implies the exercise of the masculine traits of organizational ability, rational analysis, and the application of theory to practice.

The extent to which male and female activities have been separated and classified according to sex is demonstrated by the fact that a man can take part in traditionally feminine activities only at the cost of diminishing his masculine image. Interior decorators, dress designers, art critics, etc., are automatically classified as "faggots." Even men who like ballet or classical music are considered suspect and usually compensate for any such demoralizing affinities by loudly proclaiming their prowess in more acceptable areas such as hunting or sports. And what would be the "image" of a man who chose to stay at home and care for his home and children?

In pre-supermarket times, the woman played a key role in the survival of those who depended on her to preserve the food that kept them alive. Her energy was channeled but she knew she was indispensable. Women today are no more than custodians of consumer goods, vacuuming the latest thing in wall-to-wall carpeting with the latest thing in vacuum cleaners. People don't need her any more, but those ugly stains on the kitchen sink require her constant vigilance. Objective conditions—dirty dishes, children's clutter, cavities, clean clothes every day for everyone—combine with the pressures generated by advertising (for whiter washes, softer hands, streak-free windows, odorless armpits) to wear women down to a point where change becomes literally inconceivable.

Until this is changed, there will be no revolution.

Consumerism serves as an agent of sexual oppression, and thus of counter-revolution, in that it seeks to tie the totality of women's energies to the care of products through which she is supposed to feel "fulfilled." She feels fulfilled when she looks at herself in the mirror and sees that those grey hairs have vanished. She feels fulfilled when the kids go off to school in their tumble-dried clothes and come home with fewer cavities. She feels this way because she has been too tired for too long (what is boredom, after all, but a symptom of repression?) to do anything other than what she is told by those who control her time.

Revolution will not take place until women reject and redefine their position in a society that must keep them under control by directing their search for fulfillment into the inexhaustible realm of consumption. Nothing could be more beneficial to a profit-based economy than a large population whose sole measure of its own worth lies in internalizing the concept of "marketable goods." It pays to keep the little woman alone at home with her children, visiting and being visited by other women against whom she can measure her "progress" by the yardstick of accumulation. What keeps her here is the sense of power she derives from her position in the family, the sense that it is she and she alone who teaches the children to brush after every meal, she and she alone whose market preferences determine what is on the super-market shelf, she and she alone who feeds them their portion of "culture," she and she alone who can have babies. And for this she is exalted above the God who makes a tree. Who could ask for anything more?

Not she, that's for sure. Not when everything she associated with "becoming a woman" fills her with gratitude toward her oppressors. What has she done to deserve all these things? Her husband even washes the dishes for her sometimes, and takes the kids to the park on Saturdays so that she can do her hair and her nails in peace. What will it take to turn her against those who exploit her by offering, for no money down, all the things through which she has been taught to find her fulfillment? What is it that a liberated, post-revolutionary society must offer in their stead? Our goal must be to rediscover our real needs now, if in fact we have ever known what they are, and make these the basis of actions that would serve as a model for the movement as a whole.

Stabilizing the System: Civilization and Its Discontents

Discussion of objective economic and social conditions implies collective solutions to social problems. However, capitalism both causes and feeds on alienation, a false consciousness of individuality. For women, the situation is underlined by isolation and fragmentation in our lives as workers—whether at home or on the job. Economic forces are bolstered by cultural forces that serve to stabilize the system of oppression. Both religion and psychoanalysis, for instance, function to co-opt the energies of women and reconcile them to the status quo.

Religion provides a complete mythological framework to explain the oppression of women. In the Judeo-Christian myth of creation, Eve was made from nothing more than Adam's rib, and then revealed her true colors by committing the First Sin and condemning man to eternal damnation beyond the walls of Eden. In the myth of Adam and Eve are contained the seeds for every theory of the degradation and moral corruption of women. Orthodox Jews thank God every morning that they were born men instead of women. In Jewish practice, women are segregated from men in public worship and do not even qualify as people in making up the necessary *minyan* of ten worshippers required to establish a congregation or hold a religious service. For centuries the Christian church has seen women as an embodiment of the sins of the flesh. Women are a temptation to men to abandon "higher" pursuits and principles for corrupting pleasures. Any men of real integrity and strength of character must shun the corrupting influence of women. The most obvious example of this attitude is that in the Catholic Church, priests, representing the highest earthly calling for men, must remain celibate. Priests were teachers and politicians as well as religious leaders, and the laws that were created in Western Christian countries reflected their view of women as a debased species of humanity. The best known (but not the most extreme) expression of the Christian attitude comes from St. Paul, who reluctantly conceded that women were necessary for the propagation of the species and saw this as the beginning and end of their right to existence. He counsels both men and women to remain celibate if possible, "but if they cannot contain, let them marry, for it is better to marry than to burn" (1 Corinthians, VII, 9) "But if thou marry, thou hast not sinned: and if a virgin marry, she hath not sinned. Nevertheless, such shall have trouble in the flesh; but I spare you."

Christianity, a religion founded on paradox, also contains a tradition that is the converse of this one, centering on the mystification of female chastity. Medieval Mariolatry is but one symptom of a long-standing condition that endows female virtue with mysterious powers of purification and edification. Obviously, the myth of "moral" superiority (consisting in keeping one's legs crossed) is as much a weapon to keep women from realizing themselves in society as the myth of degradation.

Women's work in connection with the church has become increasingly less socially oriented as women's function in the larger society has become less necessary. At one time, the church was an integral part of society—often, indeed, its social and political as well as religious center. Its activities were fundamental to the functioning of the community, and women did work for the church which was needed in the community and they were therefore involved in meaningful ways with it. They ran schools and taught in them; they worked as visiting nurses, bringing medicine, food and comfort to the sick; they offered advice on personal and medical problems; they ran orphanages and provided the same purposes as the modern social worker. Now, these functions are performed by professionals who, although they are often women, are not part of the communities they serve; and married women are not expected to be a permanent part of these professions.

As the traditional and necessary services have been taken over from the church, women in church and synagogue groups have not had work of real social significance to replace their former tasks. They organize bazaars and fairs at which they sell their hand-made matchbook covers, crocheted baby blankets, and patchwork quilts. The proceeds are then contributed to the organ fund or perhaps used to buy an automatic coffee machine for the ladies to use at church functions. In this way, the energies of the women are completely contained within the institution of the church itself, and the church has become more and more a self-contained unit rather than a center from which socially significant activities radiate into the larger society. Just as the world of the house-wife has contracted to include finally only her nuclear family unit, so the role of the churchwoman has contracted to include only the church and its members, almost isolated from the outside world. Conversely, the church itself is increasingly identified as a "feminine" activity, to which it is suspect for a man to give real attention, and thus, "like a woman," it too is trivialized.

The prevalence of psychotherapy in American life is another force working to stabilize oppression by reconciling women to their condition. (And the clientele of psychiatry *is* largely female). All of us—women in particular—are encouraged to believe that our individual "hang-ups," although they are the results of objective social conditions, are to be treated as isolated, idiosyncratic cases. Liberation is defined as freedom from these "hang-ups," but all too often is interpreted as adjustment to the status quo. Freedom from guilt about sexual activity reverses the mystique of female chastity, but equates erotic pleasure with human self-realization. What the "Sexual Revolution" has actually done is to establish a new bartering system, on the premise that one kind of free-dom can only be won at the sacrifice of another; fulfillment "as a woman" (orgasm, childbearing, motherhood) is made from fulfillment as a person.

In America, psychiatry continues to rely upon a Freudian model of sexual relationships, which means definition of women's behavior in terms of penis envy. All female children, Freud claims, are destined to make the "momentous discovery" that they are naturally inferior to males because they lack a penis. (*Some Psychic Consequences of the Anatomical Distinction Between the Sexes.*) It is women's sense of being born castrated that makes them wish to do things that require exercise of "masculine" aggressivity. To Freud, our actions have only form, not content, so it does not matter what goals a woman is working for. It is the *fact* of her "competitiveness" that demonstrates her penis envy. A little girl might, of course, wish she were a boy because it seems to her that boys and men have better lives than girls and women. For her, the possession of a penis might symbolize that better life and not vice versa. But Freud rationalizes this by maintaining that female attempts to take issue with his theory are only further demonstrations of the castration complex.

A great many of the highest human pursuits require use of what Freud considers "masculine" qualities. A woman who competes in these areas is said to be sacrificing her "femininity" in a very concrete form, by lessening her capacity for a fully mature (that is, vaginal) sex life. To Freud's mind, the clitoris is a truncated masculine organ, and concentration on it as center of erotic satisfaction is immature, because it indulges the castration complex. An adult woman, one who accepts her role, has her sexual pleasure centered in the vagina, and experiences vaginal orgasm, a much "better" form of expression. From which it "follows" that if a woman displays penis envy in her social actions, she will endanger her chances for mature sexual fulfillment. (Q.E.D.)

The trouble is that no one knows what a vaginal orgasm *is:* physiologists cannot detect it, Freudians cannot describe it except by theological analogy. Psychoanalytic theory thus provides one more mythology to sweeten oppression. Isolde, extrapolated, is the Clairol girl. Only her hairdresser knows for sure. Not even the Clairol girl knows. Is there or isn't there a vaginal orgasm? And whose task is it to determine (if such a thing in fact can be determined) whether or not it exists? Enlightened liberal, post-Freudian men (hotly) contend that it does and that their manhood depends on revealing to woman this chief pleasure of her basic function. Most women do not know and, accepting the evidence of others for it, are enslaved.

While encouraging women to live a fully mature sex life, Freud would also question our fitness for a broader range of human experience, not only because we should eschew self-assertive competition, but also because we cannot maintain a moral standard established for men. Freud suggests that "for women the level of what is ethically normal is different from what it is in men." (*Some Psychic Consequences.*) His reasoning is that in boys the Oedipus complex is destroyed by the castration complex. This means that girls lack the incentive to destroy the Oedipus complex, with devastating results:

> Their super-ego is never so inexorable, so impersonal, so independent of its emotional origins, as we find it in men. Character traits which critics of every epoch have brought up against women—that they show less sense of justice than men, that they are less ready to submit to the great exigencies of life, that they are more often influenced in their judgments by feelings of affection or hostility—all these would be amply accounted for by the modification in the formation of the super-ego which we have inferred above. We must not allow ourselves to be deflected from such conclusions by the denials of the feminists who are anxious to force us to regard the two sexes as completely equal in position and worth; but we shall, of course, willingly agree that the

majority of men are also far behind the masculine ideal and that all human individuals, as a result of their bisexual disposition and of cross-inheritance, combine in themselves both masculine and feminine characteristics, so that pure masculinity and femininity remain theoretical constructions of uncertain content. (Ibid.)

Here again, as in the case of possible feminist objections to his analysis of penis envy, Freud puts into operation a kind of psychic "uncertainty principle" intended to discredit disagreement. For if we point out that many women are no more unjust or emotional than many men, a Freudian can always fall back on the master's notion of our bisexuality; the important thing to remember is that the weaker side, the one functioning on the lower ethical level, is the feminine one, so that a woman's strengths come from the masculine admixture in her personality, while a man's flaws are from the presence of feminine traits in his.[1]

The Freudian myth of the vaginal orgasm, empirically undetectable and described in the language not only of self-annihilation but of submission, is itself an oppressive device. Similarly, the mystifications of science are used by Freudians to reinforce conventional beliefs and to solidify, to justify, the oppressive treatment of women. Psychoanalysis offers a philosophical system that makes a virtue of barbaric conventions. And the psychiatric bias of our culture pits even non-Freudian therapy against collective struggle to change the social conditions that inform our individual pathologies.

Sex and Sexuality: Notes Towards a Supreme Fiction

In a Freud-dominated culture, we are freer to enjoy sex, but jeopardize our capacity for enjoyment if we try to do anything else as well. Which may explain why the Sexual Revolution is not only a failure, but is neither essentially sexual nor a revolution. Often, in fact, it serves a counter-revolutionary function, for to perpetuate oppression, society has made of female sex identity either a construct of elaborate myth and mystification, or a bawdy joke. Women's bodies have long and continuously been defined by men as playthings: play, as distinguished from work, is unserious, even frivolous, and therefore (to complete the syllogism) so are women. Thus, by masculine, self-interested definition, as well as by the child-bearing function, we are reduced to a physicality. For one group of people so to enslave another, so to rob them of the

---

[1] This material is expanded in Lillian S. Robinson, *Who's Afraid of a Room of One's Own? Ripsaw* #4.

possibilities of a full and untrammeled awareness of their human potentials, talents and capacities, is outrage of the profoundest sort. The reason people smile when the phrases "women's movement" or "women's liberation" are voiced is because they have accepted such a reification as natural and unquestionable. Comedy, says Bergson, depends on robbing human beings of full control over their physical circumstances: surely this works in the case of woman, on whom the bitterest cultural joke of all time has been played. If our brothers in "The Movement" smile when we talk about women's liberation, they are quite simply accepting and perpetuating the reification society practices most continually and profoundly on women, but finally on us all.

The objective locus of our oppression having been made our very bodies, our movement must necessarily differ from the American radical movement to date. The reason that Women's Liberation can serve as a model (indeed, as the basis) for a revolutionary movement is that we have no choice *but* to consider the most basic fact of the most elemental oppression of all: our bodies, whose enslavement depends on the mystification built up around them. As long as women's bodies are not theirs to control, such myths will be used to perpetuate the servitude.

We may say that the single most important goal for a women's movement is the control by women of their own bodies. This does not mean free f---ing, for free f---ing is simply a more enlightened form of the old snare: it is Freudian pseudo-liberation. The phrase "to control one's own body" is most largely symbolic, and means control over all areas of our lives, since all the conditions of our servitude proceed from the false physical premise. What we are saying is that at such time as we control our physical destinies, we also will be able to enjoy a full work identity as well.

Towards a Radical Women's Movement

No one knows what female nature really is. What are "feminine" characteristics? Is there any scientific reason to associate female qualities with weakness, dishonesty, stupidity and mindless labor except for the fact that male domination has forced women into centuries of humiliation? These qualities are not male or female, but qualities of the oppressed. White male imperialism has always had its eager white male intellectuals to create lies justifying the "inferiority" of oppressed peoples. Because labor is necessary to human survival, yet by its very nature alienating in a capitalist society, it is relegated to "inferior" types—Third World peoples, blacks, and women. This leaves the realm of work as the unchallenged realm of white males, whether they be right

or left wing in political persuasion. But work necessary to human fulfillment; this is the essence of the black liberation struggle. We don't want
a piece of the capitalist pie; we don't want to be integrated into a system
that offers us little beyond the labor awaiting us in the nuclear family or
the system. Rather, we want freedom to realize our identities as women
and as individuals. This freedom, for us and for blacks, can come only
through transforming the white male economic system.

The transformation of society which women's liberation movements are seeking is more far-reaching than merely overthrowing capitalism and establishing socialism in its place. Before capitalism existed,
oppression of slaves and women formed the economic basis for society.
Slavery has been expanded to de facto apartheid and imperialism by
capitalist societies. Women have been systematically made empty,
commercial products whose sole human function is to flatter, feed and
f--- the imperialist white male. Not only must the distribution of
wealth be made just, but also distribution of labor: property-based
relationships between the sexes result in the oppression of women. If
female oppression is incorporated into the "revolutionary" state, fundamental abuses of capitalism reassert themselves. Any revolution based
on male chauvinism is doomed to failure, as is any revolution based on
racism. The untapped revolutionary potential of this country (the
untapped hatred for the white men who run the society) resides in
women.

Obviously, women's liberation movements do not cite the male
per se as the enemy. For "to treat comrades like enemies is to go over to
the side of the enemy." (Mao.) A tendency among some women's
liberation groups is to treat all men in the movement as enemies, or to
advocate "making it" professionally—a concept conceived of and dictated by men. This tendency works against women's liberation in the
long run because it means certain co-optation. But Mao's dictum works
the other way round: for men to treat women in women's liberation as
enemies is to go over to the side of the system. Male "supremacy" is in
many ways the basis of capitalism, and it is as important to the cause of
revolution in this country to root out this as it is to root out racism. Just
as blacks are the initiators of the anti-racist movement, having known its
oppression in their daily lives, so women must instigate the struggle
against male chauvinism, since they experience daily its oppressive
power. Women must realize that their own, real interest lies not only
with individual "success," but with transforming and finally overthrowing the oppressive regime. Only when struggle comes out of conscious
political self-interest can it succeed.

Many "radical" men, affirming the priority to our struggle of the
fight against racism, are annoyed when we draw an analogy between
racial and sexual oppression. No one with a sense of proportion claims

that the two evils are identical, and no one is attempting to drain the sympathy generated by one form of suffering into another form. What we do maintain is that the differences are in degree, not in kind and that male chauvinism is just as incompatible with revolutionary principles as racism.

Socialists recognize the economic basis of both black and female oppression. Not only is racial and sexual oppression coetaneous with private property, but both groups have historically *been* property themselves. Under capitalism both groups constitute a "marginal" source of cheap labor on which the system feeds. When capitalism becomes strained, both groups swell the ranks of the unemployed and the allegedly unemployable. Both are channeled into alienated labor service jobs with no intrinsic meaning and little material gain. Exploitation of both women and blacks is necessary to support the contradictions of the capitalist system, which cannot produce both profits and full employment, let alone provide meaningful work for all members of society.

The psychic consequences of economic conditions are also similar for members of both groups. For most of us, our race and our sex are unequivocal, objective facts, immediately recognizable to new acquaintances. Thus, an immediate reaction occurs, as whatever stereotypes one has about either group go into operation mechanically, without regard to whether an individual conforms to the stereotype. Self-hatred in both groups derives not from anything intrinsically inferior about us, but from the treatment we are accustomed to. For middle-class white women, that treatment takes a less ugly form—at least there are material comforts along with the degradation—but that doesn't increase respect for oneself. The self-images of both groups are defined and manipulated by the cultural media, and both are made the victims of the consumer mentality, so that capitalism exploits us at both ends of the productive process.

Women and blacks have been alienated from their own culture; they have no historical sense of themselves because study of their condition has been suppressed. We understand that our historical function has been that of pawns, but we are given no basis on which to construct any other view of what people like us have done, no tools with which to destroy the existing mythologies about ourselves. Both women and blacks are expected to perform an economic function as service workers. Thus members of both groups have been taught to be passive and to please white male masters in order to get what we want.

Unusually gifted members of an oppressed race or sex are treated as exceptional and made to feel their "superiority" to the group of which they must remain an inalienable part by virtue of an objective fact. The group is thus deprived of some of its natural leadership. Similarly, we all recognize that racial conflict between black and white workers redounds chiefly to the benefit of those who exploit labor. A racist white worker is substituting his "white skin privileges" and the sense of superiority they entail for real power. Similarly, the male chauvinism that is most blatant in the working class provides the exploiter with an immediate and permanent division in that class. Oppressed groups are thus cut off from their natural allies, as well.

Perhaps the greatest irony in the situation is that so many black men—including workers in the black liberation movement—are hostile to women's liberation. They have looked at the matriarchal history of American Negro society and blamed black women for destroying their manhood, rather than their true castrator, the white man. They have thus attempted to replace black women in their "natural," that is, oppressed, condition. But both they and the white men who reject the race-sex analogy seem to forget that more than half the black race is female and that you cannot liberate a people by keeping half of it in bondage. Black male chauvinism, supposed by many to be more tolerable on political grounds than white, is counter-revolutionary. While ignoring the potential strength of black women, it also maintains the myth of "the white man's women" as most desirable. This caters to white supremacist conceptions of the black while damaging the political power of the black movement. Even Eldridge Cleaver, who is responsible for the male chauvinist phrase "pussy power," arrives at this conclusion in *Soul on Ice*. White women are oppressed because of their sex; those who are workers are oppressed because of class and sex. Black women are oppressed because of race, sex and class. We cannot struggle for the liberation of society by tolerating, much less encouraging, the greatest injustices of the existing order.

Too much movement activity has been based on organizing about other people's needs. For instance, ERAP failed because it was founded on, if not false, at least misdirected consciousness. Although correctly recognizing and assessing the effects of an exploitative society on poor people, it incorrectly assumed that outsiders not of the same class could organize them. In many places in the country SDS is now up against the same fact. In order to build a strong and profound movement, it is the task of all of us to begin to consider the difficult realities of our own circumstances.

The revolution we seek is very far off, but we can begin to act on our ideas in our own lives, NOW. We must begin now, because we must raise consciousness in all men and women of the objective conditions of their oppression. We have formulated immediate and specific goals related to our roles as college and university students and teachers, but we must realize and remember that these "goals" are only tools, a means to the ultimate goal of real liberation for all people. The immediate aims are means of survival which will give us time and space for immediate ends. Radicals have often been confused on this point. We are so afraid of being co-opted by satisfaction of demands that *can* be met that we refuse to tempt our purity by articulating immediate goals at all. But if we trust our own ideology, we must realize that the capitalist system cannot provide justice for all.

The Political Economy of
Women's Liberation

Margaret Benston

Margaret Benston is Assistant Professor of Chemistry at Simon Fraser University in
Canada. She holds a Ph.D. from the University of Washington. She has been an
active member of the Vancouver women's movement since its beginning and a
member of the Vancouver Women's Caucus since the summer of 1968. This paper
grew out of the discussions in the Women's Caucus.

> The position of women rests, as everything in our complex society, on
> an economic base.
>
> Eleanor Marx and Edward Aveling

The "woman question" is generally ignored in analyses of the class
structure of society. This is so because, on the one hand, classes are
generally defined by their relation to the means of production and, on
the other hand, women are not supposed to have any unique relation to
the means of production. The category seems instead to cut across all
classes; one speaks of working-class women, middle-class women, etc.
The status of women is clearly inferior to that of men,[1] but analysis of
this condition usually falls into discussing socialization, psychology,
interpersonal relations, or the role of marriage as a social institution.[2]
Are these, however, the primary factors? In arguing that the roots of the
secondary status of women are in fact economic, it can be shown that
women as a group do indeed have a definite relation to the means of
production and that this is different from that of men. The personal
and psychological factors then follow from this special relation to
production, and a change in the latter will be a necessary (but not
sufficient) condition for changing the former.[3] If this special relation of
women to production is accepted, the analysis of the situation of women
fits naturally into a class analysis of society.

The starting point for discussion of classes in a capitalist society is
the distinction between those who own the means of production and
those who sell their labor power for a wage. As Ernest Mandel says:

> The proletarian condition is, in a nutshell, the lack of access to
> the means of production or means of subsistence which, in a society

of generalized commodity production, forces the proletarian to sell his labor power. In exchange for this labor power he receives a wage which then enables him to acquire the means of consumption necessary for satisfying his own needs and those of his family.

This is the structural definition of wage earner, the proletarian. From it necessarily flows a certain relationship to his work, to the products of his work, and to his overall situation in society, which can be summarized by the catchword alienation. But there does not follow from this structural definition any necessary conclusions as to the level of his consumption . . . the extent of his needs, or the degree to which he can satisfy them.[4]

We lack a corresponding structural definition of women. What is needed first is not a complete examination of the symptoms of the secondary status of women, but instead a statement of the material conditions in capitalist (and other) societies which define the group "women." Upon these conditions are built the specific superstructures which we know. An interesting passage from Mandel points the way to such a definition:

> The commodity . . . is a product created to be exchanged on the market, as opposed to one which has been made for direct consumption. *Every commodity must have both a use-value and an exchange-value.*
>
> It must have a use-value or else nobody would buy it. . . . A commodity without a use-value to anyone would consequently be unsalable, would constitute useless production, would have no exchange-value precisely because it had no use-value.
>
> On the other hand, every product which has use-value does not necessarily have exchange-value. It has an exchange-value only to the extent that the society itself, in which the commodity is produced, is founded on exchange, is a society where exchange is a common practice. . . .
>
> In capitalist society, commodity production, the production of exchange-values, has reached its greatest development. It is the first society in human history where the major part of production consists of commodities. It is not true, however, that all production under capitalism is commodity production. Two classes of products still remain simple use-value.
>
> The first group consists of all things produced by the peasantry for its own consumption, everything directly consumed on the farms where it is produced. . . .
>
> The second group of products in capitalist society which are not commodities but remain simple use-value consists of all things produced in the home. Despite the fact that considerable human labor goes into this type of household production, it still remains a production of use-values and not of commodities. Every time a soup is made

or a button sewn on a garment, it constitutes production, but it is not production for the market.

The appearance of commodity production and its subsequent regularization and generalization have radically transformed the way men labor and how they organize society.[5]

What Mandel may not have noticed is that his last paragraph is precisely correct. The appearance of commodity production has indeed transformed the way that *men* labor. As he points out, most household labor in capitalist society (and in the existing socialist societies, for that matter) remains in the pre-market stage. This is the work which is reserved for women and it is in this fact that we can find the basis for a definition of women.

In sheer quantity, household labor, including child care, constitutes a huge amount of socially necessary production. Nevertheless, in a society based on commodity production, it is not usually considered "real work" since it is outside of trade and the market place. It is pre-capitalist in a very real sense. This assignment of household work as the function of a special category "women" means that this group *does* stand in a different relation to production than the group "men." We will tentatively define women, then, as that group of people who are responsible for the production of simple use-values in those activities associated with the home and family.

Since men carry no responsibility for such production, the difference between the two groups lies here. Notice that women are not excluded from commodity production. Their participation in wage labor occurs but, as a group, they have no structural responsibility in this area and such participation is ordinarily regarded as transient. Men, on the other hand, are responsible for commodity production; they are not, in principle, given any role in household labor. For example, when they do participate in household production, it is regarded as more than simply exceptional; it is demoralizing, emasculating, even harmful to health. (A story on the front page of the *Vancouver Sun* in January 1969 reported that men in Britain were having their health endangered because they had to do too much housework!)

The material basis for the inferior status of women is to be found in just this definition of women. In a society in which money determines value, women are a group who work outside the money economy. Their work is not worth money, is therefore valueless, is therefore not even real work. And women themselves, who do this valueless work, can hardly be expected to be worth as much as men, who work for money. In structural terms, the closest thing to the condition of women is the condition of others who are or were also outside of commodity production, i.e., serfs and peasants.

In her recent paper on women, Juliet Mitchell introduces the subject as follows: "In advanced industrial society, women's work is only marginal to the total economy. Yet it is through work that man changes natural conditions and thereby produces society. Until there is a revolution in production, the labor situation will prescribe women's situation within the world of men."[6] The statement of the marginality of women's work is an unanalyzed recognition that the work women do is *different* from the work that men do. Such work is not marginal, however; it is just not wage labor and so is not counted. She even says later in the same article, "Domestic labor, even today, is enormous if quantified in terms of productive labor." She gives some figures to illustrate: In Sweden, 2,340 million hours a year are spent by women in housework compared with 1,290 million hours spent by women in industry. And the Chase Manhattan Bank estimates a woman's overall work week at 99.6 hours.

However, Mitchell gives little emphasis to the basic economic factors (in fact she condemns most Marxists for being "overly economist") and moves on hastily to superstructural factors, because she notices that "the advent of industrialization has not so far freed women." What she fails to see is that no society has thus far industrialized housework. Engels points out that the "first premise for the emancipation of women is the reintroduction of the entire female sex into public industry. . . . And this has become possible not only as a result of modern large-scale industry, which not only permits the participation of women in production in large numbers, but actually calls for it and, moreover, strives to convert private domestic work also into a public industry."[7] And later in the same passage: "Here we see already that the emancipation of women and their equality with men are impossible and must remain so as long as women are excluded from socially productive work and restricted to housework, which is private." What Mitchell has not taken into account is that the problem is not simply one of getting women into *existing* industrial production but the more complex one of converting private production of household work into public production.

For most North Americans, domestic work as "public production" brings immediate images of Brave New World or of a vast institution— a cross between a home for orphans and an army barracks—where we would all be forced to live. For this reason, it is probably just as well to outline here, schematically and simplistically, the nature of industrialization.

A pre-industrial production unit is one in which production is small-scale and reduplicative; i.e., there are a great number of little units, each complete and just like all the others. Ordinarily such production units are in some way kin-based and they are multi-purpose, fulfilling religious, recreational, educational, and sexual functions along with the economic function. In such a situation, desirable attributes of an individual, those which give prestige, are judged by more than purely economic criteria: for example, among approved character traits are proper behavior to kin or readiness to fulfill obligations.

Such production is originally not for exchange. But if exchange of commodities becomes important enough, then increased efficiency of production becomes necessary. Such efficiency is provided by the transition to industrialized production which involves the elimination of the kin-based production unit. A large-scale, non-reduplicative production unit is substituted which has only one function, the economic one, and where prestige or status is attained by economic skills. Production is rationalized, made vastly more efficient, and becomes more and more public—part of an integrated social network. An enormous expansion of man's productive potential takes place. Under capitalism such social productive forces are utilized almost exclusively for private profit. These can be thought of as *capitalized* forms of production.

If we apply the above to housework and child rearing, it is evident that each family, each household, constitutes an individual production unit, a pre-industrial entity, in the same way that peasant farmers or cottage weavers constitute pre-industrial production units. The main features are clear, with the reduplicative, kin-based, private nature of the work being the most important. (It is interesting to notice the other features: the multi-purpose functions of the family, the fact that desirable attributes for women do not center on economic prowess, etc.) The rationalization of production effected by a transition to large-scale production has not taken place in this area.

Industrialization is, in itself, a great force for human good; exploitation and dehumanization go with capitalism and not necessarily with industrialization. To advocate the conversion of private domestic labor into a public industry under capitalism is quite a different thing from advocating such conversion in a socialist society. In the latter case the forces of production would operate for human welfare, not private profit, and the result should be liberation, not dehumanization. In this case we can speak of *socialized* forms of production.

These definitions are not meant to be technical but rather to differentiate between two important aspects of industrialization. Thus the fear of the barracks-like result of introducing housekeeping into the public economy is most realistic under capitalism. With socialized production and the removal of the profit motive and its attendant alienated labor, there is no reason why, *in an industrialized society*, industrialization of housework should not result in better production, i.e., better food, more comfortable surroundings, more intelligent and loving child-care, etc., than in the present nuclear family.

The argument is often advanced that, under neocapitalism, the work in the home has been much reduced. Even if this is true, it is not structurally relevant. Except for the very rich, who can hire someone to do it, there is for most women an irreducible minimum of necessary labor involved in caring for home, husband, and children. For a married woman without children this irreducible minimum of work probably takes fifteen to twenty hours a week; for a woman with small children the minimum is probably seventy or eighty hours a week.[8] (There is some resistance to regarding child-rearing as a job. That labor is involved, i.e., the production of use-value, can be clearly seen when exchange-value is also involved—when the work is done by baby sitters, nurses, child-care centers, or teachers. An economist has already pointed out the paradox that if a man marries his housekeeper, he reduces the national income, since the money he gives her is no longer counted as wages.) The reduction of housework to the minimums given is also expensive; for low-income families more labor is required. In any case, household work remains structurally the same—a matter of private production.

One function of the family, the one taught to us in school and the one which is popularly accepted, is the satisfaction of emotional needs: the needs for closeness, community, and warm secure relationships. This society provides few other ways of satisfying such needs; for example, work relationships or friendships are not expected to be nearly as important as a man-woman-with-children relationship. Even other ties of kinship are increasingly secondary. This function of the family is important in stabilizing it so that it can fulfill the second, purely economic, function discussed above. The wage-earner, the husband-father, whose earnings support himself, also "pays for" the labor done by the mother-wife and supports the children. The wages of a man buy the labor of two people. The crucial importance of this second function of the family can be seen when the family unit breaks down in divorce. The continuation of the economic function is the major concern where children are involved; the man must continue to pay for the labor of the woman. His wage is very often insufficient to enable him to support a second family. In this case his emotional needs are sacrificed to the necessity to support his ex-wife and children. That is, when there is a conflict the economic function of the family very often takes precedence over the emotional one. And this in a society which teaches that the major function of the family is the satisfaction of emotional needs.[9]

As an economic unit, the nuclear family is a valuable stabilizing force in capitalist society. Since the production which is done in the home is paid for by the husband-father's earnings, his ability to withhold his labor from the market is much reduced. Even his flexibility in changing jobs is limited. The woman, denied an active place in the market, has little control over the conditions that govern her life. Her economic dependence is reflected in emotional dependence, passivity, and other "typical" female personality traits. She is conservative, fearful, supportive of the status quo.

Furthermore, the structure of this family is such that it is an ideal consumption unit. But this fact, which is widely noted in Women's Liberation literature, should not be taken to mean that this is its primary function. If the above analysis is correct, the family should be seen primarily as a production unit for housework and child-rearing. *Everyone* in capitalist society is a consumer; the structure of the family simply means that it is particularly well suited to encourage consumption. Women in particular *are* good consumers; this follows naturally from their responsibility for matters in the home. Also, the inferior status of women, their general lack of a strong sense of worth and identity, make them more exploitable than men and hence better consumers.

The history of women in the industrialized sector of the economy has depended simply on the labor needs of that sector. Women function as a massive reserve army of labor. When labor is scarce (early industrialization, the two world wars, etc.) then women form an important part of the labor force. When there is less demand for labor (as now under neocapitalism) women become a surplus labor force—but one for which their husbands and not society are economically responsible. The "cult of the home" makes its reappearance during times of labor surplus and is used to channel women out of the market economy. This is relatively easy since the pervading ideology ensures that no one, man or woman, takes women's participation in the labor force very seriously. Women's real work, we are taught, is in the home; this holds whether or not they are married, single, or the heads of households.

At all times household work is the responsibility of women. When they are working outside the home they must somehow manage to get both outside job and housework done (or they supervise a substitute for the housework). Women, particularly married women with children, who work outside the home simply do two jobs; their participation in the labor force is only allowed if they continue to fulfill their first responsibility in the home. This is particularly evident in countries like Russia and those in Eastern Europe where expanded opportunities for women in the labor force have not brought about a corresponding expansion in their liberty. Equal access to jobs outside the home, while one of the preconditions for women's liberation, will not in itself be sufficient to give equality for women; as long as work in the home remains a matter of private production and is the responsibility of women, they will simply carry a double work-load.

A second prerequisite for women's liberation which follows from the above analysis is the conversion of the work now done in the home as private production into work to be done in the public economy.[10] To be more specific, this means that child-rearing should no longer be the responsibility solely of the parents. Society must begin to take responsibility for children; the economic dependence of women and children on the husband-father must be ended. The other work that goes on in the home must also be changed—communal eating places and laundries for example. When such work is moved into the public sector, then the material basis for discrimination against women will be gone.

These are only preconditions. The idea of the inferior status of women is deeply rooted in the society and will take a great deal of effort to eradicate. But once the structures which produce and support that idea are changed then, and only then, can we hope to make progress. It is possible, for example, that a change to communal eating places would simply mean that women are moved from a home kitchen to a communal one. This *would* be an advance, to be sure, particularly in a socialist society where work would not have the inherently exploitative nature it does now. Once women are freed from private production in the home, it will probably be very difficult to maintain for any long period of time a rigid definition of jobs by sex. This illustrates the interrelation between the two preconditions given above: true equality in job opportunity is probably impossible without freedom from housework, and the industrialization of housework is unlikely unless women are leaving the home for jobs.

The changes in production necessary to get women out of the home might seem to be, in theory, possible under capitalism. One of the sources of women's liberation movements may be the fact that alternative capitalized forms of home production now exist. Day care is available, even if inadequate and perhaps expensive; convenience foods, home delivery of meals, and take-out meals are widespread; laundries and cleaners offer bulk rates. However, cost usually prohibits a complete dependence on such facilities, and they are not available everywhere, even in North America. These should probably then be regarded as embryonic forms rather than completed structures. However, they clearly stand as alternatives to the present system of getting such work done. Particularly in North America, where the growth of "service industries" is important in maintaining the growth of the economy, the contradictions between these alternatives and the need to keep women in the home will grow.

The need to keep women in the home arises from two major aspects of the present system. First, the amount of unpaid labor performed by women is very large and very profitable to those who own the means of production. To pay women for their work, even at minimum wage scales, would imply a massive redistribution of wealth. At present, the support of a family is a hidden tax on the wage earner—his wage buys the labor power of two people. And second, there is the problem of whether the economy can expand enough to put all women to work as a part of the normally employed labor force. The war economy has been adequate to draw women partially into the economy but not adequate to establish a need for all or most of them. If it is argued that the jobs created by the industrialization of housework will create this need, then one can counter by pointing to (1) the strong economic forces operating for the status quo and against capitalization discussed above, and (2) the fact that the present service industries, which somewhat counter these forces, have not been able to keep up with the growth of the labor force as presently constituted. The present trends in the service industries simply create "underemployment" in the home; they do not create new jobs for women. So long as this situation exists, women remain a very convenient and elastic part of the industrial reserve army. Their incorporation into the labor force on terms of equality—which would create pressure for capitalization of housework—is possible only with an economic expansion so far achieved by neocapitalism only under conditions of full-scale war mobilization.

In addition, such structural changes imply the complete breakdown of the present nuclear family. The stabilizing consuming functions of the family, plus the ability of the cult of the home to keep women out of the labor market, serve neocapitalism too well to be easily dispensed with. And, on a less fundamental level, even if these necessary changes in the nature of household production were achieved under capitalism it would have the unpleasant consequence of including *all* human relations in the cash nexus. The atomization and isolation of people in Western society is already sufficiently advanced to make it doubtful if such complete psychic isolation could be tolerated. It is likely in fact that one of the major negative emotional responses to women's liberation movements may be exactly such a fear. If this is the case, then possible alternatives—cooperatives, the kibbutz, etc.—can be cited to show that psychic needs for community and warmth can in fact be better satisfied if other structures are substituted for the nuclear family.

At best the change to capitalization of housework would only give women the same limited freedom given most men in capitalist society. This does not mean, however, that women should wait to demand freedom from discrimination. There *is* a material basis for women's status; we are not merely discriminated against, we are exploited. At present, our unpaid labor in the home is necessary if the entire system is to function. Pressure created by women who challenge their role will reduce the effectiveness of this exploitation. In addition, such challenges will impede the functioning of the family and may make the channeling of women out of the labor force less effective. All of these will hopefully make quicker the transition to a society in which the necessary structural changes in production can actually be made. That such a transition will require a revolution I have no doubt; our task is to make sure that revolutionary changes in the society do in fact end women's oppression.

Bibliography and Notes

1. Marlene Dixon, "Secondary Social Status of Women." (Available from U.S. Voice of Women's Liberation Movement, 1940 Bissell, Chicago, Illinois 60614.)
2. The biological argument is, of course, the first one used, but it is not usually taken seriously by socialist writers. Margaret Mead's *Sex and Temperament* is an early statement of the importance of culture instead of biology.
3. This applies to the group or category as a whole. Women as individuals can and do free themselves from their socialization to a great degree (and they can even come to terms with the economic situation in favorable cases), but the majority of women have no chance to do so.
4. Ernest Mandel, "Workers Under Neocapitalism," paper delivered at Simon Fraser University. (Available through the Department of Political Science, Sociology and Anthropology, Simon Fraser University, Burnaby, B.C., Canada.)
5. Ernest Mandel, *An Introduction to Marxist Economic Theory* (New York: Merit Publishers, 1967), pp. 10–11.
6. Juliet Mitchell, "Women: The Longest Revolution," *New Left Review*, December 1966.
7. Friedrich Engels, *Origin of the Family, Private Property and the State* (Moscow: Progress Publishers, 1968), Chapter IX, p. 158. The anthropological evidence known to Engels indicated primitive woman's dominance over man. Modern anthropology disputes this dominance but provides evidence for a more nearly equal position of women in the matrilineal societies used by Engels as examples. The arguments in this work of Engels do not require the former dominance of women but merely their former equality, and so the conclusions remain unchanged.
8. Such figures can easily be estimated. For example, a married woman without children is expected each week to cook and wash up (10 hours), clean house (4 hours), do laundry (1 hour), and shop for food (1 hour). The figures are *minimum* times required each week for such work. The total, 16 hours, is probably unrealistically low; even so, it is close to half of a regular work week. A mother with young children must spend at least six or seven days a week working close to 12 hours.
9. For evidence of such teaching, see any high school text on the family.
10. This is stated clearly by early Marxist writers besides Engels. Relevant quotes from Engels have been given in the text; those from Lenin are included in the Appendix.

Appendix

Passages from Lenin, *On the Emancipation of Women*, Progress Publishers, Moscow.

Large-scale machine industry, which concentrates masses of workers who often come from various parts of the country, absolutely refuses to tolerate survivals of patriarchalism and personal dependence, and is marked by a truly "contemptuous attitude to the past." It is this break with obsolete tradition that is one of the substantial conditions which have created the possibility and evoked the necessity of regulating production and of public control over it. In particular, . . . it must be stated that the drawing of women and juveniles into production is, at bottom, progressive. It is indisputable that the capitalist factory places these categories of the working population in particularly hard conditions, but endeavors to completely ban the work of women and juveniles in industry, or to maintain the patriarchal manner of life that ruled out such work would be reactionary and utopian. By destroying the patriarchal isolation of these categories of the population who formerly never emerged from the narrow circle of domestic family relationships, by drawing them into direct participation in social production, . . . industry stimulates their development and increases their independence (p. 15).

Notwithstanding all the laws emancipating woman, she continues to be a *domestic slave*, because *petty housework* crushes, strangles, stultifies, and degrades her, chains her to the kitchen and the nursery, and she wastes her labor on barbarously unproductive, petty, nerve-racking, stultifying and crushing drudgery. The real *emancipation of women*, real communism, will begin only where and when an all-out struggle begins (led by the proletariat wielding the state power) against this petty housekeeping, or rather when its *wholesale transformation* into a large-scale socialist economy begins.

Do we in practice pay sufficient attention to this question, which in theory every Communist considers indisputable? Of course not. Do we take proper care of the *shoots* of communism which already exist in this sphere? Again, the answer is *no*. Public catering establishments, nurseries, kindergartens—here we have examples of these shoots, here we have the simple, everyday means, involving nothing pompous, grandiloquent or ceremonial, which can *really emancipate women*, really lessen and abolish their inequality with man as regards their role in social production and public life. These means are not new, they (like all the material prerequisites for socialism) were created by large-scale capitalism. But under capitalism they remained, first, a rarity, and secondly —which is particularly important—either *profit-making* enterprises, with all the worst features of speculation, profiteering, cheating and fraud, or "acrobatics of bourgeois charity," which the best workers rightly hated and despised (pp. 61–62).

You all know that even when women have full rights, they still remain downtrodden because all housework is left to them. In most cases, housework is the most unproductive, the most savage, and the most arduous work a woman can do. It is exceptionally petty and does not include anything that would in any way promote the development of the woman (p. 67).

We are setting up model institutions, dining-rooms and nurseries, that will emancipate women from housework. . . .

We say that the emancipation of the workers must be effected by the workers themselves, and in exactly the same way the emancipation of working women is a matter for the working women themselves. The working women must themselves see to it that such institutions are developed, and this activity will bring about a complete change in their position as compared with what it was under the old, capitalist society (p. 68).

Index